RESEARCH METHODS FOR SPORTS STUDIES

Research Methods for Sports Studies is a comprehensive, engaging and practical textbook that provides a complete grounding in both qualitative and quantitative research methods for the sports studies student. Leading the reader step-by-step through the entire research process, from identifying a research question and collecting and analysing data to writing the research report, it is richly illustrated throughout with sport-related case studies and examples from around the world.

Now in a fully revised, updated and expanded third edition, the book includes completely new chapters on using social media and conducting on-line research, as well as expanded coverage of key topics such as conducting a literature review, making the most of statistics, research ethics and presenting research.

Research Methods for Sports Studies is designed to be a complete and self-contained companion to any research methods course, and contains a wealth of useful features, such as highlighted definitions of key terms, revision questions and practical research exercises. An expanded companion website offers additional material for students and instructors, including web links, multiple choice revision questions, PowerPoint slides and additional learning activities for use in and out of class. This is an essential read for any student undertaking a dissertation or research project as part of their studies in sport, exercise and related fields.

Ian Jones is the Associate Dean for Sport at Bournemouth University, UK. His teaching and research interests focus upon the areas of sport behaviour, and research methodology for sport. He is the author of several research methods texts, and has published his research in a variety of journals.

www.routledge.com/cw/jones

'Understanding the research process and the value of sport research should be a responsibility for all those engaged in the sport enterprise; academicians and practitioners alike. Ian Jones has provided a text that creates a common link between the two, so that researchers and sport practitioners can communicate in the theoretical and practical.'

Ronald W. Quinn, Associate Professor, Department of Sport Studies, Xavier University, Cincinnati, USA

'*Research Methods for Sports Studies* is structured in an easy to follow, clearly written format providing a step-by-step roadmap for research. This is an essential text for students in how to do sport studies research. The supplementary resources will assist lecturers who are teaching sport studies research, and provide students with value adding learning resources.'

Tracy Taylor, Business School Deputy Dean, University of Technology, Sydney, Australia

'Ian Jones has written a highly accessible introductory text for undergraduate sports students from a range of sport disciplines, who are about to embark on a substantial piece of research for the first time. Likewise, the book provides a structure by which lecturers and tutors can shape the delivery of research methods modules. The case study and supplementary material brings to life what can sometimes be a rather mundane endeavour.'

Jimmy O'Gorman, Senior Lecturer in Sports Development, Edge Hill University, UK

RESEARCH METHODS FOR SPORTS STUDIES

THIRD EDITION

IAN JONES

 Routledge
Taylor & Francis Group

LONDON AND NEW YORK

First published 2004
by Routledge

Second edition published 2007
by Routledge

This edition published 2015
by Routledge
2 Park Square, Milton Park, Abingdon, Oxon OX14 4RN

and by Routledge
711 Third Avenue, New York, NY 10017

*Routledge is an imprint of the Taylor & Francis Group,
an informa business*

© 2015 Ian Jones

British Library Cataloguing-in-Publication Data
A catalogue record for this book is available from the British Library

Library of Congress Cataloging-in-Publication Data
Jones, Ian, 1970-
Research methods for sports studies / Ian Jones. -- Third edition.
pages cm
Previous edition main entry Gratton, Chris.
Includes bibliographical references and index.
1. Sports--Research--Methodology. 2. Leisure--Research-
-Methodology. 3. Qualitative research. I. Gratton, Chris,
1948- Research methods for sports studies. II. Title.
GV706.8.G726 2015
796.07--dc23
2014022338

ISBN: 978-0-415-74932-9 (hbk)
ISBN: 978-0-415-74933-6 (pbk)
ISBN: 978-1-315-79622-2 (ebk)

Typeset in Melior
by GreenGate Publishing Services, Tonbridge, Kent

Printed and bound by CPI Group (UK) Ltd, Croydon, CR0 4YY

Contents

1 WHAT IS RESEARCH?   1

6 THEORIES, CONCEPTS AND VARIABLES   85

7 RESEARCH DESIGNS   111

8 COLLECTING DATA I: THE QUESTIONNAIRE SURVEY   145

viii

13 ANALYSING DATA I: QUANTITATIVE DATA ANALYSIS — 245

14 ANALYSING DATA II: QUALITATIVE DATA ANALYSIS — 273

List of figures and tables

Figures

Tables

Foreword

I first got involved with Research Methods for Sports Studies in 2002. I had chaired the Sports Studies Panel during the 2001 Research Assessment Exercise (RAE) and was invited to Luton University to give a talk on the RAE process. Ian Jones was then at Luton University. He had already written the first draft of *Research Methods for Sports Studies*, but was having some difficulty getting it published as it was his first book. It had been suggested to him that having a co-author with a longer track record of book authorship would be a good idea. Ian asked me while I was in Luton if I was willing to do that. I agreed to read through the first draft and suggest changes and/or additions. In the end, I suggested very few changes and added little more than a few case studies and examples from our own research projects at the Sport Industry Research Centre at Sheffield Hallam University. The book that was eventually published under our joint authorship was hardly any different from Ian's original first draft. It was always essentially Ian's book.

I have been immensely proud, however, to have been associated with what I believe to be one of the best books published on research methods in the sports social science field. It has been one of Routledge's bestselling books in sport and in my own university library there are over 10 copies, whereas the other books I have co-authored just have the one or two copies. Since the first edition was published in 2004 I have recommended it to all my PhD students and also to all the masters students whose dissertations I was supervising. The feedback from them on the book has always been exceedingly positive and I do point out to them that this was a compliment to Ian rather than to me.

Ian did all the changes for the second edition and I did suggest at that stage that it should now have just his name on the cover. However, it was decided to keep it as joint authorship at that stage. In this third edition, the change has now been made and finally Ian Jones gets to put his name as the sole author of the book, which was the real case all along.

I retired in 2012, two years after the second edition of the book was published, and Routledge suggested that in this foreword I could suggest my retirement as the reason for my stepping down as joint author. However, this would create the belief that when academics retire from their full-time position they also retire from writing. The opposite is the case. In retirement, I have more opportunity to write than ever before. The ideas do not stop coming, which is actually quite wonderful. I continue to work and continue to write. Why should I stop doing the things that give me pleasure? What I do not do anymore is attend committee meetings, strategy meetings, executive meetings, and all other the time-consuming activities academics do that often take them away from students, learning and research. As with so many academics I retired to work on the things I really enjoy. As Emeritus Professor of Sport Economics at Sheffield Hallam University, I am immensely grateful to Sheffield Hallam University and the Sport Industry Research Centre for providing continuing support for me in this work.

As I indicated earlier, I have been really proud to be associated with this very successful book and wish Ian the best of luck in what I believe will be many future editions.

Chris Gratton

Preface to the third edition

The first two editions of *Research Methods for Sports Studies* were written to fill a perceived need for an accessible text that would provide new researchers with a guide to some of the key issues in sport and social science research. Over this time, there has been an impressive growth in the nature and diversity of research within the broad field of 'sport studies', and also in terms of the research methods literature to accompany this development. At the time of writing the first edition, there were no subject-specific texts. Now, over 10 years later, there are a variety of books focusing on research in specific areas such as sport management and sports coaching, as well as texts focusing upon aspects such as qualitative research in sport. Despite this changing landscape, the objectives of this third edition remain largely the same as the first two:

1 To stimulate interest in sports research, to inform the student as to the importance of research in developing knowledge, and to encourage the student to both read further research and, more importantly, to carry out their own research into their own areas of sporting interest.
2 To act as a practical handbook for researchers. Rather than to be read in one go, the text acts as a resource that the researcher can refer to at different times during the research process.
3 To relate elements of the research process to actual examples of sports research, so that the theory introduced can be related to actual practice.

The text, although providing a full introduction to research methods in sports studies, is not exhaustive, and you are encouraged to read further into particular areas of interest or specialisation. Thus, for example, there is not an extensive description of the various interpretivist approaches, or a full description of different types of statistical analysis. I have, however, provided an overview, which will be enough for some students. Others, depending on their research interests, will require further or more advanced information, and for such students I would recommend the use of one of the many excellent specialist texts available for a much fuller account than I could provide here. These are outlined at the end of the relevant chapters under 'further reading'.

The intended audience for this edition also remains the same. Its primary audience will be students undertaking courses in sports-related studies, including sport management, sport development, the sociology of sport, sports marketing, sport-related tourism, coaching, physical education, recreation management and other similar degrees. It is not aimed, however, at those undertaking research into the natural sciences and their application to sport, for those whose interests lie more in the physiology or anatomy of sport. This text may also be of interest to those working in the sport industry, where research may be a requirement of the position.

One theme that is central to the text is that there is no one correct way of doing research. The 'best' way of undertaking research depends on several factors, such as the nature of the research question, the skills of the researcher, the intended outcomes of the research, the availability of time and resources and so on, so that each research question has its own unique characteristics that need to be taken into account. A good researcher will have the flexibility to adapt to such factors, rather than being constrained by a particular approach or doctrine. A second theme is the need to view research as integral to knowledge about sport, rather than as 'abstract', or removed (from my experience, it is sometimes the case that students cannot always see the relevance of a research methods course to their own personal interests or agenda). A number of examples are provided within the text to link knowledge about sport to research methods, and to demonstrate the links between the research process and our academic understanding of sport.

The structure of the book

This book is based upon the concept of the 'research process'. While it could be argued that the conceptualisation of the research process presented here is perhaps too neat and tidy, and that 'real life' research rarely follows such a structured approach, it is nevertheless a useful framework upon which to develop an understanding of sport research. The first chapters introduce the concepts and traditions of research, and are concerned with the underlying theory and philosophy of sports research. Chapter 1 introduces the concept of 'research', and its role within sports studies. Chapter 2 outlines some of the differing approaches to the nature and acquisition of knowledge. Chapter 3 then introduces the concept of the 'research process', around which the remainder of the book is based.

The first stage of the research process is that of selecting an appropriate topic for investigation, and Chapter 4 outlines some of the strategies that can be used to identify and assess suitable research questions, aims and objectives. Chapter 5 introduces the concept of the literature review, the actual processes of finding and reviewing the literature, and writing this review in an appropriate format. Chapter 6 then introduces the importance of identifying the appropriate theories, concepts and variables within a research project. Chapter 7 describes some of the different designs you can use to carry out your research. Together, these first seven chapters provide you with the 'background' information essential to understanding the nature of research itself, and the issues specific to the development of your own research project. The second part of the text is concerned with the issues related to actually undertaking a research project. Chapters 8–12 look at some of the data collection methods that you can use to collect your own data. I examine the use of questionnaires, interviews and unobtrusive methods in these chapters, as well as introducing a particular methodological approach, that of sports ethnography, in Chapter 11, and introduce the nature of online research in Chapter 12.

The third part of the book is concerned with the analysis of the data that you will collect, and the reporting of the research. Chapter 13 outlines some of the techniques of analysing quantitative data, and introduces SPSS for Windows as a tool for the analysis of quantitative data. Chapter 14 describes how to analyse and make sense of the qualitative data that you may collect. Chapter 15 discusses putting it all together, in terms of writing up your research report. Chapter 16 is of interest for those undertaking research as part of a taught course, for example those undertaking a final-year dissertation as part of a degree course in sports studies, where some of the specific issues of student research are covered.

Using the book

It is likely that you will be using this book in one of two ways. First, you may be undertaking a research methods course as part of a wider programme in a sports-related subject. If so, the content of the book is designed to be consistent with a typical teaching schedule (schedules will vary considerably; however, the content tends to remain relatively constant). In this case, you may well find yourself reading the book sequentially. Second, you may be using it as a handbook to assist you with an actual research project, in which case you may be more selective in your approach. For example, you may wish to read the chapter on student issues (Chapter 16) at an early stage. There is also an accompanying website (www.routledge.com/cw/jones) that provides a number of additional resources and activities, as well as questions to test your own understanding of the various elements of the research process.

Whatever your situation, I have provided a number of activities at the end of each chapter. The general activities will be suitable for those learning about research, and provide valuable experience of some of the elements of the research process. Other activities will be more appropriate to help you while you are actually carrying out the research, and will help you in assessing your own research.

Finally, it is important that you view research as an opportunity, whether it is an opportunity to engage with an area that attracts you, an opportunity to develop your own interests, an opportunity for personal development, or even as a personal challenge that will test your abilities to the full. Whichever it is, I hope that you will enjoy the research process and be successful in your research career.

Changes to the third edition

There have been a number of changes to the third edition. The more noticeable are those of a new chapter on online research, to reflect the growing opportunities (if not actual practice) provided by the internet. Otherwise, the structure of the text remains the same, but with each chapter being updated in light of constructive feedback received from reviewers. The final change is perhaps the most obvious one. The co-author of the first two editions, Professor Chris Gratton, has entered a well-deserved retirement, and thus this third edition is a sole effort. I would like to take this opportunity to thank Chris for all of his help and support in the past, not just with this text, but also the way that he has positively contributed to sport research in general. His influence has been immense.

Ian Jones
Bournemouth University
May 2014

1

What is research?

This chapter will:

- Introduce the concept of 'research'.
- Discuss some of the reasons why we undertake **research**.
- Outline the different types of research.
- Describe how to approach the reading of research articles.

Any honest attempt to study a problem systematically or to add to man's knowledge of a problem may be regarded as research.
(Theodorson and Theodorson 1969, cited in Reber 1995, p.663)

The aim, as far as I can see, is the same in all sciences. Put simply and cursorily, the aim is to make known something previously unknown to human beings. It is to advance human knowledge, to make it more certain or better fitting ... the aim is, as I have said, discovery.
(Elias 1986, p.20)

Introduction

We know a lot about sport. The fact that you are reading this book suggests that you have already begun to develop an understanding of sport, and its varied nature, impacts and experiences, whether focusing upon factors that influence performance at an individual level, the relationship between sport and well-being, or the broader impacts of sport at a global level. As with any social science, however, the study of sport involves the examination of constantly changing behaviours, which take place within a largely unpredictable, complex and dynamic social environment. It is within this context that research becomes, as Daniel Wann (1997, p.17) suggests, 'the lifeblood of any scientific discipline. Without it, disciplines would stagnate, failing to advance past their current limits and understanding.' Our understanding of sport is therefore never complete. Changing social, political, technological and economic contexts all influence, and are influenced by, sport. Thus, our knowledge is never absolute, and it is only through continual research that our understanding of sport is maintained and enhanced. This understanding, in turn, informs teaching and practice. Research therefore underpins every aspect of sport as an academic subject, and everything you have learned about sport to date has been, and will continue to be, based on research.

Research is not only for academia, however, and the skills associated with research are not important only for those wishing to publish in academic journals, or to write a dissertation. The growth in sports employment in recent years has led to countless professions where a knowledge and understanding of research methods is important. Those employed in the sports marketing industry, for example, may need to

2

be able to assess the effectiveness of a particular promotional strategy. Sport development officers may need to assess the reasons for non-participation in physical activity by members of a particular community. Coaches may wish to identify the impact of a change in leadership style upon team cohesion. Governments may wish to measure the economic impacts of a particular sporting event, and so on. Thus, you shouldn't see research as simply a part of academia. Doing research also helps you develop a number of more generic skills such as critical thinking, the ability to analyse data to draw conclusions, and the ability to communicate ideas to a wider audience.

What is 'research'?

Before embarking on the various methods and techniques of research, it is important to spend a bit more time considering what is actually meant by the term 'research'. A brief examination of different research methods textbooks will soon demonstrate the variety of different definitions. However, the quotes at the beginning of this chapter suggest that, although the process of research itself may be complex at times, defining 'research' is actually much more straightforward. Rather than spend time debating the merits of others' definitions, I shall use a relatively simple definition at this stage, suggesting that:

> *Research is a process of discovery and advancement of human knowledge.*

I am aware that this definition itself – like any other – is open to criticism. Through undertaking the process of research yourself, however, you will develop much more of an understanding of what research actually is than by reading and debating the validity of various textbook definitions. Even through simply reading research articles, you will soon develop your own understanding of research, without necessarily being able to produce a clear, unambiguous definition yourself. It is this understanding, as well as a personal interest in research, that is more important to you as a researcher.

The characteristics of research

Leedy (1985) and Walliman (2001) note a number of characteristics of research. These include the following:

- Research is generated by a specific research question, hypothesis or problem.
- Research follows a specific plan or procedure – the research process.
- Research aims at increasing understanding by interpreting facts and reaching conclusions based on those facts.
- Research requires reasoned argument to support conclusions.
- Research is reiterative – it is based on previous knowledge, which it aims to advance, but it may also develop further research questions, which in turn are answered by further research.

Research is therefore more than simply searching for facts. As suggested earlier, research is a systematic investigation to answer a question. Many people associate research simply with methods of data collection such as interviews and questionnaire surveys. Such data collection is just one part of a wider process, however, and other stages are equally important. Five general stages can be identified:

1 The stage before data collection, where the researcher decides upon the research question, the aim of the research, the research objectives and, in most cases, the theoretical framework that underlies the research through engaging with the relevant literature.
2 The stage of designing how to collect the data to answer the question, using which methods, and with what sample.
3 The actual data collection stage, where the data are collected by one or more research methods.
4 The analysis of the data – either with reference to the theoretical framework adopted or to generate new theory – to achieve the overall aim of the research.
5 The reporting of the research to communicate the findings to others.

These are all part of what can be termed the research process. The research process refers to the various parts of the overall process that guides a research project. This will be dealt with in more depth in Chapter 3.

4

Why undertake research?

As I have already suggested, much of our knowledge about sport is based upon research carried out by others. By undertaking systematic investigation into certain areas, we have increased our knowledge about sport dramatically in recent years, and can also maintain such understanding in a rapidly changing environment. The ways in which knowledge can be advanced by research are outlined by Hussey and Hussey (1997), who summarise the different purposes of research as follows:

- To investigate some existing situation or problem.
- To provide solutions to a problem.
- To explore and analyse more general issues.
- To construct or create a new procedure or system.
- To explain a new phenomenon.
- To generate new knowledge.
- A combination of two or more of any of the above.

Each of these can be fruitfully applied to many different aspects of sport. A further – and equally valid – purpose of research is to allow you to engage with some aspect of sport that interests you, so that you can add to existing knowledge as a personal achievement. Carrying out research into a specific area is one of the best ways to develop your own understanding of a particular area of interest. Finally, you may also wish to enhance your employment prospects in a particular area of sport. Undertaking a detailed piece of research, for example in the form of a dissertation, is often a good way to convince an employer that you have both interest, competence and the ability to undertake sustained independent research in a certain area.

JOURNAL

Although the term 'journal' may describe a number of different types of publication, I will generally be referring to academic journals within this text. Academic journals are generally published several times a year and report the most up-to-date research on a particular discipline or area of interest, such as the economics of sport, or sports marketing. Most academic journal articles have undergone some form of peer review process, whereby the quality and rigour of each article is assessed by a number of reviewers, each of whom will be an expert in their field. This ensures that the articles within such a journal are of an appropriate standard. Some sports-related journals include:

- *Sociology of Sport Journal*
- *Journal of Sport Management*
- *Journal of Sport Behavior*
- *Journal of Sport and Social Issues*
- *Journal of Sport and Tourism*
- *International Review for the Sociology of Sport*
- *European Journal of Sport Management*
- *European Sport Management Quarterly*
- *Sport in Society*
- *Qualitative Research in Sport and Exercise*

This is not an exhaustive list, and there are also a number of non-sport-specific journals that publish sport-related articles, so you shouldn't focus entirely on the ones listed above. These journals are all published in paper form, but you can also access them, and many other journals, electronically through your library as well as through search engines such as Google Scholar.

The different types of research

There are a number of different ways of classifying research, depending upon the purpose of the research, the data that are collected, and how such data are analysed. Three general types will be outlined here, these being referred to as exploratory, descriptive and explanatory.

6

Exploratory research

Exploratory research takes place where there is little or no prior knowledge of a phenomenon. Thus, there is a need for an initial exploration before more specific research can be undertaken. This type of research looks for clues about the phenomenon, attempts to gain some familiarity with the appropriate concepts and looks for patterns or ideas emerging from the data without any preconceived ideas or explanation. An example of this would be the study of Hing *et al.* (2014), who investigated the impact of gambling promotions during televised sports events upon subsequent gambling intentions of young people, an area where there had been little prior research. The nature of exploratory research means that clearly defined research questions or hypotheses are inappropriate, and often the direction of the research will emerge as the study progresses. Exploratory research is generally followed up by further research that tests any ideas or hypotheses generated.

Descriptive research

Descriptive research describes a particular phenomenon, focusing upon the issue of what is happening, or how much of it has happened, rather than why it is happening. The study of Martinent *et al.* (2012), for example, which described the differences in the frequency, direction, duration and co-occurrence of emotions among table-tennis players, was a good example of this. With descriptive research, there is little or no attempt to explain the results obtained, they are simply reported. Descriptive research is often used quantitatively to track changing patterns of sport, such as monitoring participation over time, or to assess or evaluate the outcome of something, such as an economic impact study of a mega event, or, as is often the case with qualitative research, to present a 'rich' evocative picture of an aspect of sport to the reader.

Explanatory research

This type of research is involved in explaining why something happens, often assessing causal relationships between variables. Thus, a researcher interested in why sport advertising might lead to body image concerns in adults would be undertaking explanatory research. The study of Scelles *et al.* (2013), which developed an explanation of the factors affecting attendance in French Ligue 1 football, is another example.

Explanatory research requires some sort of theoretical framework so that explanation may be deduced from the data (theoretical and conceptual frameworks are discussed in more depth in Chapter 6). Explanatory research allows us also to forecast future phenomena, based on the explanations we generate.

Pure and applied research

Each of the types of research I have identified above can also be placed on a continuum between pure and applied research depending upon its context. At one end of the continuum, pure research takes place to explore a particular concept, or issue, without regard for a specific problem, and may be carried out to simply gain a better understanding of the overall concepts, for example the development of a general model of coaching behaviour. Such research in itself has no immediate value beyond contributing to an area of intellectual inquiry. Applied research, on the other hand, is undertaken to solve a specific problem or provide a solution to a practical question. An example of this may be a particular sports organisation that wishes to explore potential markets, and commissions research to determine demand for a sports-related service or product, or research to explain why individuals drop out from a particular fitness programme after a short period of time.

Primary and secondary research

There is also a distinction that can be made between primary and secondary research. Primary research refers to research that has involved the collection of original data specific to that particular research project, for example through using research methods such as questionnaires or interviews. Secondary research refers to research where no such original data are collected, but the research project uses existing (or secondary) sources of data, for example census or archive data, or data that have been collected for another study but that can be reanalysed to answer a different research question.

8

Theoretical and empirical research

It is also possible to distinguish between theoretical and empirical research. Theoretical research generally uses the findings from existing works to develop new insight, theory and explanation. These new ideas are not tested through collecting evidence in the form of primary data, but instead have a focus on the theory itself. Empirical research, on the other hand, supports the development of new ideas through the collection of data, and the research is 'data driven' (empirical means based upon observation or measurement rather than theoretical reasoning). Thus, a researcher who develops a theory of sport fan violence through visiting a library and developing their own explanation through reading existing work will be undertaking theoretical research. The researcher who takes this one step further and collects data to test their explanation will be undertaking empirical research. Although theoretical research has its merits, I would suggest that you should – if at all possible – support your findings empirically through the collection of primary data.

Disciplinary approaches to sport research

It is also worth introducing the idea of disciplines at this stage, and the range of disciplines within which sport research is undertaken (I discuss this in Chapter 6 as well). A discipline focuses upon a particular way of looking at a subject using its own distinctive theories and explanations, such as the disciplines of history, education, geography and economics. Sociology, for example, focuses upon our behaviour as social beings, and the impact of social forces upon the way we behave, whereas psychology focuses upon the mind, its associated mental functions, and their impact upon behaviour. Sport itself is not a discipline as such (calling it a 'field' would be more accurate), but is studied within a discipline, for example sport psychology, or the sociology of sport. It's a good idea to identify your disciplinary approach, as it will help guide you through the various approaches associated with that discipline. Sometimes this will be clear. If you are reading this book while undertaking a sport psychology degree, for example, then your discipline will be psychology. If you are undertaking a programme in 'sport studies', however, then it may be more of an issue.

You may also come across terms such as 'multidisciplinary' (approaching your research from two or more disciplines), 'cross-disciplinary' (using approaches from other disciplines to inform your own approach) and 'interdisciplinary' (where your approach does not fit into a specific discipline, but generally takes elements, theories and approaches from varied disciplines to create a new approach).

DISCIPLINE

A discipline refers to a particular approach to the study of an aspect of sport, and the approaches, techniques and theories used to study and explain that particular aspect. Thus, sociologists are interested in the relationship between sport and society, and have developed particular sociological theories to explain sports behaviour. The discipline of psychology, however, is more interested in intrinsic influences upon sports behaviour. Each discipline will have a number of sub-disciplines, so sociology, for example, would encompass feminist sociology, cultural studies and so on. Understanding your 'home' discipline is helpful in guiding your approach, finding literature, and understanding the methods associated with that discipline.

Some misconceptions about research

As well as being able to define what is meant by research, it is also useful to describe some of the misconceptions often associated with research.

- Research in the way that I have conceptualised it is not simply the gathering of existing information. Reading an article on the economic impacts of major sporting events and making notes is not research. Neither is collecting existing information to write an essay or paper on the economic impacts of the Summer Olympics. Gathering existing information is simply one part of the wider research process.

10

- Nor is research simply the collection of new data. You may be interested in the reasons why individuals take up competitive tennis. Simply going to a tennis club and asking them is not research. Again, this is simply one part of a broader process.

- Research is not setting out to prove an opinion, based on personal experience. For example, if you do not attend major sporting events because of ticket prices, and decide to set out to prove that ticket prices are the most important deterrent to attendance, you are not carrying out research.

- Research is not the production of something completely original. Often students are daunted by the suggestion that they are required to produce some original findings, and often overestimate what is meant by 'original'. Even at the highest academic level, there are very few 'breakthrough' pieces of research within the social sciences, and almost all research involves adding to existing knowledge, rather than creating new knowledge, for example the testing of existing theories on new situations, which would still produce original findings. As Veal and Darcy (2014) note, there are a number of different ways to make a piece of research original, such as testing an existing theory in a different geographical area, or replicating an existing study using a different methodology (see Chapter 4). The production of a significant level of original knowledge is generally a requirement only of postgraduate degrees such as MPhil or PhD.

- Research does not always involve a problem. Many textbooks – including this one – do use the term 'research problem' frequently. Although research often involves the solving of a problem, it can, as is often the case in theoretical research, simply be done to advance the scope of human knowledge or to explore an issue where the researcher has a personal interest.

Understanding sports research

By far the best way to begin to develop your initial understanding is to read a variety of actual research located in sport-related journals. While research textbooks will provide the necessary theoretical grounding, Worsley (1992, p.79) notes that they do tend to 'present an unreal and idealised account of research'. He goes on to suggest that:

The best way to learn about research methods, apart from conducting research under supervision, is also, alas, the one requiring most effort. Most students ... reading a book or article pay most attention to the theories or concepts used and the overall argument, some attention to the actual substantive findings, and very little heed to the methods used. This is particularly so if the results are statistical or presented in tabular form. Yet simply paying more attention to how a study was done, what the substantive results were, and assessing whether they support the conclusions, will teach more than reading a dozen texts.

The suggested activity at the end of this chapter involves you reading and assessing some sports research. This is an activity that should not just be done once you have read this particular chapter, but you should ensure that reading and evaluating research is done on a continual basis. You will find that, as your research knowledge increases, you will be able to evaluate the research more confidently, assess the methodologies and methods adopted, and be able to more clearly identify the strengths and weaknesses within a piece of research. At first, this may seem a difficult and daunting task, especially if you are reading research undertaken by experts in a particular field. You should persevere, however, as the benefits will be worthwhile. Try not to be put off by the complex statistical analyses employed, or by the seemingly impenetrable academic writing that is often used (especially in some of the more sociologically based pieces of research). You should try initially to find some less complex articles, especially if the research is in an area with which you are not overly familiar.

How to read research

As I suggested above, you may find reading research articles a difficult task at the beginning of your research career. Thomas and Nelson (2010) and Baker (1994) provide a few useful pointers to bear in mind while you are reading a piece of research.

1   Locate and read a few articles from within a field you are comfortable with. By doing this, the concepts involved and the technical

language often used may not be as big a stumbling block as otherwise may be the case. It is also more likely that you will be able to understand the overall aims of the research. In the same way, avoid disciplines with which you lack familiarity, so if your expertise lies in sport management, then avoid sport psychology research.

2   Read studies that are of interest to you. Do not feel obliged to read through every article at first. Neither should you be afraid to stop reading after you have started if the article is not of interest – do not attempt to plough through it! Think of the areas that you enjoy, and focus on them at the beginning. If you have decided to focus on sociological research, and have an interest in the Olympics, for example, then search for articles related to the sociology of the Olympic Games. If you play a particular sport, then search for articles on an aspect of that sport.

3   Read the abstract first. The abstract will help you decide whether the article is relevant without having to read the entire paper. If the article doesn't seem of interest after you have read the abstract, then move on to another article.

4   Identify the research question and objectives. Is the research question a clearly defined hypothesis, or a vague area for investigation? What is the overall aim of the research? What about the objectives? Why is it important that this topic is researched?

5   Why did the researcher(s) choose a particular setting or sample? Where were the data collected? Who from? If a particular sample was chosen, such as children, or the elderly, then can you relate that choice to the overall research question? What were the strengths and/or limitations of this choice?

6   What were the methods chosen to collect data? How were the data collected? Were people interviewed, given a questionnaire, or observed? Why was this method or methods chosen?

7   What were the most important findings? Identify the most important findings made by the author, and identify the contribution to knowledge or understanding that the research has made. Who are the findings important to, and why? Do the findings suggest any further research that should be undertaken?

8   Do not be over-concerned with any statistical analysis you might encounter at this stage. Do not pay too much attention to what tests were used, and the level of significance at first. Try simply to determine the general meaning of the results.

13

9   Be critical but objective. You may find it difficult to evaluate the research critically, especially considering that it is likely that the reviewing process adopted by most journals would screen out most examples of questionable research. Try to assess, however, the strengths and limitations of the research. What would you have done differently, if anything?

KEY TERM

ABSTRACT

Research reports often commence with an abstract. The abstract is a short section, generally of about 150–250 words, outlining the aims of the research, the background to the study, the methods employed to collect data, the sample from which the data were collected and a summary of the main conclusions and the contribution of the research to knowledge or understanding. Abstracts allow researchers to identify whether a piece of research will be valuable in their own studies without having to read the entire article.

The second way of learning about research is to undertake it yourself. This is especially useful if, for example, you are to undertake a one-off piece of important research, such as a final-year undergraduate or postgraduate dissertation. Try to undertake a small research project beforehand, ideally during your training in research methods, so that you do not approach your research 'cold', but with some awareness of the research process, its potential pitfalls and the time and effort required to undertake a research project.

Summary

1   There are a number of definitions of research. Defining research is perhaps less important than understanding its nature.
2   Research is important for the advancement of any academic field or discipline.

14

3   Research can be classified as exploratory, descriptive, or explana-
    tory, depending upon its purpose. It can also be classified as either
    theoretical or applied, depending upon the level of application of
    the findings to 'real life' situations.
4   Research may involve the collection of new data (primary research)
    or the use of existing data (secondary research).
5   The best way to begin to develop your understanding of research, its
    role, and the types of research is to undertake some reading. Choose
    some appropriate articles, and begin to read!

Activity

You should familiarise yourself with the key academic journals in your
area of interest. If you are interested in sport management, for example,
ensure that you locate and read at least one article from the *Journal of
Sport Management, European Sport Management Quarterly*, or another
appropriate journal. When you have located an article that you are comfortable with, read it with the following questions in mind:

- What is the question being asked in the research?
- What is the underlying discipline?
- What type of research is being undertaken – exploratory, descrip-
  tive, explanatory or predictive? Is it pure or applied?
- Once you have become more familiar with research methods
  outlined in Chapters 8–12, reread the article. Try to identify the par-
  ticular strengths and weaknesses of the methods chosen.
- How has the research added to our knowledge about sport?

You should also begin your research diary. In this diary you should be
recording everything of importance to your own research, from your initial ideas to contact details of potential informants. Such a diary can be
an extremely useful resource, and you should ensure that it is as detailed
as possible. Some of the things you may include in such a diary are:

- Summaries of your meetings with tutors/supervisors.
- Ideas relevant to the research, for example in terms of potential
  information sources, or possible directions for the research.

- Problems that have arisen and ideas as to how to deal with such problems.
- Short- and long-term objectives.
- General thoughts about the research process.

Further reading

Rather than suggest any particular reading for this chapter, the activity above should be sufficient. At this stage, however, you should also be reading around your own subject area and beginning to develop a few ideas about your own research. Make sure you record these in your research diary!

2

Research traditions

This chapter will:

- Outline the general philosophical approaches underlying the research process, explaining what is meant by ontology and epistemology.
- Describe the characteristics of, and relationships between, positivist, interpretivist, qualitative, quantitative, mixed methods, and deductive and inductive research.

Introduction

In Chapter 1, I suggested that one of the aims of sport-related research is to advance our knowledge of the field. Unfortunately, while the term 'knowledge' may seem relatively straightforward, there are a number of issues related to what 'knowledge' actually is, and, as a consequence, how it can be acquired. The study of the philosophy of knowledge, or 'what knowledge actually is', is referred to as *ontology*, and the philosophical study of how such knowledge is acquired is referred to as *epistemology*. Although you may consider that philosophical debates may lack immediate relevance to your research project, an awareness of ontology and epistemology is important for three reasons:

1   The issues related to the differing philosophical approaches are important to some extent in all research that you will encounter. Thus, a broad ontological and epistemological awareness is important so that you have a framework within which you can understand the assumptions inherent in the different research that you will read, the position of the researcher, their key decisions during the research process, and how they analyse, interpret and discuss their findings.

2   This understanding may help you to determine the most appropriate design to answer your own research question. Thus, if you are interested in understanding why something happens in an area where there is limited knowledge, then an interpretative approach using an inductive methodology may be more suitable. If, however, you are interested in describing, comparing or measuring, or researching a well-established concept, then a positivistic, deductive approach may be more appropriate.

3   Alternatively, your own inclinations may allow you to focus on questions more suited to your ontological and epistemological preferences.

ONTOLOGY AND EPISTEMOLOGY

Ontology refers to the philosophy of the existence and nature of phenomena. Is knowledge a 'thing' that can be observed, or is it something that is experienced? You might, for example, be thinking about doing a study on coach effectiveness. What is the study actually about? Is it about the observable, measurable performance of the team, or the experiences of those being coached, experiences that are constructed at the individual, subjective level? Each concept will have a different ontology, and your answers to these types of question will form your ontological position.

Epistemology ('the study of knowledge') is the branch of philosophy that deals with how knowledge of such phenomena is acquired, and what counts as knowledge. Thus, are the perceptions of the players actually evidence that can be used to answer the question? Or would some form of objective measurement be more appropriate? These are issues of epistemology.

It is important, however, to note that you should not become overly concerned with the issues contained within this chapter at the expense of other aspects of the research process, especially if you are relatively new to research. You should rather have a general awareness and understanding of them. Also, it is worth revisiting this chapter after you have developed your research question, when some of the issues will be more relevant to you.

The nature of knowledge

Our ontological and epistemological positions will underpin our approach to research. Three broad approaches to the nature of knowledge are outlined in this chapter:

- positivism
- post-positivism
- interpretivism.

Each has differing epistemological and ontological assumptions, and each has differing implications for the types of research questions that

19

are asked, the subsequent methodology adopted, the nature of the data that are collected, and the analysis and interpretation of such data.

Positivism

Positivism refers to the school of thought that the only 'true' or valid form of knowledge is that which is 'scientific', that is where the principles and methods of the natural sciences (such as chemistry or physics) are used to study human behaviour, which in itself is objective and tangible in nature. In the same way that a chemist can observe the effect of adding one chemical compound to another, make precise observations or measurements, and develop laws of nature, the social researcher can observe human behaviour and measure 'facts', and 'laws' or theories of behaviour can be developed. These 'laws' could then be applied to other contexts to explain or predict future behaviour (one of the early goals of sociologists was to be able to develop a number of such laws that would one day be able to predict all aspects of human behaviour). Positivists would assume that the sports environment is relatively stable across different times or settings. Within such a stable context, the precise measurement and analysis of observable, concrete 'facts' allows the development of theories, which can then be tested through further measurement. Measurements themselves should be objective and not subject to the influence of the researcher's values or interpretation; others could see the same evidence and reach the same conclusions based on that evidence. This approach to obtaining knowledge involves precise measurements, which can be controlled or manipulated by the researcher. Such exact measurement allows statistical analysis which provides an impartial and precise answer. Careful research designs can show causal relationships. Finally, the whole process of investigation is objective: the researcher has no influence on the findings, and has no personal influence on the results. Concepts such as feelings, emotions or beliefs have a limited place in research as they cannot be directly observed or measured, they are unreliable and they are not constant over time. Such an approach has a number of characteristics, including:

- Control. The researcher is able to control one variable, and assess the influence that it has on another variable, for example the presence of a crowd upon shooting performance in a particular sport. The

20

researcher can control the size of the crowd, measure both the crowd size and performance, and draw inferences from the data.

- Replication. To explain a phenomenon, the same results would need to occur if the experiment was to be repeated, that is an increase in crowd size would always lead to a decrease in performance.
- Hypothesis testing. Positivistic research involves the creation of a hypothesis, which can then be systematically tested.

The positivist approach has its undoubted strengths, notably in terms of precision, control and objectivity. Through precise control and measurement, objective information is created, which can then be subject to statistical analysis, removing the need for intuitive interpretation. As a result, 'scientific' conclusions can be drawn.

HYPOTHESIS

Generally associated with quantitative research, a hypothesis is essentially a predicted result, based on existing knowledge that can be tested through the collection of data. For example, a hypothesis may be that 'Higher income is positively related to higher participation levels in outdoor sports'.

As well as a hypothesis, research projects will also present a null hypothesis. A null hypothesis suggests that there is no relationship between the variables under investigation. It is the null hypothesis that is tested by statistical analysis (Chapter 13 will examine this issue in more depth).

Post-positivism

Post-positivism is an approach closely aligned to, and generally not considered distinct from, positivism (Brustad 2002). The first of the general tenets of post-positivism is that it is, in reality, not possible to gain a truly objective understanding through measurement and observation, such as advocated by a totally positivist stance, and that there are limitations inherent within an approach that attempts complete objectivity which need to be recognised, such as the influence of the researcher, and their own values and biases. Second, there is a rejection of dualistic thinking in terms of things being

21

either subjective or objective, or correct or incorrect, and acknowledging the complexity of the subject under investigation. Third, post-positivism is characterised by the researcher adopting a 'learner role', learning with and about participants, rather than adopting a 'tester role', as is the case with hypothesis-driven research. Finally, post-positivist approaches are characterised by a much greater openness to different methodological approaches, and will often include qualitative, as well as quantitative methods, with a greater emphasis upon the use of multiple methods to look at a single phenomenon using a variety of means.

Interpretivism

Although the positivist approach is clearly well suited for research into aspects of sport such as biomechanics, anatomy or other disciplines more aligned with the natural sciences, sport is, for many, a social phenomenon. That is those who participate in, watch or manage sports are acted upon by a number of external social forces, but also have free will to respond to such forces in an active way, and are not inanimate objects, whose behaviour can be understood in terms of causal relationships. When examining sport we cannot predict whether X will always cause Y as – unlike the subject matter of the natural sciences – we all have, to differing extents, freedom to act in, and experience sport in different, subjective ways. This subjectivity forms the basis of the interpretative approach. We do not measure this subjectivity numerically – such an approach would argue that these concepts are too complex to be reduced to numbers. Rather, they are 'measured' using words, statements and other non-numerical measures, collecting data from the viewpoint of the participant. The data are then interpreted by the researcher, who attempts to uncover meanings, values, explanations and so on. It is the study of processes rather than the outcomes that is generally of importance to the interpretative researcher. This approach also avoids any search for a single 'truth', instead seeking understanding, and acknowledging that there are multiple truths. The interpretative approach allows the researcher to gain an insider's perspective, to try to understand the subjects 'from within', and to explore and uncover explanations, rather than deduce them from measurements. Thus, whereas a positivist approach may statistically identify a relationship between X and Y, an interpretative approach may be able to describe and explain that relationship from the viewpoint of those being investigated.

You may also come across alternative paradigms. Thus, you may see approaches labelled critical theory, phenomenology, constructivism, critical realism, feminist theory and critical interpretivism, to name just some. Critical theory emphasises the relationship of social 'reality' within historically situated social structures. Constructivist and phenomenological approaches suggest that multiple realities exist, formed within a particular context. The researcher studies how reality is 'constructed' by the individual within this context. Realism suggests that there is actually a 'real' truth to be discovered, albeit with limitations, and that this truth can be discovered using elements of both the positivist and interpretive approaches. Feminist theory applies feminist principles to research, suggesting that women will experience sport differently to men, and seeks to use this idea to avoid gender bias in research. Critical interpretivism is a blend of several overlapping elements: historiography, ethnography, comparison, investigation, critical sociology and 'gonzo' ('gonzo' refers to a particular type of approach that involves the researcher taking a position that is as close as possible to the subject without becoming part of it, and using that position to present a vivid and personalised account). If you do need further information, then we would suggest you read a more specialist text, such as Lincoln and Guba (1985) for information on the first four approaches, Olive and Thorpe (2011) for an interesting application of feminist theory, or Sugden and Tomlinson (1999) for an account of critical interpretivism.

Quantitative and qualitative research

In the preceding discussion, it was noted how differing assumptions could be made about the nature of knowledge, and how such knowledge is to be obtained. These differing assumptions are translated into the use of different types of data. As outlined above, Positivists assume that behaviours can be observed and objectively measured and analysed. Such objective measures are generally, although not always, numerical in nature. The use of numerical measurement and analysis is referred to as a quantitative approach, that is research that involves measurable 'quantities'. Thus, you may be interested in the relationship between economic investment in sport and subsequent success. You may approach this by measuring how much money has been invested into a particular sport, and measuring performance in that sport in terms of medal counts at major events such as the Olympics. This would give you a set of numerical data, which could be analysed to determine any relationship. This is quantitative research. Both variables are directly measurable, and easily converted into numerical form, which can then be statistically analysed. Quantitative data are thus closely aligned to the positivist approach.

A POSITIVIST QUANTITATIVE STUDY:
THE RELATIONSHIP BETWEEN SPORT ACTIVITY
AND EXPERIENCE IN WINTER SPORT TOURISM

Hallmann *et al.* (2012) were interested in the relationship between sporting activities and behaviour, and how these influenced the overall winter sport tourist experience. They noted that, as objectivity was important, and cause and effect were to be studied, the study was positivist in nature. To determine the relationship, elements of the experience such as hedonism, novelty, interaction, local culture, comfort, safety, and stimulation were all measured quantitatively on a five-point rating scale (from 1 = strongly disagree to 5 = strongly agree). Through statistical analysis, the researchers were able to determine that only two single winter sport activities (alpine skiing and sledge) influenced the winter sport experience, and a combination of activities (such as alpine skiing and sledging) seemed to be particularly important in increasing the sport tourist experience.

Qualitative research, on the other hand, aims to capture meanings or qualities that are not quantifiable, such as feelings, thoughts and experiences, that is those concepts associated with interpretative approaches. Qualitative research uses non-numerical data – often collected over an extended time period – to describe and understand concepts. Such concepts are difficult to meaningfully convert into numbers, and thus it is data in the form of words that have to be interpreted by the researcher that are relevant. Unlike quantitative research, the issue of 'how many' is not relevant, as Krane *et al.* (1997, p.214) suggest:

24

*Placing a frequency count after a category of experiences is
tantamount to saying how important it is; thus value is derived by
number. In many cases, rare experiences are no less meaningful,
useful, or important than common ones. In some cases, the rare
experience may be the most enlightening one.*

The characteristics of quantitative and qualitative research are summarised
in Table 2.1.

Table 2.1 Characteristics of quantitative and qualitative research

Quantitative	Qualitative
Uses numerical analysis to measure social phenomena to provide 'facts'	Relies on non-numerical analysis to provide understanding
Assumes a single, objective social reality	Assumes social reality is a subjective experience
Assumes social reality is constant across different times and settings	Assumes social reality is continuously constructed and related to the immediate social context
Uses statistical analysis to determine causal relationships	Objectives are description, understanding and meaning
Studies samples with the intention of generalising to populations	Uses smaller samples, or 'cases'
Researcher is objective, and 'detached' from the subjects under investigation	Data are rich and subjective
The setting is often contrived	The location of the research is often natural
Data are collected using inanimate objects, for example pen and paper, tablet or laptop	The researcher is the data collection instrument; flexible approach to data collection
Associated with the positivist approach	Associated with the interpretative approach
Generally deductive	Generally inductive

In certain areas, for example sports psychology, early research was dominated by positivist, quantitative approaches. Controlled experiments were
undertaken in laboratory settings to measure behaviour, and develop 'laws'
of human activity. Much of this research did provide useful information;
however, the need to understand the underlying experiences, feelings and
emotions related to such behaviour has been acknowledged in recent years,
and as a consequence qualitative research is taking on increasing importance
within sports studies. Previous arguments as to the relative merits of each
approach have largely diminished, to the extent that qualitative research
is now no longer seen, as has been in the past, as 'inferior' to quantitative
research.

AN INTERPRETATIVE, QUALITATIVE STUDY: FACTORS AFFECTING MOTIVATION IN ELITE ATHLETES

To achieve success, elite athletes need to be highly motivated over a long period of time. Keegan *et al.* (2014) were interested in the question of how key social agents – coaches, team-mates and parents – influence such motivation. To understand this, they collected qualitative data that explored the subjective beliefs of 28 elite athletes in the athletes' own words through interviews and focus groups. This data suggested that, by exploring the athletes' own perspective, rather than simple casual relationships, there were 'complex contextual interactions between the immediate behaviours of social agents and the impact on the athlete's motivation' (p.97), with coaches and peers being focal influences. Only the coach–athlete and peer–athlete relationships appeared to be important in influencing motivation towards sport, with parents being more limited to emotional and moral support.

Choosing quantitative or qualitative approaches

The decision to collect either quantitative or qualitative data depends upon the nature of the research question and the objectives of your research. Obviously if you are interested in the measurement of a particular phenomenon then you will need to collect quantitative data. If you are more interested in the thoughts or feelings of people, then these are difficult to quantify, and qualitative data will be more appropriate. Or, if your own particular epistemological preferences lead you to an interpretative study, then you may want to use that approach to develop the research question. There is no one 'better' approach; rather the approach should be linked to, and appropriate for, the research question. Do not, for example, decide to collect qualitative data simply because you are uncomfortable with statistical analysis. It is also important, as Buckley (2007) notes, not to view a 'softer' qualitative route as an easy option, as qualitative research is often extremely complex, and can be less straight-forward than some quantitative options. For many students, especially those whose initial exposure to sport has been through more 'conventional' report writing, qualitative research is very much a learning process. He adds that 'making mistakes and learning through problem solving are a natural feature of most people's first experiences with qualitative research' (p.91).

Mixing quantitative and qualitative data

You may also decide to mix quantitative and qualitative data through a mixed method (MM) approach. While some academics suggest that the two forms are incompatible, relying on differing epistemological assumptions and others suggest that time constraints, the need to limit the scope of a study, and the difficulty of publishing such findings are also factors against mixing qualitative and quantitative data (Creswell 1994), mixed approaches are becoming increasingly influential within social sciences as a whole. Their use within sport, however, is more limited, with Van der Roest *et al.* (2013) suggesting that they are still underused, poorly legitimised, and often weakly designed in sport research. If well designed, however, mixed approaches can lead to strong research. As Nau (1995, p.1) suggests, 'blending qualitative and quantitative methods of research can produce a final product which can highlight the significant contributions of both'. For example, qualitative data can be used to 'support and explicate the meaning of quantitative research' (Jayaratne 1993, p.117) in terms of providing some explanation to quantitative measurements. Henderson *et al.* (1999, p.253) noted with reference to their study of physical activity and culture that:

> *Linking types of data provides a way to use statistics, the traditional language of research, along with anecdotes and narratives for further clarity in understanding physical activity involvement. Descriptive statistics do not tell the meanings of physical activity. In-depth interviews alone are not necessarily representative of the sample. Together, however, linking the data gives a bigger picture of some of the issues that described and mitigated the physical activity of these women of colour.*

As I have already suggested, however, it is important that your approach is suited to the research question, rather than your own particular preferences. You can mix quantitative and qualitative methods in the following ways:

1 One may facilitate the other (sequential mixed methods). Thus a piece of quantitative research may identify the existence of a particular occurrence that could then be explained through the collection of qualitative data.
2 Both approaches investigate the same phenomenon concurrently. Quantitative methods may be used to collect numerical data from a large sample, whereas qualitative methods may collect 'rich' data from a smaller sample.

Five purposes of mixed methods research

Greene *et al.* (1989) have identified five purposes of mixed method studies:

1 Triangulation (seeking convergence and corroboration of results from different methods studying the same phenomenon).
2 Complementarity (seeking elaboration or clarification of the results from one method with results from another).
3 Development (using the results from one method to inform another method).
4 Initiation (discovering paradoxes and contradictions that lead to a reframing of the research question).
5 Expansion (i.e. seeking to expand the breadth and range of inquiry).

One thing you should consider at the outset is whether you have the time and resources to carry out multiple methods (the use of different methods to address different research questions regarding the same phenomenon) or mixed methods (where two methods are used to address the same research question) study. Often, such approaches require more in the way of time and money and this can be an important consideration, especially if you have constraints related to time and resources!

28

A MIXED METHODS STUDY: COMBINING QUANTITATIVE AND QUALITATIVE DATA TO EXPLORE THE EXPERIENCES OF OLDER ADULTS USING THE WII VIDEO GAME SYSTEM

Keogh *et al.* (2014) examined whether the use of a Nintendo Wii video game could have any impact upon the functional ability, physical activity levels, and quality of life older adults. They were able to determine through quantitative analysis that there were actual benefits, such as increases in muscular endurance, physical activity levels and psychological quality of life. In addition, however, qualitative data collected through a focus group allowed them to determine how participants actually experienced such changes, finding out that the experiences revolved around three main themes (feeling silly, feeling good; having fun; and something to look forward to), suggesting that participants developed a sense of empowerment and achievement after some initial reluctance and anxiousness, feeling that using the Wii was fun and an opportunity for greater socialisation.

Deductive and inductive research

There is one final distinction that can be made between different approaches to research in terms of deductive and inductive research. Deductive research is more generally associated with positivist and quantitative research. It involves the development of an idea, or hypothesis, from existing theory which can then be tested through the collection of data. A hypothesis is a statement of the relationship between two variables that can be tested empirically; for example, a hypothesis could be that 'children with parents who participate regularly in sport are more likely to have positive attitudes towards sports participation themselves'.

Deductive research progresses through the following stages:

1   A statement regarding the theory used to underpin the research.
2   A statement deduced from that theory that would suggest, if the theory is true, the relationship between two or more variables – your hypothesis.

29

3   Collecting data to test this hypothesis.
4   Using the results to confirm, modify or refute the theory used to develop the hypothesis.

Inductive research is more often associated with interpretative or post-positivist studies. Here, the pattern is to collect data, and analyse that data to develop a theory, model or explanation. For example, you may be interested as to the usage of social media by sports fans. You may find that there is not enough existing evidence to develop a hypothesis. You could undertake a content analysis (see Chapter 10) of social media usage, analyse how social media is being used, and subsequently develop an explanation. This theory can then be tested and refined if necessary through further data collection.

Two broad research traditions

We can summarise two general research traditions in Table 2.2. It is important to realise that these summaries are not concrete, and that it is entirely possible to carry out inductive research using quantitative methods, or vice versa.

Table 2.2 Two broad research traditions

Approach 'A'	Approach 'B'
Positivist	Interpretative
Quantitative	Qualitative
Deductive	Inductive
Questions such as 'what' 'when' and 'how many'	Questions such as 'why' and how'
Follows a pre-determined design	Follows a flexible research design that may be continually adapted
Establishes causality	Explains causality
Confirms theory	Develops theory

30

What approaches are suitable for my research?

Although it is important to have an awareness of the research traditions and approaches described above, it is also important not to be too constrained by them when undertaking your research. You should not consider any approach as necessarily better than any other, and choose the approach that best suits the objectives of the research. For example, if you are interested in describing what is happening in an area where there is a considerable amount of existing theory, then a deductive approach may be appropriate. If you are interested in explaining why something is happening, and the area is relatively new, or under-researched, then an inductive approach may be better. It is relatively easy to become immersed within the complex issues of ontology and epistemology. In reality, the key question to ask is what approach will best suit my research?

Second, time and resources can be a major issue. Inductive research tends to take longer and takes more resources than deductive research, as theories have to gradually emerge from the data, rather than be tested by data collected in one go. A third consideration is that deductive research is often lower risk than inductive research, where it can be possible for many hours of data collection to prove fruitless.

A final – and often overlooked – consideration is that of your own stance. You may – as many experienced researchers do – develop your own preferences towards a particular approach. Some of the questions that you may want to consider to get you thinking about your choices are:

1   Can I measure the phenomenon I am interested in numerically? Or is this inappropriate?
2   Am I concerned only with measurable 'facts'?
3   Am I concerned with the individual's views or explanations of what is happening?
4   Do I think that the 'truth' is different for each individual, and I cannot develop scientific 'laws' of behaviour?
5   What would I be happier doing in terms of positivist or interpretative research?

If you answer 'yes' to the first two and 'no' to the next two questions, then you are likely to follow a positivist, quantitative approach. If you responded 'no' to the first two and 'yes' to the next two, then you are likely to follow an inductive, qualitative approach.

Summary

1   Three broad approaches to the nature of knowledge exist – positivism, post-positivism and interpretivism.
2   Positivists adhere to the tenets of the natural sciences and view behaviour as directly measurable and explainable via laws.
3   Post-positivism, although often aligned with positivist approaches, has a more flexible view to the nature of knowledge, and how such knowledge is developed.
4   Interpretivists suggest that individuals have freedom to act in particular ways, and that they experience things differently. Thus, the researcher has to interpret 'reality' from each individual's experiences.
5   Distinctions can also be made between quantitative and qualitative research. Quantitative research is based upon numerical measurement and analysis. Qualitative research is based upon non-numerical analysis of words, feelings, emotions and so on.
6   Research may follow a deductive or an inductive process. Deductive research involves the testing of a pre-determined theory, explanation or hypothesis. Inductive research generates the explanation from the data collected.

Activity

Reread some of the research articles that you used at the end of Chapter 1. For each article, try to identify:

1   Is the research positivist, post-positivist or interpretative in nature? What are the key factors that lead you to this decision?

32

2   What type of data are collected? Quantitative, qualitative or a combination of both?

3   Does the research follow an inductive or a deductive approach? If the research is deductive in nature, try to identify: (a) what is the underlying theory used by the researcher(s), and (b) what is the hypothesis?

Locate a journal that publishes a range of positivist research, such as *Sport Management Review*, for example, and compare and contrast those studies with those published in a journal such as *Qualitative Research in Sport and Exercise*, which focuses upon interpretative work. Look at the different types of questions asked in each, the type of data collected, and the methods used. Also try and locate a study that uses mixed methods. Is the rationale for mixing methods clear? What has the mixed methods approach added to this study above that of the use of a single method?

ABOUT YOUR RESEARCH PROJECT

- Is your own research positivist, post-positivist or interpretative in nature? Can you justify your approach in terms of its appropriateness to the research objectives?
- Are you collecting quantitative or qualitative data? Can this be reconciled with your choice of a positivist or interpretative approach?
- Are you following a deductive or an inductive design? Can this be reconciled with your answers to the above questions?

3

The research process

This chapter will:

- Introduce the concept of the 'research process'.
- Outline the different stages of this process.
- Describe how the different stages interrelate as part of one overall process.

Introduction

When we initially consider the idea of research, our first thought is often to think of the collection of quantitative or qualitative data through interviewing, questionnaires or other methods. While such primary data collection is an important part of many research projects, it is much more involved than simply collecting data, and it is generally more appropriate to consider data collection as part of a wider process involving important stages both before and after. This chapter introduces this concept of the 'research process', describes the elements within the process, and the relationships between the elements. It is important that you have an understanding of all elements of the research process before commencing your research project so that you have an idea of the 'big picture'. At this stage I would strongly recommend reading the excellent text by Neil *et al.* (2014), which, through reference to a number of varied examples from a varied range of disciplines, shows how different sport researchers have navigated this process through reference to real-life accounts of research, and the key decisions that were made during the process.

The research process

The research process described in the following section is a particularly sanitised model of carrying out research. In reality, the process is much less neat, and you will find that you will not usually follow the process stage by stage, but will often move continually back and forth between the elements, or carry out two or more of the elements concurrently, especially if you are undertaking a more interpretative or qualitative study (see Chapter 2). Although different models of the research process exist, each containing different numbers of stages, most include the same general elements. The research process that we will refer to consists of nine elements (Figure 3.1).

1. Selection of topic

2. Reviewing the literature

3. Development of theoretical and conceptual frameworks

4. Clarification of research question/hypothesis

5. Research design

6. Data collection

7. Data analysis

8. Drawing conclusions

9. Dissemination

Figure 3.1 The research process

It is important to remember that these are not isolated, discrete stages, but are actually part of one overall process. It may also be the case that for certain approaches the order of the stages may be somewhat different; for example, a qualitative research project may involve a continual integration of reviewing the literature and data collection, and the development of a conceptual framework after data collection. Thus, you should be prepared to be flexible, depending upon the nature of the research being undertaken. Whatever approach you take, however, it is important that you maintain a sense of coherence within the overall research project, or what some refer to as a 'golden thread', or 'vertical thread'. This thread should be the research question, and everything within the research process should be related to answering that question. This chapter will briefly outline the stages of the research process. Each of the areas will be covered in more depth in later chapters of the book.

Stage 1. Selection of topic

The stage that will take up most (if not all) of your time at the beginning of your research is that of actually selecting a topic, and developing a preliminary research aim and set of objectives. The selection of your research question is a crucial stage, as an inappropriate topic or question will often lead to irretrievable difficulties later in the research, so it is worth dealing with this stage carefully. It is unlikely that you will develop a final question and set of objectives at this stage of the research process, and further work, as outlined in stages 2 and 3, are important in developing and assessing your question more fully. I will discuss some of the issues related to coming up with a research question in more depth in Chapter 4.

Stage 2. Reviewing the literature

This stage is covered in more depth in Chapter 5. A literature review essentially consists of critically reading, evaluating and organising existing literature on the topic to assess the state of knowledge and understanding in the area, and identifying how your proposed question relates to that state of knowledge. During this stage you should aim to become an 'expert' in your field of research. The literature review is generally done alongside the development of the theoretical and conceptual frameworks (stage 3 of the research process). Reading widely may also alert you to other helpful factors, such as whether similar research has already been carried out, the findings that you could expect, or provide descriptions of the theoretical frameworks and previous methodologies adopted by others doing similar research.

Stage 3. Development of theoretical and conceptual frameworks

As you read the literature, you should be continually developing and refining your theoretical and conceptual frameworks. This is a stage that can often be overlooked in the haste to collect data. It is, however, a vital part of the research process, and is important in alerting you to potential problems before they occur. Your theoretical framework refers to the underlying theoretical approach that you adopt to underpin your study, for example social learning theory, or self-determination theory. The conceptual framework defines and organises the concepts important within your study. These issues are covered in more depth in Chapter 6.

Stage 4. Clarification of the research question

Stages 1, 2 and 3 of the research process will initially, in many cases, become a circular process, whereby initial research questions are chosen, investigated and amended or rejected for a number of reasons. For example:

- The question lacks sufficient focus.
- The conceptual framework has identified problems in either defining and/or measuring the appropriate concepts.
- There are too many moderating or intervening variables.
- The project is lacks feasibility in terms of complexity, access, facilities or resources.

Stages 1–3 can take longer than initially anticipated, and you may well become discouraged by a lack of success in identifying a good research question. There are no easy methods to come up with an appropriate question, and it can be very much a case of perseverance. Once you have developed a good, focused research question, then the rest of the research process is based upon answering that question. A common fault is the lack of clarity over the overall aim of the research, and the importance of developing a clearly focused aim and set of research objectives at this stage cannot be overstated.

Stage 5. Research design

Once the focused research question has been ascertained, the next stage is to consider two questions:

1 What data do I need to collect to answer this question?
2 What is the best way to collect the data?

This stage considers more than just the practical methods of collecting data, such as choosing questionnaires or interviews, but also a number of broader issues. The typical issues considered by the researcher might include:

- What overall research design should I use? Will I, for example, use a cross-sectional, experimental or longitudinal design?
- Will I need to collect primary data, or will there be suitable secondary data to use?
- What methods, for example interviews, questionnaire surveys and so on, will be the best ones to collect the primary data?
- Who should participate in the research, and how will I gain access to them?
- What are the exact procedures that I should adopt in my data collection to ensure reliability and validity?
- Are there any ethical issues associated with the research?

These issues are covered in depth in Chapter 7, as well as throughout much of the rest of the text.

Stage 6. Data collection

Once the issues identified in stages 4 and 5 of the research process have been addressed, then you should have a clear idea of what data to collect, and how to collect them. You have to consider which methodology to choose, and which methods to utilise within the methodology. The background to this is dealt with in more depth in the next chapter, and the actual practical issues of collecting data are dealt with in Chapters 8–12.

Stage 7. Data analysis and discussion of the findings

The data you collect in stage 6 need to be analysed to provide answers to your research question. Methods of data analysis should always be related to the objectives of the research, that is, your analysis should answer the research question or hypothesis. In your discussion of the results, reference should also be made back to the literature reviewed in stage 2; for example, how do the findings add to this literature? Do they support the literature? If not, what are the possible reasons why? A common fault is to discuss the findings with no reference back to the literature reviewed as part of stage 2 of the development of the conceptual framework. Chapter 13 deals with issues of quantitative analysis, and Chapter 14 discusses some of the methods of qualitative data analysis that you may use.

Stage 8. Drawing conclusions

This should relate back to the focused research question. Here, the answer to the research question(s) should be clearly stated. You can evaluate how successful you have been in achieving your research objectives, and highlight the strengths and weaknesses of the research. You may also want to make recommendations for further research.

Stage 9. Disseminating the findings

An essential part of the research process is actually communicating the findings to a wider audience wherever possible. For some, this audience may be limited to just the examiners of the research, but there are also a number of other options, such as publishing your work in journals, presenting it at conferences, and more informally through social media. The various ways in which you can share your research are discussed in more depth in Chapter 16.

Planning the research process

At this stage, it is also worth emphasising that this process will not be a smooth one for much of the time, and it's a good idea to consider some of the things that will make the research process as positive an experience as it's possible to be.

1   Start the research process early. You may well have a timescale of a number of months, or longer to complete the research, but remember – it will take you all of this time. Set a number of precise and measurable goals in terms of what you want to achieve, and when, and ensure you monitor your progress continuously. Make sure you

40

build in enough time to allow for contingencies, and also for any other assessments that you are required to do during this time. You might be someone who thinks that they work best under pressure by leaving things later than necessary and working to unnecessarily tight deadlines. You don't.

2   Start writing as soon as possible. Don't worry about word counts, and don't worry that not everything you write will end up in the final submission. Your writing will improve significantly as you progress through the research process, provided you are writing on a regular basis.

3   You will find the process at different times enjoyable, exciting, frustrating and stressful. You will also go through stages where you lack motivation, doubt the quality of the work and find it hard to see an end product. Be prepared for this, particularly when the research becomes difficult. At such times, make full use of your research supervisor, and utilise their experience and advice. They will have supervised a number of research projects, and they are there to help you.

4   Make sure you make the most of your supervisor throughout the research process. They are there to work with you, and help you produce the best piece of work of which you are capable, but this requires you to take control of the relationship. It is your responsibility to arrange meetings, and set the agenda for discussion. Don't expect your supervisor to tell you what to do; they are there to advise you on the decisions you have made and the ideas that you have developed. Often, your supervisor will not have specific expertise in your particular topic area. Don't worry about this; it is far more important that they are able to guide you through the research process as a whole. If you are unhappy with your supervisor, though, ask to change. In many cases – provided that you make the request early enough and have a valid reason – this should be possible.

5   Do not talk to friends about the progress they are making, the support they are receiving, or listen to rumours about what is expected. In reality, there is very little correlation between what others say they have done, and what they have actually achieved. There are also a number of different ways of approaching the research process, so others might well be doing things in a different way. If you have any queries about the requirements, you should only consult sources such as any handbook that you might have been provided with, or your supervisor.

Summary

1   Research is not just about the collection of data. Data collection is important, but it is simply part of a wider process – the research process.
2   The research process follows nine steps: selection of topic, reviewing the literature, developing your theoretical and conceptual frameworks, clarifying your research question, developing a research design, collecting data, analysing data, drawing conclusions, and disseminating your findings.
3   Relating your project to the research process will allow you to develop and answer your research question in a logical and systematic manner.

Activity

1   Locate a copy of Neil *et al.*'s *The Research Process in Sport, Exercise and Health* (see below), and choose one of the chapters most closely related to your own discipline or interests. Try to get an idea of the process that the author went through from the initial formulation of the research problem, to the final dissemination of the research.
2   Reread one of the pieces of research from the activity suggested at the end of Chapter 1. Can you relate this research to the research process? Does the research follow this process? Are the steps easily recognisable?

Further reading

Neil, R., Hanton, S., Fleming, S. and Wilson, K. (2014) *The Research Process in Sport, Exercise and Health: Case Studies of Active Researchers*, London: Routledge.

Do try and read this text. It illustrates the research process through a number of different cases, including those related to sport management, sport ethics, coaching, sport development and the sociology of sport, each relating the research to the wider research process, explaining the key elements of the research process, and how they were addressed by the author.

At this stage, it can also be a good idea to catch up on your reading to get you thinking about the different ways in which the study of sport has been approached, and the various, diverse aspects of sport within society. Try to locate some of the key textbooks and journals in your particular field and try to get a feel for the range of topics that are covered, and some of the key theories and ideas that exist within those topics. The following are texts that you may want to browse through:

Coakley, J. (2009) *Sport in Society: Issues and Controversies*, Boston, MA: McGraw-Hill.
Coakley, J. and Dunning, E. (eds) (2002) *Handbook of Sports Studies*, London: Sage.
Houlihan, B. (2007) *Sport and Society: A Student Introduction* (2nd edn), London: Sage.
Jarvie, G. (2012) *Sport, Culture and Society*, London: Routledge.

Alternatively, you may want to browse through some peer-reviewed journals. Try journals such as *Sociology of Sport* or the *Journal of Sport Management*, for example, or any journals published in your particular areas of interest. Start thinking about the areas of sport that really interest you, and try to get a feel for some of the research that has been undertaken in those areas.

4 Research questions, aims and objectives

This chapter will:

- Describe some of the ways by which you can identify and develop a potential research area or research problem into a research question.
- Outline some ways by which you can focus your research question.
- Discuss some of the means by which you can assess the strengths and weaknesses of your research question.
- Describe the content of a research proposal, and identify some of the common weaknesses in research proposals.

Introduction

The starting point for any research project is to decide upon your initial research topic, and develop this topic into a focused research question. This is an important stage – a poorly thought out research question can lead to irretrievable difficulties in your research project later on. It can also be a difficult task, and one that can be extremely time consuming. In this chapter I will describe some of the strategies that you can use to develop your research question, focus the aims and objectives of your research, and also outline some of the means by which you can assess your research question.

Before you start considering your research question, it is worth revisiting the concept of research outlined in Chapter 1. As noted there, a feature of research is that it adds to knowledge. Often, however, students over-estimate the extent of originality required in a research project, and feel that they have to produce something completely new. In reality, this is unrealistic in almost all cases. Nearly all research builds upon work done by others, and uses existing knowledge. It is highly unlikely that you will come up with a completely original piece of research, and building upon the work of others through using existing knowledge provides the framework for a more realistic research proposal. Thus, you should not be concerned if your research topic does not seem as original as it could be. It should have some degree of originality, but often this can be achieved in a number of ways, as I will discuss later in the chapter.

Coming up with a research question

It is extremely unlikely that you will identify a clearly focused research question straight away, and before you even begin to develop and focus your research question, you will generally need to identify a broad topic. You may find that coming up with this initial topic proves difficult. Veal and Darcy (2014) and Saunders *et al.* (2000) provide a number of possible sources to help you:

- Existing sport literature. Past research projects are a useful source of ideas. By looking at past research, for example reading journal articles, you may develop an idea of the types of questions being researched in your field of interest and assess the types of subjects that are at the forefront of research. Alternatively your institution may have an archive of past dissertations or theses. From such reading you may encounter a certain idea, argument or theory that interests you, and that you would be interested in developing further. Choose a range of the most recent editions of a number of sport-related journals, and see what cutting-edge research is being done, and how it could be extended or applied to a new context.
- Literature from other disciplines. Alternatively, you could look at journals from outside sport, and see if there is current research that could be applied to a sporting context. Journals from the 'home' discipline (such as sociology, psychology and so on) can be useful here; for example, you might browse through the *Journal of Management*, and come across Ireland and Webb's (2007) paper on entrepreneurship. This is an aspect that has considerable importance in sport management, yet limited research, and might encourage you to look at the area of sports entrepreneurship further, or you might encounter the work of Hoobler *et al.* (2014) in the same journal, exploring the idea that managers' biased evaluations of women as being less career motivated was an explanation for their lower managerial aspirations than men in US Fortune 500 organisations, and think about whether this could be examined with reference to sport-related organisations.
- Social concerns. You may wish to explore certain contemporary social concerns and problems related to sport; for example, you may be interested in sports provision in deprived inner-city areas, or the sports experiences of minority groups. Other contemporary social concerns, such as violence or cheating in sport, or the impact of terrorism on sport, may also interest you. Think about the concerns that you are interested in, and whether they could lead to a research question.
- Popular issues. There may be certain popular issues that are worthy of investigation. An examination of newspapers or social media sites may indicate such issues. Choose a quality newspaper or magazine and identify the relevant sporting issues of the moment, and explore those issues as a basis for your research. Often you may be able to explore such issues from an academic perspective. You will find that the media will tend to report on what is happening, so you could

develop that by exploring why it is happening. You don't have to focus on the national media; often local or regional media will provide you with rich sources of ideas. Alternatively have a look to see what is popular on social media and what relevant blogs are discussing.

- Your own history and personal characteristics. What are your own strengths and interests? In what subjects are you both knowledgeable and interested? What about your own career aspirations? If you are interested in a career in sports marketing then it would be a logical idea to undertake research in this area. If you would like to become a coach or teacher, then undertaking a related piece of research will not only give you valuable experience, but will also be beneficial for your CV. In terms of your own history, do you have an in-depth knowledge of a particular sport for example? Maybe you have acted as a sports volunteer, and would like to use that knowledge.
- Brainstorming. Brainstorming is a good way to develop topics. Discuss potential ideas with others, and use this interaction to develop, critique and refine possible questions. Write down as many words as you can think of related to the areas of sport that interest you. Then write words such as 'why', and 'how', and see if any questions emerge. Do not critique or judge ideas while going through the process, the aim is simply to generate as many areas as you can.
- Your tutors. Your tutors will have their own research areas and areas of expertise, and they will generally be extremely happy to supervise in these areas. Talk to your tutors, and see if they can guide you in the right direction (although it is not necessarily their role to provide you with a question). Read some of their publications, and think about whether you could make your own contribution to their research. This approach has the advantage that your tutor will have an extensive knowledge of the subject area, and working with them in their specialist area can be a particularly rewarding experience.

When you have identified a topic and have undertaken some preliminary investigation, it may well seem that your topic has already been explored in some depth, and there may be little scope for original research. If this is the case – and it is very likely that it is – you should not be discouraged. As I noted earlier, almost all research builds upon and uses existing theories and ideas. Often, your originality comes not from generating new ideas and theories, but in using existing ones in an original way. Veal (2006) provides a number of examples of how you could do this:

- Geographically. Certain theories may have been developed and empirically tested in one area but have not received the same attention elsewhere. Thus, you may find research focused on sport in the USA. Undertaking similar research in the UK would provide you with the basis for an original study. Alternatively, existing research may have examined sports provision in an urban context. You may wish to carry out similar research in a rural setting, which again would form the basis for an original study.
- Socially. You may find that certain social groups have not received as much attention as others. Existing work may focus exclusively upon men, and exclude women, or you may find a certain theory that has not been applied to the elderly, or to the physically disabled, for example.
- Temporally. A theory may have been developed a number of years ago, thus its relevance in contemporary society could be investigated. Comparing the findings would be an original study in itself. You may also come across a study that took place some years ago. Collecting more up-to-date data may also form the basis for an original project.
- Contextually. You may find existing theories from outside the field of sports studies that have yet to be applied to the sport context. Alternatively, you could revisit existing research using new theories and assess whether such theories have greater explanatory power.
- Methodologically. You could collect different data to explore a phenomenon. An example may be if you find a theory that has been tested quantitatively, and apply a qualitative research design, or if you collect data using in-depth interviews rather than questionnaire surveys. Thus the issue of originality should not be a major stumbling block to your choice of topic. What you should be careful of, however, is undertaking research where the theories are so well established that you are certain as to your findings before you even start the research!

The next stage, after deciding upon the initial topic, is to begin developing a focused research question. One of the continual complaints of examiners of research projects is that the research question chosen is too broad. Stating that 'I would like to research the growth of Western sports in China', for example, is too broad and lacks direction. Which sport are you interested in? All sports, or just one of them? What exactly is it about the growth that you are interested in? Are you interested in the whole of China, or a particular region? What is the timescale of the research? The research question is vital for a good piece of research. Without a good, focused question, it is almost impossible to carry out research successfully. De Vaus (2001) suggests some guidelines to focus your question that can be applied to sports research, and these are outlined in the following section.

DEVELOPING A RESEARCH QUESTION: ALCOHOL USE BY SPORT STARS AND THEIR STATUS AS ROLE MODELS

Jones (2014) provides an interesting account of how his research question about the relationship between alcohol use by sport stars and their status as role models emerged from both his academic and personal interests. He explains how he initially found questions related to ethics and morals to be the most interesting he encountered during his early studies, leading him to specialise in the ethics of sport. He then became interested in negative and sensationalised newspaper coverage of sport stars within the press. Through being able to apply his own academic background to a current issue that was receiving a lot of media attention, he was able to identify first a broad research problem – that of the effect of vices on sport stars' ability to be role models – and second a number of specific research questions, such as the extent to which individuals were morally responsible for their actions.

Focusing your research question

1   Define your core concepts. If you are discussing participation in sport, what exactly do you mean by participation? Do you mean participation in all sport? Or just organised sport? Does it mean regular or sporadic participation? The term regular itself is problematic: for example, participation once a year or once a day could both be

termed 'regular'. Unless you can clearly define or specify your core concepts, you cannot develop your research question. Any ambiguity over your key concepts needs to be removed.

2   What is your timeframe? Are you interested in the contemporary picture, or do you want to measure changes? If so, over what time period?
3   What is the geographical location? One community, facility or sports team? Are you going to compare one or more locations?
4   What aspect of the topic are you interested in? If you are researching the commercialisation of the Olympics, for example, are you interested in the economics, the experiences of the athletes, or the impact of commercialisation upon spectators?
5   What is your unit of analysis (i.e. the 'thing' that you collect data about and from which you draw conclusions)? Is this a person (e.g. sports participant or fan), an organisation (e.g. a sports team) or an event?

The following is an alternative process that you may find useful in helping you to focus your research question:

1   Write out your provisional research question. For example, you may be interested in leadership styles, and whether different types of coaches demonstrate different leadership styles in a coaching situation. This leads you to a provisional question such as 'Do coaches have different leadership styles depending upon whether they are coaching team or individual sports?' While the area is appropriate, it is, as it stands, far too broad as a question. There are, for example, many different types of coach, and the term 'sport' is so broad as to be essentially meaningless in this case. The question clearly needs more focus.
2   Identify the key terms (or 'concepts' – more about them in Chapter 6) in the research question, for example 'coaches', 'leadership styles' and 'sports'.
3   Try to identify whether you can break down each of your key terms into more focused categories or make them more specific through a clear definition. The first thing to do is to focus the subject of your research, in this case the concept of a coach. Either through exploring the literature, or developing your own thoughts and ideas, you may break down coaches into 'male and 'female' (see Figure 4.1). Knowing that there may well be gender differences in leadership styles (Eagly and Johnson 1990), you could make the decision to focus on male coaches to remove this variable. This still leaves a very broad concept, so you may then decide to focus through making the decision to concentrate

on amateur coaches, as you may well have greater access (see 'CAFE', page 52). Finally, you could focus on experienced, rather than novice coaches, as measured by their total number of coaching hours.

4   The next stage is to do the same with any other key terms. As noted above, the concept of 'sport' needs much more clarification. There are several ways to do this, one of which may be to identify which sports you are focusing on, for example golf and squash as individual sports, and soccer and hockey as team sports, or, you may simply decide to take a broad sample from a range of sports. More focus can then be achieved by following the process above, for example deciding to focus on non-elite sport (again due to access issues). As before, gender issues lead you to focus on one area (female sport), and a further variable might occur – that of the level of the team being coached, so to remove that, the decision is made to focus on junior (i.e. under 18) sport. You can then identify a number of alternative research questions.

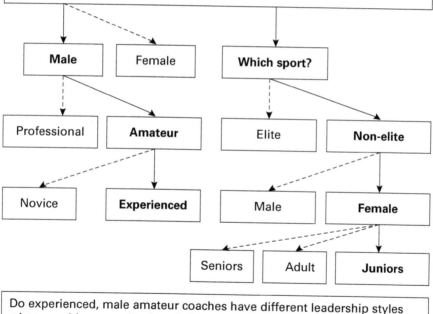

Figure 4.1 Focusing a research question

Thus, by identifying alternative categories, and making choices between categories, the question has been focused from:

Do coaches have different leadership styles depending upon whether they are coaching team or individual sports?

to

Do experienced male amateur coaches have different leadership styles depending upon whether they are coaching team or individual non-elite female junior sport?

Which is considerably more focused, and will lead to a much greater chance of success in terms of the overall research project. Don't ever look at your research question and think it's too focused. This is incredibly rare, and by far the most common issue is too little focus. It's very tempting when developing your research question to look at the expected word count of the submission (for example 10,000 words) and worry about how you are ever going to write that many words about a focused topic. Don't worry. Your problem is more likely to focus upon keeping it *within* the word count.

Even when you have decided upon a research question that you think is appropriate, it is not always possible to undertake the research to answer that question. You will also need to consider the 'CAFE' acronym (Clarke *et al.* 1998) to ensure that it is feasible. CAFE refers to four considerations, these being complexity, access, facilities and resources, and expertise.

- Complexity. A particular topic may involve several competing theories, or just one complex theory. Could you do the topic justice within your research if this is the case? This may be the case if you are limited by time or resources, or in terms of your own personal background. Do you have the ability to undertake a research project in the chosen area? A good research question involves writing a lot about very little, rather than the other way round, and an overly complex question will make this difficult. A simple, focused question is often better, as it allows you much greater depth.

- Access. How easy will it be for you to collect the data? How realistic is it, for example, to send questionnaires to professional sports club owners or elite athletes and expect a response? There is often a tendency to be over-optimistic in terms of response rates and so on, and you need to consider this carefully. Generally you are better advised to use more accessible samples. There is no correlation between the level of sport and the quality of research at all, so a study on casual amateur basketball players is just as worthy as a study on Olympic athletes. Simply having access to an elite sample doesn't necessarily make it a good area to research.
- Facilities and resources. Consider the demands of your research. Will you, for example, require extensive travel to carry out interviews? Will you require any specialist video or IT equipment? You need to identify any specialist resources at this stage.
- Expertise. Consider your expertise. Would you be happy undertaking a research project that necessitated the use of complex multivariate analysis? If you are undertaking a sport management programme, then do you have the relevant sociological or psychological expertise to examine group behaviour in sport? If you are undertaking a dissertation as part of a taught programme, it may well also be wise to consider the expertise of your tutors, especially if they are particularly renowned in a certain field.

Gill and Johnson (1997) note that your topic should have, if possible, a symmetry of potential outcomes. What this means is that your research will have value no matter what your findings are. You may be interested to find out whether there is a relationship between the anxiety of umpires before a game and how many years they have been umpiring. If there is no such relationship, then the findings may have little interest or relevance. One solution is to amend the research question, for example to investigate the causes of stress among umpires. In this way, the findings will have relevance and interest whatever they are. In this instance, you need also to confirm any assumptions; for example, you are assuming that umpires actually experience stress! You should also avoid research questions that can be answered with a simple 'yes' or 'no'.

CHOOSING YOUR RESEARCH QUESTION

When you are developing your research question, you should continually refer to the following list:

- You must have a focused research question. Vague statements of intent such as 'I would like to investigate violence in sport' are inappropriate. If you cannot clearly state your research question, then you will need to revisit your intended research.
- The research question must be of interest to you. Research projects take a considerable length of time and effort, and you should ensure that you have sufficient interest in the research to be able to read extensively around the topic, spend time, effort and resources collecting data, and write a substantial research report at the end. If you lack sufficient interest, then your chances of completing the research project are correspondingly reduced.
- The research question must be feasible – especially in terms of time and resources. Most projects have a limited time allocation, and you should ensure that yours is achievable within the time.
- The data must be obtainable – you should not assume that by sending questionnaires you will get a response. Sport governing bodies, for example, are often inundated with requests from researchers, and may be unlikely to respond.
- You must have the appropriate skills to undertake the research.
- You must be able to cope with the relevant theoretical and conceptual issues related to the research.

You will also need to develop a number of research objectives. These are the objectives that you will need to achieve to answer the overall research question. They are essential in guiding your approach. Your research question may be something like:

Are there any gender differences in the extent to which sport fans identify with their favourite team?

Your objectives may be as follows:

- To determine and apply a suitable operationalisation of (or a way to measure) fan identification.
- To measure the identification of a representative sample of male fans.
- To measure the identification of a representative sample of female fans.

- To compare the identification of both groups to ascertain whether there is a statistically significant difference.

The objectives thus set the scene for the project, and identify the key tasks that need to be undertaken. They are also useful in providing a measurable set of targets for the researcher. Note that they about what will be achieved, rather than the processes that you follow, so something like 'to distribute a questionnaire among fans' is not an objective. When setting your objectives, remember the 'SMART' acronym. Thus, your objectives need to be:

- Specific. You must be clear about what is to be achieved.
- Measurable. You must be able to identify when such objectives have been achieved.
- Achievable. You must have a likelihood of success in achieving your objectives.
- Realistic. The objectives must be realistic in light of any constraints that you may face, such as time, money or access.
- Time bound. You should be able to set specific targets for when each objective is to be accomplished.

Thus, if you are interested in the cultural impacts of professional sport, you may set yourself an objective 'to review the literature on the cultural impacts of hosting a mega-event'. While the review of literature is a necessary process, by relating it to the above list, we can see that it is, in fact, not an objective. The outcome needs to be clear with any of your objectives, rather than the process.

**SETTING AIMS AND OBJECTIVES:
SPORT ENGLAND AND ECONOMIC ANALYSIS**

Sport England (2002) wanted to evaluate the economic impact of sport in a number of regions. To achieve this, they set a number of aims:

- To develop a standard economic model that can be applied to all of Sport England's regions to enable comparability between regions and provide a relatively easy mechanism whereby the assessments can be updated to enable us to measure change over time.
- To conduct economic impact of sport assessments in all nine Sport England regions.
- To report the economic value of sport in these regions.

To achieve these aims, a number of research objectives were developed. These included:

- To identify the regional sources of relevant economic data.
- To identify where relevant economic data is not available at the regional level.
- To collect relevant regional economic data.
- To apply an appropriate model to the regional economic data, initially from three pilot regions, in order to ascertain the overall economic impact of sport in each region.
- To modify the model, as necessary, based on its application to the three pilot regions.
- To apply the modified model (if modifications are required) to the regional economic data from the remaining six Sport England regions.

These objectives can all be related to the SMART concept, and, as such, provide a clear, focused and measurable set of objectives that together allow the aims of the research to be achieved.

Writing a research proposal

An important part of many research projects, and a key element for anyone wishing to secure funding for research, is that of writing a research proposal, or a plan of the intended research programme. Even if it is not a formal requirement, it is still a useful exercise to undertake during the early stages of your research. You should try to produce your own research proposal as soon as you have determined your research question even if one isn't needed. This proposal can be very effective in clarifying in your own mind the overall aim of the project, and how you intend to achieve that aim, and to identify potential problems with the study. Requirements for a research proposal will depend upon its purpose. However, there is certain information related to the research process that will generally be required:

- A clear statement of the overall aim and associated objectives of the research.
- A statement outlining the originality, relevance and importance of the research.

- A brief description of existing work in the area.
- A clear link to be demonstrated between the aim of your research and that existing work highlighted previously.
- How the research is to be conducted, the research design to be adopted, anticipated methods, and an indication of the likely sample group, sample size and recruitment methods.
- How the data collected are to be analysed.
- The anticipated timescale for the research.
- Any specific requirements in terms of access, financial requirements, etc.
- Any ethical issues that may be relevant to the study.

Weaknesses in research proposals

In many cases, your research proposal will be assessed, by either your institution or funding body. If it is not, then you need to assess it yourself, which can be a difficult task. One way to do this is to compare your proposal against a set of criteria or headings. Leedy (1985) has listed the weaknesses commonly found in research proposals, and by comparing your proposal with his list, you may be able to identify weaknesses in your own proposal. The most relevant weaknesses identified are as follows:

1 The research problem:
   - The problem is of insufficient importance or unlikely to produce any new or useful information.
   - The hypothesis upon which the research is based is unsound, or is not based on any existing evidence.
   - The problem is more complex than the investigator appears to realise.
   - The research is overly complex, with too many elements.
2 The approach:
   - The proposed methods are not suitable to achieve the research objectives.
   - The description of the approach lacks specificity and clarity.
   - The research design has not been carefully considered.

- The statistical aspects/details of the means by which qualitative data are to be analysed have not received sufficient attention.
3   Personal characteristics:
- The researcher does not have adequate experience or ability to undertake such a project.
- The researcher seems unfamiliar with recent or important work in the area.

Even if you are not required to produce a research proposal for assessment, it is essential that you consider the points raised above, and critically assess your own research proposal. Even better, get a colleague to play 'devil's advocate' and critically question your proposal. It is much better that problems are identified at this stage, when you can change your approach, than after you have begun to carry out the research.

Summary

1   The first stage of the research process is to identify a research topic for investigation. This can be a difficult task, but it is important to the success of the subsequent research project.
2   There are a number of sources of ideas for research topics, the main ones being existing literature, social concerns and popular issues, personal characteristics and preferences, brainstorming, and debate with your tutor.
3   Although some degree of originality is desirable, the extent of this originality is often overestimated. There are a number of ways by which research can be seen to be original; for example, through applying existing theory to new situations, or using different approaches.
4   The topic should lead to a focused question, which forms the 'vertical thread' of the research.
5   Answering the research question must be achievable, in terms of the personal abilities of the researcher, access to an appropriate sample, and the availability of any specialist resources or equipment.

58

Activity

You should come up with two or three possible research questions. Assess each question, and for each:

1 Identify whether you feel that it is a good research question. Try to identify the limitations of each of the questions and rewrite accordingly if necessary. Apply the principles of Figure 4.1 to your own questions to see how they could be focused.
2 Identify a series of objectives that would need to be met to answer each question.
3 Assess those objectives in terms of SMART; that is, are they specific, measurable, achievable, realistic and time bound? Again, rewrite if necessary.

ABOUT YOUR RESEARCH PROJECT

The activities above are all important to your research project and you should carry them out with reference to your proposed question. You should also undertake the following tasks:

- Refer to the criteria mentioned earlier in the chapter (see the box 'Choosing your research question'), and assess whether your research question fulfils these criteria.
- Can you relate your question to the four elements of CAFE outlined in this chapter?
- Is your question sufficiently focused, or can you focus your question further in any way?

5 Reviewing the literature

This chapter will:

- Introduce the role of the literature review, and outline why it is an important part of any research project.
- Describe some of the sources of literature available to you.
- Describe some guidance for assessing the quality of the literature that you identify.
- Provide guidance on writing and presenting the literature review.

Introduction

Before commencing data collection, and before you have even considered your research design, it is important that you become knowledgeable in your chosen subject, understanding not only the appropriate concepts, but also the work that has previously been done on the subject. As Jankowicz (1995, pp.128–9) notes:

> *Knowledge does not exist in a vacuum, and your work only has value in relation to other people's. Your work and your findings will be significant only to the extent that they are the same as, or different from, other people's work.*

Reviewing the literature is an essential task in all research. No matter how original you think the research question may be, it is almost certain that your work will be building on the work of others, often from outside the field of sport. It is here that your review of such work is important. A literature review is the background to your research, where you demonstrate a clear understanding of the relevant theories and concepts, the results of past research into the area, the types of methodologies and research designs employed in such research, and areas where the literature is deficient. This reading will then form the basis for a significant element of your research report, where your understanding of this literature is presented in a written form. Thus, the literature review can be seen to consist of two different aspects:

1 The actual process of locating, reading and organising the appropriate academic literature.
2 The presentation of the information collected above as part of the research report.

Thus, you will need to read and report the literature critically, demonstrating an awareness of the state of knowledge on the subject, both in terms of the strengths of existing literature, and any weaknesses, or omissions. You also need to place your own research question within this context. The reader of your research needs to understand and appreciate your research in the light of existing work. This understanding will come from your definitions and explanations of key terms and concepts, and your review of the research that has been undertaken, and the key findings emerging from that review.

Purposes of the literature review

You should consider the purposes of the review of the literature before you start, as this will make it easier for you to identify the things that you should be looking to do. These are as follows:

- To demonstrate your familiarity with, and knowledge of, the subject.
- To determine the extent of past research into the subject matter. It is important to determine at an early stage whether you have identified an original research question, or whether you are simply repeating past research. The review of literature will enable you to identify gaps in existing research, which can be filled through new research.
- To provide an outline of the relevant theories and concepts important within your research project. Using an appropriate theory is important to allow you to have a framework within which to explain your findings. Concepts are important so that others may share and understand your findings in the knowledge that the often rather abstract phenomena under investigation are clearly outlined. The literature will be able to help you gain a clear understanding and definition of appropriate concepts, as well as provide an indication of how they have been used in past studies.
- To focus the research question. As I noted in the previous chapter, one of the biggest problems faced by researchers is they struggle with the research because they have not sufficiently focused or delimited their research question. By reading how others have focused their research and gaining an understanding of the types of questions that have been tackled in the past you will be able to gain ideas on focusing your own research question, and get an indication of the type of research questions that have been successfully answered in the past. This will help you if you undertake the activity based on Figure 4.1 (page 51).
- To develop a hypothesis, if appropriate. Your hypothesis is the predicted outcome of the research based upon logical reason or existing evidence. The literature will help you to develop this hypothesis. Otherwise your hypothesis is likely to be no more than educated guesswork! Hypotheses are generally associated with positivist, deductive and quantitative research, and normally not a feature of qualitative research.

- To help ensure all relevant variables are identified. A thorough search of the literature should identify all the moderating variables that may have an influence upon the research programme. Identifying such variables allows you to ensure that they can be addressed within your methodology.
- To identify methodologies and methods that have been successfully utilised in the past. You may be able to gain valuable insights into how others have approached similar questions, for example in terms of sampling methods, data collection instruments, methods of analysis and so on (although you should avoid simply replicating existing methodologies without careful consideration).
- To allow comparison of your findings with the findings of others. You may wish to compare your findings with the findings of other researchers, thus you will need to identify these. You will also need to identify how your work builds on the work and adds to knowledge.
- To inform the reader that you are competent to undertake research in that particular area.

Quantitative and qualitative studies – the differing nature of the literature review

One of the differences between a quantitative and qualitative study is in their use of the literature. Generally (although not always), this is in terms of the scope of literature presented within the review itself. Quantitative studies tend to have a more extensive review that covers the full range of relevant literature, and are guided very much by the content of the review in terms of what is measured, the formation of hypotheses, and the subsequent analysis of data. It is rare for new literature to be brought in to any discussion. It is perfectly acceptable, however, for a qualitative study to present a briefer 'overview' of the literature, and to allow the relevant literature to emerge from the themes developed from the data (see Chapter 14 on qualitative analysis), demonstrating an 'ongoing dialogue with the literature' (Jones *et al.* 2013, p.32), allowing new literature to be presented within the discussion. Indeed some qualitative researchers see the inclusion of too much literature at the start of a project as bad practice, potentially biasing the subsequent research. The literature review is still, however, important in identifying a gap within knowledge, and to locate the research question within that gap within qualitative research provide that the data maintain primacy.

Sources of literature

One worry that researchers beginning a project often have is that there will be insufficient literature available, especially if the question is tightly focused. In practice, this is rarely (if ever) the case. A search through library databases and search engines will soon demonstrate the large amounts of information available to you. The problem tends to lie in where to find the appropriate information, and what to do with the information when you have found it. There are a number of varied information sources, of which the main ones available to you are as follows.

Books. These are an obvious source of information, and often are the first information resource to be utilised. Books are good for providing a broad overview of the topic, and describing the key research that has been undertaken. However, they are unlikely to be sufficient, as they will often lack depth or focus upon the topic being researched, especially if they are general textbooks. Another potential problem is that books may become out-dated, especially in a rapidly developing field such as sports studies. Thus you should ensure that you are looking at the most recent texts available. Books will often provide you with a list of further useful sources in their reference section or bibliography. I would strongly recommend using books to develop your initial understanding of the topic, before focusing on more specialist journals as your understanding develops.

Peer-reviewed journals. These will be an important source of information to you. You should be using contemporary articles from peer-reviewed journals wherever possible. Peer reviewing is a process whereby the work submitted for such journals is assessed by independent, expert reviewers, who ensure that the publication is of the appropriate standard. Such journals will show the up-to-date research being carried out in the area, and you should ensure that you have identified relevant articles

64

within them. Most journals will now publish their latest articles online before the print copy, and it's always worth having a look through these.

Conference papers. These are often more difficult to obtain, and the quality may not always be as high as with journal articles, as they might not have gone through any peer review process. However, they do often provide useful insights into the type of research being carried out in the field, especially in terms of work in progress, or developing fields of study. If you can actually attend conferences in your subject area, then this is an excellent method of identifying the most up-to-date research being carried out.

Past theses. These can provide large quantities of detailed information. You can search relevant indexes, such as the Index to Theses (www. theses.com). Once you have identified relevant theses, they can be obtained using interlibrary loans, or they are becoming increasingly available to download from university digital repositories, or EThOS (Electronic Theses Online System). Older studies will often be provided in microfiche form, so you will need access to a suitable reader.

Newspapers/magazines. Newspapers and magazines can provide useful and up-to-date factual data. Back issues of quality newspapers are also widely accessible, either online or stored on CD-ROM. Care needs to be taken with such sources, however, as reports may be distorted in some way, and such sources generally do not provide a bias-free perspective.

Trade journals. Trade journals will provide useful data on current trends and developments in the area; however they are not aimed at an academic audience. They may not be available as widely as academic journals in libraries, and you may need to contact the relevant association directly if you require particular issues.

Finding the literature

Much of the relevant literature will be indexed within various databases or search engines, which can then be searched using one or more keywords. The search will provide information about articles containing that keyword so you can decide whether the article is relevant to your research, and enough detail will be given for you either to locate the article in your library, or to obtain it from other sources. You may also be able to use a citation index, which will identify which other works have cited a particular article themselves. Searching electronic sources is not a guarantee of being able to find all of the relevant literature. It requires careful planning. You should, beforehand, write down all of the key terms that may be appropriate to your research project, including variations. Identify alternative words for each key term (for example 'coach' and 'instructor', or 'fan' and 'spectator'), and note variations in spelling (for example 'behaviour' and 'behavior', 'organisation' and 'organization').

There are a number of databases and search engines that you can use to search for relevant literature. This is not an exhaustive list, so check with your librarian for any other sources of information. Some of the databases will be freely accessible; others will require you to log on using a username and password. If this is the case, see your librarian to find out how to get these details.

- Google Scholar. This provides a straightforward way to search for literature across many disciplines and sources, including journal articles, books, abstracts and theses, from academic publishers, professional societies, online repositories, universities and other web sites. This is an excellent starting point for your literature search. Google Scholar also ranks results based on factors such as where they were published, and how often and how recently they were cited. There is the option to see who has used the articles you find as well, using the 'cited by' function, which provides both further relevant literature for you, as well as also providing some clues about the worth of the research (although remember that more recent articles will be cited less than those that are older).
- SportDiscus. This contains references to journal articles, books and conference papers from a variety of disciplinary approaches, such as sociology, psychology, physical education and so on, from 1975 onwards.
- ASSIA. This is a general database focusing on health, psychology, sociology, economics, politics, race relations and education; however it does contain a number of useful sports-related articles.

- PsychInfo. If you are undertaking research into the psychological aspects of sport, then you should access this database. It contains psychological abstracts from key journals from as early as 1887.
- Sociological Abstracts. This will help you locate articles that have approached sport research from a sociological perspective.
- Pro Quest. This will enable you to locate articles in the areas of business, management, economics and finance.
- British Humanities Index. This is a general index covering a variety of newspapers and journals. It will be of interest to those studying sport from a humanities perspective, such as those researching sports history.
- Zetoc. This provides access to the British Library's Electronic Table of Contents (ETOC), and provides details of a range of journal articles and conference proceedings.

You can also search:

- Library catalogues. You can search for items on library catalogues. However, such searches are less detailed. They are a good means to locate appropriate books, but generally less useful to locate journal articles.
- Internet searches. There is a wealth of information on the internet. However, searching the internet can be a difficult and time-consuming task. As I suggested earlier, there is also less 'quality control' of sources, and you need to be extremely cautious in your use of the internet.
- Publishers' web pages. These can be a valuable resource, and will often list journal contents pages as well as relevant books. For example, *http://www.routledge.com/sport* will provide up-to-date information on the sports-related books produced by Routledge.
- Reference lists. One method to quickly develop your bibliography is to locate a relevant, up-to-date book or article. Read the list of references at the end of the work, and identify important sources from the references. Obtain those references, and repeat the process looking for new sources. Using this method, you can build up a substantial bibliography in a relatively short period of time. Be aware, however, that this is unlikely to identify very recently published sources.

Faced with this wide range of sources in a number of different formats, beginning the literature review will seem a daunting task. Unfortunately there is no one best way of finding the literature to begin with. The important advice to be aware of before you start is as follows:

- Start as soon as you possibly can. If, for example, you are undertaking a final-year undergraduate dissertation, then you should be looking to begin your literature search towards the end of the preceding year if at all possible. Be systematic as far as possible, but always be on the lookout for relevant literature that you may uncover by accident.
- Have a search strategy – don't randomly enter search terms in an ad hoc manner.
- Don't restrict your search to sport related sources. Use the wider discipline or other fields to help you, for example explore the wider literature from management if you are researching leadership in sport, or some of the more generic literature on consumer behavior if you are interested in peoples' decision making processes when buying sports equipment.
- Keep careful records of your searches and of any literature that you uncover from the beginning of the search. Do not imagine that you will be able to locate relevant details later (see the box on page 70 on maintaining your references).

Focusing your literature search

A common error, especially in student research, is to focus too early in the initial review of literature, and become discouraged at the apparent lack of available sources. Thus, the student who is interested in why women begin to play rugby union, may – quite correctly – identify theories of socialisation as a possible theoretical framework. The student may then carry out a search for literature on women's socialisation into rugby, find relatively little of it, and become discouraged by the apparent lack of material. An alternative, and more appropriate, approach would be to avoid becoming too focused in the initial search for related literature, for example by undertaking a search using the following general strategy:

- Theories of socialisation in general. You may find research into the socialisation of women into many social groups seemingly unrelated to sport, such as into education, medicine and business. You must remember, however, that both the underlying theoretical frameworks used by these authors and the methodologies that have been used in such research may provide important background information to you, so do explore alternative fields of study.
- Socialisation into sport. There is a wide range of literature based upon socialisation into sport; for example you may find the work of Donnelly and Young (1988) of interest. They investigated the processes by which males were socialised into two sport subcultures, those being rugby and rock climbing. They provide a useful symbolic interactionist perspective of socialisation that you may find helpful that can then be used within your specific study.
- Socialisation of women into sport. You may now focus further by investigating the research carried out on the socialisation of women into sport, to identify any particular gender issues that may be appropriate.

By the end of this search, even if no literature has been found specifically on the socialisation of women into rugby, you should have achieved the following:

- To have gained a clear understanding of the theoretical concept of socialisation.
- To have an overview of the nature of existing research into the socialisation of women into various social groups, research into the area of socialisation into sport, and the socialisation of women into sport.
- To have identified gaps in the research, which can be used to help you develop your research question. You will then attempt to fill a gap in the literature with your own research.
- To have developed ideas about the possible findings of your own research.
- To have developed ideas on possible methodologies that could be used based on past research.

Assessing the literature

Once you have identified the literature, then the next stage is to read, digest and fully record the literature that you have found. While you read each article, you should consider both the content of the article, and the implications for your own research project. You should make notes while you are reading each article with this in mind. You should also carefully record the full reference for your bibliography. Once you have read and made notes on several articles, then you should consider organising them into a structured form, with articles taking a similar approach being placed together.

CASE STUDY

MAINTAINING YOUR REFERENCES – USING ENDNOTE

You are going to collect a lot of literature throughout the research process, and it is crucial to maintain accurate records of the literature you find on an on-going basis, and not to rely on being able to construct your reference list at the end of the project. I would strongly recommend using EndNote. This service allows you to collect, store and manage your references, either through an internet-based service (EndNote Online) or as downloadable software (EndNote Desktop). You can insert your references automatically into Word documents, and create reference lists in the required format. You can also download references from many databases straight into EndNote.

It is important that you don't assume that each piece of literature you find is of the same standard. Not every source you locate will be appropriate, for example it may lack relevance or quality. You will need to critically assess the quality of the literature that you obtain, and ensure that you pay more attention to works that are more relevant, or of higher quality, than to works that are only partially related, or of lower quality. There are a number of criteria that you can use to assess these factors, including:

- What is the source of the literature? Is it from an international, peer-reviewed journal or a trade magazine, for example? A peer-reviewed article should carry more weight than the trade journal, yet the trade journal may be more useful in identifying areas of study that are of immediate relevance and practical interest. A trade journal will, however, generally lack any sort of academic or theoretical framework.
- Who are the authors? Are they recognised experts in the field? What other work have they published in this area? What are their qualifications for writing such a book or article?
- Is that piece of literature referenced elsewhere in other articles on the subject area? If so, are such references positive or critical? How many citations has the work received elsewhere, and in what type of publication?
- When was the article published? Is it a recent article or has it been superseded by other research?
- Using your own knowledge, how good do you think the article is?

Be prepared to be critical of the research both in your reading and the write-up of the literature review if you can support your criticisms. This may especially be the case if the work is several years old, and theories and methods have since developed, or if your source has not been subject to an academic review process.

Assessing internet sites

If you are going to use internet sources in your literature review, you need to assess them in terms of their quality and usefulness. Anyone with the correct equipment can put a web page on the internet or edit existing pages (such as Wikipedia), and being available on the internet is no guarantee of accuracy or quality. Do not, however, rule out the use of such sites as many will contain valuable and high quality information. Therefore it is your responsibility to assess each site. There is no fool-proof way of doing this; however, there are a number of questions that should be asked:

- Who produced the page? Was it:
  - An academic institution or publisher?
  - An official company or organisational web page?
  - A personal web page?
- What are their qualifications or credentials for producing such material?
- What was their purpose in producing the page? Might this impact upon the content in some way?
- Who was their intended audience?
- Has the content undergone any form of refereeing process?
- When was the page last updated?

How do I know when I have collected enough literature?

The question of when you have sufficient literature is a difficult one to answer. There is no set amount of literature that you should include, and some research projects will contain much more literature than others. You should aim to reach what could be referred to as 'saturation', that is when reading new articles, you are coming across the same references again and again. If you have all of these references, then this suggests that you have covered the main literature sufficiently. Do make sure, however, that you keep an eye on the key journals in your field throughout the remainder of the research programme to ensure you don't miss anything relevant that is published after you have completed your literature search (although you would not be penalised for not including an article that was published close to your submission date). The number of sources you cite is also not always an indication of the quality of the literature review, and it is how you use the sources that is more important. A well-constructed review with fewer references is far preferable to a poorly written review with many references, and thus the question of 'how many' should be less important to you than 'how have I used them?'.

Writing up the literature review

You will need to communicate your review to readers of the research report, so that they also can judge how your research fits in with existing work. A common error is to produce an annotated bibliography, rather than a review of the literature. An annotated bibliography is a list of sources, each of which is followed by a brief note or 'annotation', stating and evaluating the content of the research, and its usefulness to your own research project. Instead, your review should demonstrate to the reader the underlying state of knowledge in the area, highlight the gaps in existing research, and demonstrate how your research fits in to the state of existing knowledge. This will involve much more of a synthesis of the literature into a coherent review rather than a list of sources.

The literature review should start with an introduction, identifying the topic under investigation and providing a context for the review. This should be followed by the main body, where the literature is reviewed. Often it is useful to begin the review with a broad overview of the relevant ideas, concepts and definitions, before narrowing down to more relevant works. Note that a literature review is not simply a list of relevant literature, but an organisation of past work into a logical structure under common themes or ideas. A literature review where each paragraph focuses upon the work of a single author is usually a sign that the researcher has produced an annotated bibliography rather than a literature review. Whereas an annotated bibliography is ordered by author, a literature review should be ordered by idea, and past research should be grouped together under appropriate categories, for example:

- Studies involving similar research problems.
- Studies involving similar methodologies.
- Studies coming to similar conclusions.

Those studies that are seen as more significant to your research should be dealt with in more depth than those that are less relevant, for example you should give information about the aim of such studies, the methodology which was employed, including details of the sample, and a clear outline of the findings. For less important works, a brief summary of the findings may suffice. It is important that the literature review is not just a generic review of the subject matter. It should, instead, be a review of the state of knowledge of the subject area of your research project, and the implications of such knowledge for your own programme of research. At the end of each section, you should summarise such implications for your research project. Finally, you should conclude the literature review with an evaluation of the current state of knowledge in the area, and summarise the relationship of your study to the literature, suggesting your anticipated findings – if appropriate – in the form of a hypothesis. You should ensure when you write up your literature review that you make it clear how the work of others is related to your study. It is also important to assess where the literature may be deficient. If your study is filling a gap in existing literature, for example, you should aim to clearly demonstrate that such a gap exists in your review, and relate your research question to this gap. I recommend that you select a highly regarded journal publishing sport-related research, such as the *Sociology of Sport Journal* or the *Journal of Sport Management*, and read as many literature reviews as possible to get a 'feel' for what a well-written review is like.

HOW NOT TO WRITE A LITERATURE REVIEW

The following is a hypothetical example of a poorly written literature review:

> There are a number of authors whose work is important in this respect. Birrell and Loy (1979) have described four functions of the media with regard to sport: providing information, integrating society, arousal, and escape. Gruneau (1989) found that entertainment was a key element in mediated sport, with the focus upon spectacle, drama and risk. These factors were emphasised by the producers of televised sport. Nixon and Frey (1996) suggested that television has affected sport in a number of ways, such as improving its popularity, increasing salaries, and enforcing rule changes to make the sport more viewer-friendly. Coakley (2009) has also described the effects of the media upon sport. This research will look at the effects of television on one particular sport, that of tennis, to determine how the sport has been affected by the media, and assess the findings in light of the works mentioned above.

Note how the review is simply a list of works, with no effort by the author to relate the works to his or her own research question, or to identify themes or patterns within the literature. Additionally, the author devotes exactly the same amount of space in the review to less important sources as is given to important sources.

74

Structuring your literature review

Effectively, in most cases, the literature review needs to tell the reader three things:

1 What is known about the subject under investigation.
2 What isn't known.
3 What the research question is, and this is how it relates to points (1) and (2) above.

When you write a literature review, you should follow the same guidelines as with any piece of academic writing. Always begin the review with an introduction, and complete it with a summary – you should also introduce and summarise any major subsections of the review. If you feel that it is appropriate, you don't have to have just one literature review chapter – break it up into two if necessary. Remember to cite all sources, and make sure that they are all included in your bibliography or reference list. Avoid statements such as 'it is a well-known fact that ...', or 'it is widely believed that ...' unless you can provide evidence to support such claims. You should also avoid the use of jargon or technical terms, and attempt to make the review as readable as possible. As with any piece of work, ensure that you check your grammar and spelling carefully, as mistakes will detract from the quality of the review.

A further point concerns the inclusion of direct quotations. It is all too easy to insert large numbers of direct quotations into a review, and this can seem a quick and easy method to boost word counts. However, it can be a debatable practice. I would recommend that you keep the use of direct quotes to a minimum, and only use them when the original author has stated a point in such a clear and concise manner that you are unlikely to be able to state the point as well yourself. Otherwise, use your own words as far as is possible. A literature review should demonstrate your ability to demonstrate an understanding of the broad state of knowledge in your area, not your ability to cut and paste from varied sources. In terms of the actual structure, it is often a good idea to follow the same sort of approach as I suggested with finding the literature. Start with a broad perspective, and introduce your key concepts and theories. Gradually focus your review so that it becomes more specific to your particular research question.

CORNWALL COLLEGE
LEARNING CENTRE

**THINGS TO CONSIDER WHEN WRITING
THE LITERATURE REVIEW**

- Gain familiarity with the subject before writing, but start writing as soon as you can.
- Construct your bibliography as quickly as possible – identify and access the key sources that you will need at the earliest possible stage.
- Allow yourself much more time than you initially think you need to write the review. It is rare to complete the review in one go, and generally a number of rewrites are necessary. You should be prepared for this.
- Work from an initial plan, but be prepared to continually refine and develop your structure as your understanding progresses.
- Include subheadings where necessary to guide the reader.
- Summarise your key findings regularly in longer literature reviews. Don't let the reader have to do the work in terms of understanding the point that you are trying to make, make it clear to them.
- Be selective – include literature that is relevant to your research, and spend more time on higher quality or important articles.
- Extract the relevant information from each study you use. Do not spend an inordinate amount of time describing each study in depth.
- Be up to date. Look at the dates from your bibliography. Are the key works recent, or are they several years old? If the latter, are they still 'cutting edge' or have they been superseded by more recent works? Do include, however, 'classic' works in your field wherever appropriate. Simply because a piece of work may be ten or more years old doesn't mean that it doesn't have value. Use your judgement!

Referencing other authors

You will need to reference the work of others throughout your literature review (as well as the rest of the report). A reference consists of three elements:

1 The text or idea that has come from the original author, whether quoted directly, paraphrased or summarised. For example, the

76

following extract from Hutchins and Rowe's (2012) book *Sport Beyond Television* discussing the image associated with the typical sport journalist may be included within a literature review (inside quotation marks, as it is a direct quote):

'The stereotypical image of a print sports journalist, though, has proven resilient. Crudely exaggerated for the purposes of argument, it is that of a star-struck, sports-loving newspaper-man who "got lucky" by being paid to do what other people who aren't celebrities or dignitaries have to pay for – watch sports events from the best seat in the house.'

2   The abbreviated reference within the text to show where the statement originated. Normally (although not always) this is placed at the end of the statement, for example: '… from the best seat in the house' (Hutchins and Rowe 2012, p.125). This shows that the authors of the quote were Hutchins and Rowe, the source was their text published in 2012, and the quotation was taken from page 125. If you had simply taken their ideas and rewritten them in your own words, then the page number is not necessary. If you had referred to two different works by the same authors, both published in the same year, then you should differentiate between them using 2012a and 2012b.

3   The full reference in the reference list or bibliography at the end of the research report. The in-text reference allows the reader to identify the full source of the quotation or idea here, for example: Hutchins, B. and Rowe, D. (2012) *Sport Beyond Television*. New York: Routledge.

The full references are then placed in alphabetical order in either a reference or bibliography section at the end of the research report. Thus, the reader can, simply by looking at the reference within the text, locate the full details of the source material.

There are a number of purposes of referencing. Jankowicz (2000) provides a useful list to outline the key purposes:

- To attribute a quotation. If you use the words of other authors, you must enclose them using inverted commas, and provide a reference, rather than claim them as your own. As I noted above, for such direct quotations you should also provide the page number, as is shown in the following example:

'until fairly recently, most sociologists, and social historians, and many anthropologists have neglected sport as a potentially fruitful object of study' (MacClancy 1996, p.1).

- To justify an important statement. If you are making an important claim, then you should support your claim with a reference. An example of this may be that you want to make the point that sport has, for a long period of time, been overlooked by many as an area of academic study, and therefore write a statement to this effect. At the end of the statement you should support your claim through providing a reference to other authors who agree:

Sport has been overlooked for many years as a legitimate area of academic study (MacClancy 1996).

This shows that you have not simply made up the statement, but that it is a statement based on a source. This source can then be checked by the reader. Note that a page number is not required, as you are not directly quoting the author.

- To justify your approach. You may wish to justify your approach to your research by referring to similar authors who have taken the same approach or used similar theories or models with successful results.
- To demonstrate breadth of reading. A further advantage of consistently referencing your sources is that you can demonstrate the breadth of your reading (although you should resist the temptation to throw in references at every available opportunity). It is tempting to include references that you have not actually read or used as a strategy to boost your bibliography, and demonstrate more reading than you have actually done. This practice should be avoided.

Wherever possible, you should use the original text or article rather than use what is referred to as secondary referencing. If in your reading of Hutchins and Rowe (2012) you find a reference to the work of Marshall and colleagues (2010) on the rise of lunchtime audiences for internet sport, for example, then it's important that you don't give the impression that you've directly accessed and read the text by Marshall *et al.* yourself, which would be misleading. To avoid such potential problems, you should acknowledge in the text that what you are citing or quoting has come from another source (which you have actually read). Thus, rather than write: 'As Marshall *et al.* (2010) note, the growth of the lunchtime audience for internet sport content is a prominent example of change in the way sport is consumed', which would suggest that you have read their work yourself, you should acknowledge the true source of your information. For example: 'As Marshall *et al.* (2010, cited in Hutchins and Rowe, 2012) note, the growth of the lunchtime audience for internet sport content is a prominent example of change in the way sport is consumed'. Thus it is clear that you have got your information from Hutchins and Rowe, rather than the study of Marshall *et al.* You should then only include Hutchins and Rowe (2012) in your list of references or bibliography.

Mistakes often made in the literature review

Many inexperienced (as well as more experienced) researchers find writing the literature review a difficult part of the research process. Unfortunately there are no easy answers, and it is the case in most instances that you will have to rewrite and restructure the literature review a number of times. Even well-known authors publishing in top journals will have rewritten their literature reviews a number of times. For this reason, I recommend that you commence the writing of the review as soon as possible, rather than leaving it to the last minute. The mistakes commonly made include the following:

- Making the review simply a list of past studies, or producing an annotated bibliography.
- Not relating the literature review to the study, and making it simply a general review of the subject matter rather than providing background to your study.
- Not taking time to identify the best sources, and give such sources due emphasis, while at the same time overemphasising weaker or less important sources.
- Failing to appreciate the relevant wider (i.e. beyond just that which is sports related) literature.
- Relying on secondary rather than primary sources of literature (textbooks rather than journal articles, for example).

- Uncritically accepting the findings of existing literature rather than critically evaluating them.

One of the most common errors with the literature review is that it reads as a stand-alone piece of work about the research topic, without relating to your research question, that is it should not be just a review of the literature per se, rather it should be a review of the literature in terms of how it relates to what you are doing. By reading the literature review, the reader should get a sense of how your research question has 'emerged' from the literature, By the end of the literature review, there should be a clear indication of what you are doing, how it is adding to existing literature, and, if appropriate, what you could expect to find.

Identifying secondary data

Using existing literature can help you not only in terms of providing the background to your own data collection, but can sometimes provide you with the actual data to answer your research question. Data can be separated into two forms: primary data – data that you have collected yourself, through your own questionnaires, interviews, observations and so on – and secondary data, which have already been collected by others. Secondary data come in a wide range of forms, such as research articles, annual reports, government publications and so on. When searching through the literature you may find secondary data which will help you answer your research question. This may be either raw data, or data that have been previously analysed. Using secondary data can save a significant amount of time and effort, and may even produce higher quality data than if you had collected it yourself. There are potential problems with using secondary data however. First, you need to ensure that the data collected was valid and reliable, and not subject to any serious methodological errors. Second, you need to be aware of when the data was collected, and whether it is still appropriate, or is dated. Remember that secondary data were collected with a different purpose from the one that you are to put them to, and you should always be aware that the original author of the data may have been subject to particular constraints, had a particular agenda and so on. You need to be

80

aware of any issues, and state them clearly in the final written report (it is no good being aware of the limitations if you don't make this awareness clear to whoever will assess your report). Things you may wish to consider when using secondary data are:

- Who collected the data? What were their qualifications for doing so?
- What was the purpose of the data collection? Were there any factors that may have influenced the collection and presentation of the data? Was the data collection sponsored by an outside organisation, for example?
- How were the data used or analysed by the original author?
- Have the data been used as secondary data in any other research project of which you are aware?

USING SECONDARY DATA TO EXPLORE PROFESSIONAL ATHLETES INVOLVEMENT IN CHARITABLE FOUNDATIONS

Tainsky and Babiak (2011) wanted to explore and profile professional athletes participating in philanthropic activity within the NBA. To do this, they were able to use existing data on the athletes including their salaries, ages and other relevant information on NBA players, gained from a number of reliable sources such as ESPN.com, often using more than one source to corroborate the data. They then used Google, the Foundations Directory and the NBA Players Association web page to identify which players had established foundations and followed relevant hits to decipher the name of the foundation, its mission, and the existence of a link to the player's team foundation. Information on which players established foundations was verified by the Sports Philanthropy project. They then examined tax forms to identify the amount of support player foundations were giving and to whom. The data allowed them to determine that older, higher-paid athletes were more likely to create foundations and that association with a charitable team also predicted athlete philanthropy.

How do I know if I have completed my literature review?

You will reach a stage where you think you are approaching the end of your literature review. If so, you need to ask yourself the following questions:

- Have I covered the key literature? If I have read recent journal articles in the field, are there any sources used by the authors of those journals that I should have used?
- Is the literature review up to date? Have I covered recent sources? Have I included any out-dated material?
- Do I relate that literature to my research question?
- Have I included literature that contradicts, as well as supports my viewpoint?
- Have I produced a critical assessment rather than a descriptive review?
- Have I organised the review into a logical and coherent structure rather than simply producing a list of literature?
- Have I identified the gaps/weaknesses in existing literature?
- Does my research question emerge clearly from the literature?

Summary

1 It is important that you develop your own expertise in the subject matter at an early stage in the research process. This is done through locating, reading and reviewing relevant literature.
2 The written review of this literature also forms an important part of your written report.
3 In your search for literature, you should not restrict yourself. Broaden your search at the beginning, and be prepared to seek out different sources. You should then gradually focus your review towards your particular research objectives.

4   Always relate your review to your own research question, rather than simply making it a review of the state of knowledge in the area per se.

5   Existing literature may, in certain cases, provide you with existing data with which you can achieve your research objectives.

Activity

The best way to get a 'feel' for what a literature review involves is to read as many reviews as possible. Choose a subject area of interest to you. Locate a number of sources pertaining to the topic using each of the search methods discussed in this chapter, including the use of a database such as Sport Discus. Ensure that at least two articles that you locate are recent pieces of research from peer-reviewed journals. Read the articles, and pay special attention to the literature reviews. You should note how the author has structured the review, what has been included, and how the review is focused towards the overall research question.

ABOUT YOUR RESEARCH PROJECT

Once the first draft has been completed, you should critically assess your own literature review. Consider the following points:

■ Have you included all the key works or are there any omissions that you are aware of?

■ Have you used a range of sources, including journal articles, or have you relied upon a few textbooks?

■ Have you synthesised your reading into a comprehensive review of the literature, or have you just listed descriptions of past research?

■ Have you related the review to your research question, and considered the implications of the literature review for your research question?

■ Have you correctly referenced all of your sources, paying particular attention to secondary referencing?

Further reading

Hart, C. (2009) *Doing a Literature Review: Releasing the Social Science Research Imagination*, London: Sage.

Ridley, D. (2012) *The Literature Review: A Step-by-Step Guide for Students*, London: Sage.

Theobald, W. and Dunsmore, H. (2000) *Internet Resources for Leisure and Tourism*, Oxford: Butterworth-Heinemann.

84

6 Theories, concepts and variables

This chapter will:

- Introduce the role and importance of theory within your research project.
- Describe how you should be able to relate your question to existing disciplines in sport.
- Describe how to develop a conceptual framework for your study.
- Introduce and define the concepts of reliability and validity, describe the relationship between the two, and outline their importance within a quantitative research project.
- Discuss the terms reliability, credibility, trustworthiness and rigour, and discuss their importance within a qualitative research project.

Introduction

For many students, the importance of theory within a research project can be a difficult issue, yet it is one of the most important considerations, and in many cases underpins the entire research project, especially if you are taking a deductive approach to your research. While it might be tempting to go into the data collection stage of the research as soon as possible, you do need to spend some time thinking about the theories and concepts involved within your study, and developing an appropriate theoretical framework within which such data can be analysed, interpreted and explained. This chapter introduces some of the issues related to choosing your theoretical framework, and relating this theoretical framework to your study. Theories themselves are constructed from concepts, and a key process here is to identify exactly what concepts are involved, their relationships to each other, and how they are to be investigated, so that your data can be related to your choice of theoretical framework. This is the process of developing your conceptual framework, and this idea will also be outlined. Finally, the issues related to how you measure your concepts, and the quality of such measurement, whether quantitative or qualitative, will be discussed.

Theories and theoretical frameworks

Theories are, simply, explanations of why things occur. If you drop an apple, it will fall to the ground at a particular speed. If you repeat the experiment, the result will be the same. All your results show is that an apple will fall to the ground at the same rate each time, and no more. This is, therefore, an example of very basic descriptive research. To explain why this is the case an appropriate theory is required. In this instance, the theory of gravity can explain your findings, that is to say why the apples all dropped at the same rate. The same theory could also be used to predict that any further apples dropped would also fall at the same rate. We can either identify the theory of gravity beforehand, and test it by dropping the apple in a deductive manner, or we could follow Sir Isaac Newton, who collected his data beforehand, according

86

to tradition, by observing the apple fall, and then developing his theory of gravity in an inductive manner, which could then be applied to other contexts (for example applying the theory of gravity to sports where it has a major impact, such as archery or gymnastics). Whichever way we choose, the data itself is of limited value. Only when it is related to theory can we explain the findings, and take our understanding beyond the basic descriptive level. It is therefore important that your research has a theoretical grounding if you want your research to be more than simply descriptive, and this will come from the theory that you choose to underpin your research project. At an early stage, you should be thinking carefully about your theoretical underpinning. As Yiannakis (1992, p.8) suggests:

> Research that is not theoretically informed, not grounded in the existing body of knowledge, or of the 'shotgun' variety that fails to raise and investigate conceptually grounded questions, is likely to generate findings of a narrow and ungeneralisable value.

Social theories, dealing with the behaviour of individuals who have free will, individual choice and who are subject to unpredictable events or occurrences, will clearly have less predictive power than those of the natural sciences. This notwithstanding, theory is significant to your research in being able to draw connections between concepts and developing explanation. Its role can be demonstrated using a relatively simple example. Imagine that you have come up with the following research question: 'Do sports fans identify more strongly with their favourite team when the team are winning?' It would be relatively easy to make the appropriate measurements (whether the team is winning and how strongly a sports fan identifies with his or her team) and collect data accordingly. The answer to the research question is likely to be 'yes', in that a sports fan is likely to identify strongly with their team when they are winning (I shall assume for the sake of simplicity that there are no other factors affecting this relationship). That, however, is the only conclusion that can be drawn from such research without a theoretical framework. You would be unable to explain this finding, that is to say why it had happened. Neither would you be able to predict the same finding in the future with any confidence. Thus, you would need to place your findings within an appropriate theoretical framework. In this instance it would be appropriate to use a theory such as social identity theory to make sense of the findings. One of the tenets of this theory is that we prefer to identify with groups that positively enhance our self-esteem, that is groups that are seen positively by others. With this theory, we could reasonably hypothesise that people would identify with their team (i.e. be a member of that particular group) if they are seen positively (i.e. by being successful). Using an appropriate theory, therefore, has allowed us to explain the findings. We could also use this theory to try to predict, to a partial extent, future behaviour in this context. Unfortunately, many research projects are examples of what Phillips and Pugh (1994) refer to as 'intelligence gathering'. This refers to the gathering and presentation of data, with no reference to any such theoretical framework. Essentially this is descriptive research, and simply describes data. For example, it would be relatively easy to collect data to answer the question 'what was the proportion of male to female participants at the 2012 Olympic Games?'. By using an appropriate theory, you may be able to propose a plausible explanation of why there were such differences.

Considering your approach

As I noted earlier in the book, sport, as a whole, can be studied from the viewpoint of a single discipline, or from an interdisciplinary or multi-disciplinary perspective. This means that there is no single academic subject that we can refer to as 'sports studies', but rather that there are a number of different ways of approaching sport academically, through the various disciplinary approaches. Thus sport can be studied from a sociological perspective, a psychological perspective, a geographical perspective, an economic perspective, as well as from multi and inter-disciplinary perspectives; the United Kingdom Quality Assurance Agency (QAA), for example, notes 29 different subject areas related to the study of sport.

Within each of these broad disciplines, there are a number of more specific fields, such as 'sport' itself, or 'physical activity', and more specific aspects of each field. Thus, sociologists may be interested in the aspect of socialisation into sport, or the relationship between sport and religion, for example. Each aspect will normally consist of a number of

88

theories, for example the aspect of socialisation into sport will include theories such as Donnelly and Young's (1988) model of group socialisation. Thus, in this particular instance we can see our broad disciplinary framework as follows:

Discipline	➤	Field	➤	Aspect	➤	Theory
Sociology	➤	Sport	➤	Socialisation into sport	➤	Donnelly and Young's (1988) model of group socialisation

If you are undertaking a deductive study, then you need to start thinking about your theoretical orientation, and to try to locate your ideas within this type of framework. Although this is something that you may develop as you read around your topic, it is important to be aware at an early stage whether you intend to approach your research sociologically, or using an economic approach, for example. If you are a keen hockey player then you may consider a proposal along the lines of 'I want to research whether the size of the crowd has an effect on the outcome of hockey matches'. If this is the case then you need to identify your disciplinary approach, in this case psychology. Through reading around the sport psychology literature you can then identify the relevant aspect (the specific application of the discipline). You can also, if possible at this stage, identify your specific theory. For example, in the above case the researcher may adopt social facilitation theory (Zajonc 1965). You should identify your theoretical orientation, and then apply it to the situation, for example:

Discipline	➤	Field	➤	Aspect	➤	Theory
Psychology	➤	Sport	➤	Crowd effects on performance	➤	Zajonc's (1965) theory of social facilitation

The thing to remember is that, rather than thinking about your research as a piece of research into 'football' for example, start thinking about the theory that you will be using in your research project. This can then be applied to the appropriate context. When you are developing this framework – what Jankowicz (2000) calls a 'provenance table' – you can work either left to right or right to left, or a combination of both at the same time using this approach. Thus you can start off intending to under-take a piece of research based on your own sport preferences, such as hockey. This is perfectly acceptable provided that you can complete the rest. Alternatively, you may consider that you would like to do a piece of research from a psychological perspective, as you may feel you have the appropriate interest and expertise. All that then remains is to iden-tify – most probably after you have begun reading around the subject – your theoretical grounding, such as social facilitation theory. Another alternative is to start with a theory that you are interested in, and then consider its application. The order of the process often doesn't matter, it's the outcome that is important, in that you identify an appropriate theoretical underpinning for the research, unless you decide to under-take a totally inductive approach to your research, but even then, an understanding of the possible theoretical approaches is always helpful, as discussed below.

Choosing an appropriate theory

At an early stage, it is likely that you may find it difficult finding appropriate theories, or deciding which theory is best for you. If you are undertaking a deductive study, you will need to have a clear idea of your theoretical framework at the outset. Even if you are undertak-ing an inductive approach, it is useful to have an idea of some of the appropriate theories that may be able to inform your study, without nec-essarily restricting yourself to any specific theories. There is no easy answer at this stage. It is generally a case of reading around the subject, and trying to identify which theories have been used in past studies. Your review of literature should alert you to the theoretical approaches adopted by other researchers in the past. Alternatively, you may want to read around some of the broader, non-sports-related literature and identify theories from these sources. As always, don't restrict yourself if possible, and be prepared to search through the wider sociological, geo-graphical, management-based literature and so on. Alternatively, you can always discuss this issue with your research supervisor or tutor, who may be able to put you on the right track. It's important to ensure that you choose your theory in because it is appropriate for your research

90

study, rather than it being, for example, one you find interesting, or easy to understand.

Concepts and conceptual frameworks

As I suggested earlier, theories are explanations with which we make sense of our findings. These explanations are built up using concepts. A concept is often easier to identify than it is to define. I would suggest that a concept is a shared representation of an object, a property, or a behaviour. Examples of concepts are age, intelligence, anxiety, self-confidence and so on. Having a shared understanding of what concepts actually are is important so that researchers may be able to understand or replicate others' work. Thus, when one researcher discusses a particular concept, such as 'intelligence', others will know exactly what he or she is referring to. By having a shared understanding of the appropriate concepts and conceptual framework this is possible. As Miles and Huberman (1994, p.18) describe:

> Categories such as 'sociocultural climate', 'cultural scene', and 'role conflict' are the labels we put on 'intellectual bins' containing many discrete events and behaviours. Any researcher, no matter how inductive in approach, knows which bins are likely to be in play in the study, and what is likely to be in them. Bins come from theory and experience and (often) from the general objectives of the study envisioned. Setting out the bins, naming them and getting clearer about their interrelationships lead you to a conceptual framework.

The conceptual framework describes and explains the concepts to be used in the study, not just those that build up your theory, but also those other concepts that may affect your findings. It outlines the relationships between concepts, and how they are to be measured. Thus it is important in helping you plan your overall methodology, what exactly you are going to explore, and why. Developing your conceptual framework requires five main steps:

1 Identifying the relevant concepts.
2 Defining these concepts.
3 Operationalising the concepts.
4 Identifying the relationship between variables.
5 Identifying any moderating or intervening variables.

We can illustrate the process with reference to a hypothetical research proposal based upon Chelladurai's (1990) work on leadership styles in sport, and the further work by authors such as Ehsani *et al.* (2012) who have subsequently built upon this body of knowledge in varied sports. Say, for example, that you are interested in whether there is any relationship between the leadership style of sports coaches, and the consequent success of the teams that they coach. Thus, your research proposal was based on the following question:

How does the leadership style of a sports coach affect the performance of their team?

The first step is to identify your concepts, or 'building blocks' within the statement.

In this instance, these are:

- Leadership style.
- Sports coach.
- Performance.
- Team.

Second, you must be able to define these concepts. This will help you clarify exactly what you are investigating. These definitions should, if at all possible, come from existing literature, and use commonly accepted definitions, so that your research can easily be compared to both existing theory and the findings of others. Here, 'leadership style' could refer to whether the coach displays autocratic or democratic leadership behaviour. 'Sports coach' could be defined as the individual with overall responsibility for the strategy, tactics and training of the team. 'Performance' could be defined as the team's win/loss record. The concept of 'team' would not have to be defined in this instance. Instead, it would be important, and more useful to the researcher, to identify the specific criteria under which teams would be included; for example, professional rather than amateur teams and so on.

At this stage, if there is sufficient evidence within the existing literature, you may want to suggest a hypothesis rather than a research question. As I noted in Chapter 2, a hypothesis is a suggested relationship between concepts to be tested empirically. A hypothesis generally requires four things:

1   It must be adequate. A hypothesis must be able to explain findings or relationships that are determined by subsequent data collection.
2   It must be testable. Unless a hypothesis can actually be tested empirically, then it has little value.
3   It should require relatively few assumptions, for example a hypothesis should not only be valid if a considerable number of conditions have to be met.
4   A good hypothesis must be better than other possible or rival hypotheses, that is it should have better explanatory power than alternative hypotheses that could be considered.

Whether you decide upon a hypothesis or a research question, the next step in developing your conceptual framework is that of operationalising your concepts. Operationalising a concept means deciding how that concept is to be measured. Being able to produce an outstanding piece of theoretical work as the background to your research is of little use if you are unable to subsequently test your theories empirically, or if your measurements of the concepts do not actually reflect what you think they do.

The term 'measurement' may suggest a purely quantitative approach. Even if you are undertaking a qualitative study, however, it is important to have a clear idea as to how you are going to 'measure' your concepts. If you were going to undertake a qualitative approach on the effects of leadership style, trying to explain why the coaching style had a certain effect on performance, then how would you identify and evaluate the qualitative data provided by the players of that sports team? Often, within a qualitative study, this is a more emergent process, and you will develop your understanding of the appropriate concepts throughout the data collection and analysis process (see Chapter 14 for a more in-depth account of qualitative analysis). This is obviously closely related to your epistemological assumptions, as outlined in Chapter 2, that is what you actually perceive to be 'valid knowledge'.

EMPIRICAL

Often you will see reference to good research as being 'empirical' in nature. This simply means that the conclusions drawn are based upon evidence (or data) rather than conjecture or speculation.

As is the case with defining your concepts, try to use generally accepted measures of a concept (you should be able to identify these when you are reviewing the literature). There are two reasons for this. First, it will allow you to compare your findings with existing literature more effectively, and second, it will give you confidence that your measures are actually valid and reliable (I will explain these terms later on in this chapter). Using the above example, leadership styles can be operationalised by using Chelladurai and Saleh's (1980) Leadership Scale for Sport, a 40-item scale that can assess the coach's leadership style. Operationalising the concepts of sports coach and team is not appropriate here, as the clear definitions provided at the first step should be sufficient, and it is simply a case of ensuring that your sample reflects these criteria. We simply need to know whether they are a coach, and of which team they are a coach. Operationalising 'performance', however, leads us into a problem of how such a concept can be accurately measured. I defined performance earlier in terms of win/loss record. This is an obvious way of measuring performance, yet is it a valid measure of performance? There are a number of factors that are of concern here, for example the obvious point that a team may perform well and yet still lose. Conversely, a team may play badly and defeat inferior opposition. Are we interested in the performance of the team as a whole or of individual players? Thus, the concept of performance is likely to be a problematic one in this research project and will need to be reconsidered.

DIFFICULT TERMS TO OPERATIONALISE

Within sports studies, there are a number of terms that are difficult to operationalise accurately, and you should critically assess your own operationalisation of your concepts. Such terms include 'performance', as noted above. Another common concept used rather vaguely is that of 'effect', such as in 'what has been the effect of commercialisation on the Olympic Games?' There are so many ways that 'effect' could be operationalised, that until you can clarify exactly what is meant by effect, and how it will be measured, the question is almost meaningless. In the same way terms such as 'change' or 'influence' are also difficult to define unambiguously. Thus, throughout stages 2 and 3 of the conceptual framework development, you should always ensure that you have clear, unambiguous and valid definitions and operationalisations.

Types of quantitative measurement

Quantitative data collection tends to involve the collection of factual or directly measurable data, yet, as I have just shown, this is not always straightforward. Although the data itself may be clear, how it is operationalised has important implications for the validity of the research (we shall discuss this concept in more depth later in this chapter), and also for how your data is to be analysed. Take the following example. You may be interested in the relationship between income and interest in sport. To determine income, a number of different questions could be asked:

1 What is your gross annual income? _____
2 Is your gross annual income:

- under £20,000   ❑
- £20,001–£25,000   ❑
- £25,001–£30,000   ❑
- above £30,000   ❑

3   Do you earn more than £20,000 per year?   Yes ❑   No ❑

These questions are asking roughly the same thing, but in a different way, and each will give you a different response. These responses will all provide accurate data, yet they may all result in different types of conclusion to your question. The questions above show respectively an example of interval level data, ordinal data and finally nominal data. Each of these types of data can be analysed differently, and may give you differing results to your research question. This will be dealt with in more depth in Chapter 13. At this stage, however, it is important for you to consider exactly what you will be measuring, and why such measurement is being adopted. Variables can be quantitatively measured in four different ways: nominal, ordinal, interval and ratio.

- Nominal scales group subjects into different categories. For instance, grouping football players on the basis of the team they play for is an example of a nominal scale. A nominal scale does not suggest any relationships between the groups, for example grouping together those playing for team X under the label '1' and those playing for team Y under the label '2' does not suggest that those in team Y are somehow different, or 'better' in any way. Nominal data is sometimes referred to as categorical data. If there is any order to the categories, however, then this becomes ordinal data.
- Ordinal data have a rank order, but do not indicate the difference between scores. Think, for example, of placement on a squash ladder. The person on top has performed better than the person second, and so on. Thus data is ordered, but there is no indication of how much difference there is between players. The player assigned a score of '1' is not necessarily twice as good as the player assigned '2'. They might be slightly better, or considerably better – there is no measure of this. The only information we have is that of the order itself.
- Interval data have equal intervals of measurement between values, for example a gymnastics scoring scale. There are equal intervals between each score, i.e. there is the same difference between an 8.00 and a 9.00 as there is between a 9.00 and a 10.00. It is not necessarily the case, however, that a 10.00 is worth twice as much as a 5.00.
- Ratio data are also based on order, with equal units of measurement, but they are proportional and have an absolute zero. For example, if a basketball team scores 50 points, then that is worth twice as much as a team that scored 25 points.

Once a concept has been operationalised, it becomes a **variable**. The two most important types of variables are independent and dependent variables. Independent variables are the presumed cause of the effect being researched; for example if gender influences attitudes towards violent sports, then it is gender that has the presumed effect upon the attitudes, therefore it is the independent variable. Dependent variables are those that can be explained by the effect of the independent variable, which in the above instance is the attitude towards violent sport. In the example I have already discussed, leadership style is predicted to influence performance. Therefore leadership style is the independent variable and performance is the dependent variable. You need to ensure that you correctly identify your independent and dependent variables, otherwise you run the risk of your conclusions becoming meaningless! One extreme example is that of the relationship between height and basketball players. You may be interested in why basketball players are taller than average. You may make the assumption that participation in basketball is the independent variable, and height is the dependent variable. It would be highly possible that you find data to support a relationship between the two variables, only by confusing the independent and dependent variables, your conclusion would be that playing basketball causes an individual to become taller! Although this is an extreme example, it highlights the dangers of incorrectly identifying your variables.

Therefore, superficially at least, it would seem that by measuring leadership style and performance we could identify whether there is a relationship between the two. Unfortunately, research is rarely this straightforward. Leadership style will not be the only influence upon performance. Other variables may also have an effect on the relationship, and we will need to identify them. These are called moderating, or extraneous variables. Thus, the next stage of developing your conceptual framework is to identify these variables. This is important, as too many unaccounted moderating variables will affect the validity of the research, in that any effect you identify may well be attributable to moderating factors. Moderating variables for our hypothetical example may include:

- Different opposition.
- Type of competition.
- Team factors (injuries, etc.).
- Weather.

- Influence of the crowd.
- Performance of the referee.

With so many moderating variables, it may be difficult to conclude that the performance has been affected as a consequence of leadership style. One option for the researcher is to systematically identify and remove as many moderating variables as possible, for example, researching teams involved in only one type of competition, using data collected from performances against one opposition team only, or to use a control group, where all variables are the same for both groups, with the exception of the independent, or treatment variable. Often, however, you won't be able to control for all variables. Therefore a further option is to measure such variables, and attempt to account for them in your analysis. However, this can often involve some very complicated statistics, and you need to consider your expertise in being able to undertake and evaluate such analyses. Generally, the more focused your research question, the fewer moderating variables you can anticipate, and this is a good reason for focusing your study as much as possible!

In some cases you will also encounter intervening variables. As the name suggests, these are variables that intervene between the independent and dependent variables. For example, rather than a direct relationship between leadership style (independent variable) and performance (dependent variable), it may be the case that there is another relationship involving a different variable:

Leadership style (independent variable) ➤ affects self-efficacy (intervening variable) ➤ affects performance (dependent variable)

You need to be able to control such intervening variables if you are to determine the true influence of the independent variable upon the dependent. Alternatively you need to assess the influence of the independent variable upon the intervening variable, and then the influence of the intervening variable upon the dependent variable. By ignoring intervening variables, you may well end up with an apparent relationship that does not actually exist; for example, there may be a strong correlation between leadership style and team performance, yet it is not necessarily the case that leadership style does affect performance.

98

Instead, it may be that self-efficacy is actually influenced by leadership style. Self-efficacy may also influence performance, with the consequence that the researcher makes a link between leadership style and performance that doesn't actually exist.

A similar, though slightly different, hypothetical case can also be provided to demonstrate some of the potential dangers in not assessing carefully the relationships between variables. You may be interested in the relationship between education and attitudes to competitive sport, i.e. education (independent variable) affects attitudes to competitive sport (dependent variable). You may well find a relationship between the two, and conclude that our attitudes towards competitive sport are shaped by our education. There may be an alternative explanation, however. Our education is often dependent upon the socio-economic class of our parents. What if our attitudes to competitive sport were also shaped by our socio-economic background? We would then have the following situation:

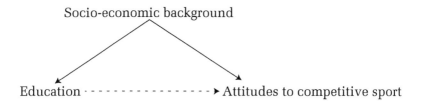

There may be no connection between education and attitudes towards competitive sport, yet your measurements would suggest there is (you may get a significant correlation between the two). This is an example of a spurious relationship, and you need to ensure that you are measuring relationships that actually exist.

Once you have identified your variables, you can graphically represent the relationships between them, as, for example, Madrigal (1995) did when he explored the idea of sport fan satisfaction (see Figure 6.1). This can be useful in clarifying the objectives of your research, and also to provide you with a framework for the analysis and interpretation of your data.

A CONCEPTUAL FRAMEWORK FOR SPORTS FAN SATISFACTION

Madrigal (1995) was interested in fan satisfaction in attending a particular sporting event. Rather than a single independent variable affecting satisfaction, he identified a number of relevant concepts from the literature that could have an effect, for example:

- Expectancy disconfirmation – or the difference between the expected and actual outcome.
- Team identification – or the extent of the involvement of the fan with their team.
- Quality of the opponent.
- BIRGing – or the tendency to 'bask in reflected glory' of the team. Madrigal suggested that this was influenced by the three factors cited above.
- Enjoyment – this was also influenced by the same three factors.

Madrigal's conceptual framework is graphically represented in Figure 6.1.

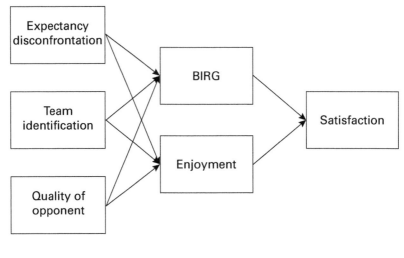

Figure 6.1 An example of a conceptual framework

Developing a conceptual framework is important for a **number of reasons.** As well as providing an overall framework to guide us through the data we need to collect, and our subsequent analysis, it also identifies potential issues before data collection commences. We can see that through developing our conceptual framework with the example presented here that our initial research question raises a number of potential problems, these being the difficulties in defining and operationalising performance, and also the issue of having too many moderating or intervening variables. By undertaking this process you can be made aware of these problems before the research commences, and can refocus your research topic.

The role of a conceptual framework does differ between quantitative and qualitative research. Whereas, in quantitative research I would always recommend developing your conceptual framework before data collection, it has more of a guiding role in qualitative research, and often, in such research, your data analysis will lead you to developing and refining your conceptual framework at the conclusion to the study.

Assessing quantitative research

The process above will allow you to identify the measurements that you are going to make. It is now a good idea to assess the extent to which your operationalisation of your concepts will actually provide a 'true' answer to your research question, that is the quality of your measures. Two key concepts by which the quality of quantitative research is assessed are those of reliability and validity, and these are often used to assess how 'truthful' a piece of research actually is.

Reliability

Suppose that you are researching brand usage of products of sports sponsors. You ask your sample whether they have used a particular brand and the affirmative response is 75 per cent. You ask the same sample the following day, and the positive response is 51 per cent. Which is the correct answer? Obviously, to be sure that you had the correct answer, you would have hoped for approximately the same answer on both occasions. Reliability generally refers to the consistency of the results obtained. A number of forms of reliability are important to the researcher, three in particular:

- Inter-observer reliability.
- Test–retest reliability.
- Internal consistency reliability.

Inter-observer reliability assesses the extent to which different observers would give similar scores to the same phenomenon, that is would two researchers measuring the same behaviour at the same time give such a behaviour equal scores? This is especially important if there are a number of people involved in collecting data for a research project; for example, if you had a team of researchers observing the ratio of hostile and instrumental acts of aggression in a sporting event, then how do you ensure that they would all assign the same interpretation to similar acts of aggression?

Test–retest reliability is the extent to which the research would provide the same measurements if repeated at a different time, thus the test would give the same score over and over again (provided what was being measured wasn't actually changing!). If a measurement was taken of an athlete's ability at a particular sporting task in week one, and then the same measurement was taken in week two resulting in a different score, then what is the athlete's true score on the task? Such a measure would be considered unreliable. One of your tasks as a researcher is to identify reliable measurements of the phenomenon under investigation. Internal consistency reliability refers to the extent to which each question within a measure is actually measuring the same phenomenon. Thus, if you are assessing an individual's commitment to sport using a five-item scale, that is five questions that are analysed together to give an overall measure, then all five questions should be assessing commitment. This is more important when you use scales as a measurement technique (I will discuss the use of scales in Chapter 8).

Threats to reliability

Reliability is a prerequisite for any successful research project. A number of potential threats to reliability exist. These include:

- Subject error. The subject may respond differently depending upon when they are asked to supply data. If you question sports participants as to their predictions of future participation, you may find that your results are different if you ask them directly before rather than directly after a match. This can be overcome by choosing a 'neutral' time to question them, for example in between matches.

- Researcher error. Two researchers may take slightly differing approaches to collecting the same data, which may result in different responses. If multiple researchers are to be used, then it is vital that each follows the same procedures. A study might involve, for example, multiple observers recording the number of aggressive tackles made by ice hockey players. If they have differing views as to what constitutes an 'aggressive tackle', then reliability will be threatened.
- Subject bias. Participants may give the response they think the researcher wants, or try and give the 'correct' answers. Anonymity should be stressed by the researcher if possible, as well as reminding the participant that there are no 'right' or 'best' answers.

Validity

A second important research issue is that of 'how do I know that the method I am using is really measuring what I want it to measure, and are my conclusions drawn from these measurements therefore valid conclusions?' This is the concept of validity. Validity has several different components. You should consider all of these components before rather than after you carry out your data collection.

Face validity – Does your method appear appropriate to measure what you want it to measure at first glance? Ask a sample from the population that you are going to research. Do they think it measures adequately the concept you intend to measure? Although establishing face validity on its own is normally not sufficient, you should not overlook this stage, as without face validity it is impossible to achieve the other components of validity. Face validity is also important to prevent participants becoming frustrated by having to answer questions that they may feel are irrelevant or unrelated to the subject under investigation.

Content validity – This is similar to face validity, except that it refers to the initial assessment from an expert's point of view. The expert should be aware of some of the more subtle issues and nuances of the concept, and be able to critically assess whether you have accounted for these.

Predictive validity – Can your measures predict future behaviour? If someone scores highly on a test of positive attitudes to sport participation, will it predict their future sporting behaviour?

Construct validity – Do your data correlate with other measures? If you have measured people's attitudes towards their own health and fitness, do the scores you obtained correlate with other scores such as attendance at health/fitness facilities, weight, diet, sports participation, etc.? This is the most rigorous form of validity, and you should aim to ensure this as far as possible.

VALIDITY AND RELIABILITY

Consider the following example. You are interested to know whether there is a link between how strongly a sports fan identifies with their favourite team, and how much they spend on merchandise in the stadium. The researcher may consider that the best measure of how committed a fan is to their team may be that of how many times a season they attend a match, and by using this as the independent variable then any relationship with spend (the dependent variable) could be determined. This, however, would not be a valid measure of sports fan identification. Fans on lower incomes may be just as committed but unable to afford to attend regularly. Time commitments with work or family may also reduce the frequency of attendance. Parents may attend regularly in order to take children to the game, but with no real interest themselves. Validity is thus likely to be low. Reliability is also an important issue here. If a different measure of identification is used, for example simply asking fans how strongly they identify with the team, then it is likely that fans would give differing responses depending whether the team had just won, just lost, or not played recently. Thus the research would lack reliability.

It is, therefore, important to find a method that is both valid and reliable. One solution to this is to use methods that have been found to be both reliable and valid by other researchers. In the above instance, it would have been appropriate to measure fan identification using the sports spectator identification scale, a scale that has been found to be both reliable and valid (Wann and Branscombe 1993).

104

The relationship between reliability and validity

Although I have looked at reliability and validity as separate concepts, they are related. A number of possible relationships exist between the two:

1   The measure is neither reliable nor valid. The lack of reliability means that sometimes the correct measurement is taken, but that measure lacks validity anyway. You may be interested in an individual's perceived competence at sport. You may wish to measure this by asking them to rate their competence on a poorly designed scale of competence. If you ask them after a heavy defeat, you are likely to get a different score than if you were to ask them after a good performance. Thus the measure is unreliable. On rare occasions valid measures may occur, although by chance. On most other occasions, however, a different, invalid score will be obtained.

2   The measure is reliable but not valid. The measure may be consistently measuring the concept incorrectly, thus reliability is achieved, but the scores are invalid. Using the example above, individuals may consistently report the same level of perceived competence in their sport after a number of separate heavy defeats using the same scale. Thus the measure is reliable as the measure results in a consistent score each time it is used.

3   The measure is valid but not reliable. Although unlikely, it is possible that the spread of unreliable scores averages out to give an overall valid score for the population. The scores for each participant may vary from test to test, but the overall mean is an accurate measure.

4   The measure is valid and reliable. This is what you must strive for in your research. Thus you need to identify a measure that accurately reflects the phenomenon, and results in the same score at different times.

Enhancing reliability and validity

As well as some of the considerations highlighted above, there are some other steps you can take to make your data as reliable and valid as possible. The first is to ensure all of the concepts to be measured are clearly defined and operationalised. If possible, use existing definitions and measures from peer-reviewed literature. Additionally, have the data collection instrument assessed by others with expertise in the subject area to obtain feedback. Think about other measures, or data that may be available to compare your findings with. Finally, consider the volatility of the context. If volatility is high, and behaviours, attitudes and so on are likely to fluctuate, then carefully consider how to account for this within your research design. Use existing studies to help you here, by seeing how other researchers have coped with such issues.

Assessing qualitative research

There has been considerable discussion regarding the means by which qualitative research is assessed, and growing consensus that the traditional concepts of reliability and validity are inappropriate. Lincoln and Guba (1985) are primary among those who have argued for an alternative view of assessing qualitative data using alternative criteria. These criteria include:

Reliability – this term is used in a different way to that normally associated with its quantitative application. Whereas, earlier in the chapter, reliability was referred to as the extent to which the results would be repeated, in qualitative research it refers more to the consistency of methods by which the data were collected. Within the interpretative perspective, interpretation may well differ between different researchers, or even between the same researcher at different times, thus concepts such as test–retest reliability become inappropriate. The key is to ensure sufficient detail is provided so that the study could be repeated by others, even if the findings would not be exactly replicated. Some authors (e.g.

Lincoln and Guba 1985) also use the term dependability to refer to this concept.

Rigour – related to the concept of reliability is rigour. Whereas reliability focuses upon the procedure, rigour examines the appropriateness of the methodological choices made by the researcher. Thus, as well as providing a detailed account of the methodology, choices such as the choice of theory, the selection of respondents, the method of data collection and analysis and so on should be justified by the researcher.

Credibility – this relates to how believable the findings and interpretations of a study are, and are related to the idea of internal validity. Do the findings accurately reflect participant's experiences? Would participants recognise the story presented by the researcher as an accurate representation? Would they see the researcher's analysis as credible? Credibility can, where appropriate, be assessed on an on-going basis by a technique known as 'member checking', where the researcher can discuss their interpretations and conclusions with participants of the study.

Authenticity – A study is authentic when the strategies used are appropriate for the true reporting of the participants' ideas, and the study actually helps participants, as well as readers, understand their social world. Authenticity consists of the following (Holloway and Wheeler 2009):

1 Fairness. The researcher must be fair to participants, gain their acceptance throughout the study and continued valid informed consent must be obtained.
2 Ontological authenticity. Both readers and participants of the study will have been educated in terms of understanding the social world that has been investigated.
3 Educative authenticity. Through the understanding from ontological authenticity, participants could develop a greater understanding of others within that social world.
4 Catalytic authenticity. Decision making by participants should be enhanced by the research.
5 Tactical authenticity. The research should empower participants.

Enhancing the quality of qualitative research

Jones *et al.* (2013) identify a number of strategies that you can use to enhance the quality of your qualitative research. These include strategies such as:

1 Keeping an audit trail of all parts of the process, including the key decisions made, and the underlying thought processes. Your audit trail should start at the very beginning of the process and cover every element, such as your search strategy for literature, your process of analysis and so on. The audit trail is something to be continually referred to, and assessed in terms of being able to help you understand your role as part of, rather than outside of the research, and how this involvement has influenced the whole process.

2 Member checking, as briefly outlined above. This is not always appropriate, for example it is difficult to discuss complex theories or ideas with participants, and some groups, such as young children, will not be able to provide feedback.

3 Triangulation within and between methods. Using interviews and observation together, for example to explore a phenomenon.

4 Searching for alternative theories and explanations. This essentially means being open to alternative ideas, theories and explanations rather than remaining focused on your initial assumptions.

5 Reflexivity, in terms of assessing your own characteristics, the relationship between you and the research, and how this relationship might impact upon all elements of the research process.

KEY TERM

REFLEXIVITY

As Brackenridge (1999, p.399) notes, 'reflexivity is becoming an increasingly important research skill'. Defined simply, reflexivity is a process whereby the effect of the researcher, and their own characteristics, background, values, attitudes and so on, upon the subject matter is taken account of. As Brackenridge notes, an assessment of the position of the researcher, and the power relations between the researcher and participants, is important in achieving an evaluation of the 'truth' of any findings.

Summary

1 Theory plays a crucial role in most research projects. Having an understanding of the importance of theory, and of the particular theories to be used in your research is an important element of the research process.

2 Developing your conceptual framework is also an important stage of the research process. Undertaking this process will allow you to clarify the important concepts within your study, their relationships to each other, and their measurement.

3 You also need to consider issues of validity (the extent to which what you are measuring actually reflects the phenomenon under investigation) and reliability (the extent to which the findings would be the same if the research were repeated). Validity and reliability are two of the key areas upon which your research will be assessed if you undertake quantitative research. If you are undertaking qualitative research, then how will you ensure your approach is trustworthy authentic, reliable, rigorous and credible?

Activity

Go back to some of the research articles that you have already read. Try to answer the following questions:

1 Can you identify the theoretical framework used by the author(s)?
2 What are the important concepts within the study?
3 How have they been defined?
4 How have the concepts been operationalised? Have the authors used their own measures or have they used existing measures from the literature?
5 Are there any moderating or intervening variables within the study? How have they been accounted for?
6 How have the authors addressed the quality of their measurements? How have the ideas of reliability and validity been addressed if the study is quantitative? Alternatively, if the study is qualitative, then are other measures of quality addressed?

Now is the time to start identifying and reading past studies that have also used the same theoretical approach. Reading such studies may help you with the next activity.

- Develop your conceptual framework, paying particular attention to the operationalisation of your concepts. How will you measure (either quantitatively or qualitatively) the necessary concepts?
- Can you identify any moderating or intervening variables? If so, how do you plan to account for these?
- What are the threats to reliability and validity in your research project if you are taking a quantitative approach? If you are taking a qualitative approach, how will you ensure the quality of the data that you collect?
- What steps can be taken to minimise the threats to the quality of your data?

7 Research designs

This chapter will:

- Describe the different types of research design that you may adopt within your research project – experimental, cross-sectional, time series, longitudinal, case study, grounded theory, action research, ethnography and autoethnography.
- Introduce the concept of sampling, and describe some of the sampling techniques that you may use.
- Describe some of the methods you may use within your research design to collect data from your sample.
- Introduce the concept of triangulation as a means of strengthening the validity of your research.
- Outline some of the ethical considerations to be made when considering your research design.

Introduction

Once you have developed your research objectives, clarified the role of theory within your research and developed your conceptual framework, two questions now need to be considered. These are:

1   What data do I need to provide me with the information to answer my research question?
2   What is the best way to collect these data?

You can approach your data collection in two ways. The first way is to go straight into a consideration of methods (the techniques of collecting data) and sample (those providing your data). The second (and far preferable) approach is to develop a carefully considered methodology that will allow you to systematically collect the data you need, while at the same time maximising the quality of those data. Your methodology is, essentially, the principles, practices and procedure underpinning the way in which you collect your data, and is thus strongly related to your epistemology, or philosophy of how knowledge is acquired. Thus, if you have taken a particular epistemological approach, then this should be reflected in your methodology.

METHODOLOGY AND METHODS

There is sometimes confusion over what is meant by methodology, and how this differs from methods. 'Methodology' is the overall research strategy that outlines how you go about answering your research question, justifying decisions about things such as what to study, who to study, what type of data to collect, what to do with that data, ethical concerns and so on. 'Methods', on the other hand, are the techniques to collect the data. Thus they are an integral part of a methodology, but a methodology consists of a lot more than just the collection of data through various methods.

The first stage in planning your methodology is to consider your research design. The research design is the overall 'blueprint' that guides the researcher in the data collection stages. In later chapters I will deal with the specifics of data collection – questionnaire design, interviewing and so on – but in this chapter I will focus upon the wider context within which such data collection occurs. Nine research designs are outlined, these being:

- Experimental.
- Cross-sectional.
- Time series.
- Longitudinal.
- Case study.
- Grounded theory.
- Action research.
- Ethnography.
- Autoethnography.

Experimental designs

Experimental designs are generally used to identify whether an independent variable has an effect upon a chosen dependent variable. The simplest form of experimental design involves the measuring of a variable (X1) from a single group (dependent variable), exposure of the group to a particular treatment (independent variable), followed by measuring the initial variable again (X2). The effect of the treatment is thus assumed to be the difference between the two measures. Obviously, you will need to be able to manipulate the independent variable to undertake such a design.

$X1$ ➤ treatment ➤ $X2$
Effect of treatment = $(X2 - X1)$

You may be interested in the effect of mental rehearsal upon shooting performance in basketball. The above design would involve you perhaps asking your participants to shoot 20 free throws. This would give you a success score of between zero and 20 (X1). You would then ask them to visualise a successful shot a number of times (the experimental treatment) before asking them to repeat the shooting task, again giving you a score out of 20 (X2). The effect of the treatment would then be calculated by working out the difference between the mean score after the visualisation and the mean score before, for example:

Mean score before visualisation = 11.25
Mean score after visualisation = 13.00
Effect of visualisation = (13.00 – 11.25) = 1.75

You may already have spotted the limitations in the above design, however. While it may be possible that any improvement may have been down to visualising the task, it may also be that simply by practice, the participants' performance on the task improved, and you have identified an apparent effect of visualisation that doesn't exist in reality. Alternatively, it may be that participants tired during the second set of shots, and the improvement caused by mentally rehearsing the shots was lost due to fatigue. One way to account for these moderating variables is to use a control group. This design compares two groups, which have been assigned on a random basis. One group is exposed to the treatment (for example being asked to mentally rehearse the shots). The other group (the control group) are not exposed to the treatment (they are not asked to rehearse the shots). The other moderating variables (such as practice, fatigue, etc.) should cancel each other out, as they are equivalent for each group. Measurements of the dependent variable are taken from each group before the treatment (pre-test), and again from each group after the treatment has been administered to the non-control group (post-test). The overall effect of the treatment is thus the overall difference in scores between each group:

Group 1
X1 ➤ treatment ➤ X2
Effect of treatment = (X2 – X1)

Group 2 (control group)
X3 ➤ no treatment ➤ X4
Effect of non-treatment = (X4 – X3)

Net effect of treatment = (X2 – X1) – (X4 – X3)

Thus, repeating our earlier experimental design, we could more accurately assess the effect of visualisation:

Mean score before visualisation (treatment group) = 11.25
Mean score after visualisation (treatment group) = 13.00
Mean score before visualisation (control group) = 11.00
Mean score after visualisation (control group) = 11.90
Effect of visualisation = (13.0 − 11.25) − (11.9 − 11.0) = 0.85

You could then test the results from the two groups to see if there were any significant differences (such issues of quantitative analysis are dealt with in Chapter 13). Experimental designs may be carried out in either a controlled (laboratory) setting, or in the natural environment. The main disadvantage with laboratory-based designs is the possibility that participants will behave differently if they are aware they are part of a research project. This may be overcome by undertaking the data collection in the natural environment. However, it may then be more difficult for you to control your variables.

Although experimental research designs are perhaps more closely associated with natural science approaches to sport, and are generally associated with the positivist paradigm, they can be used to great effect within social science research. Dijksterhuis and van Knippenberg (1998), for example, carried out an experiment where some participants spent a few minutes describing the behaviours, lifestyle, and appearance attributes of a professor, whereas others described those of a soccer hooligan. Participants then performed a multiple-choice general knowledge test. Those describing the stereotypes of the professor scored more highly on the test than those describing the hooligan.

Demonstrating causality using experimental designs

Experimental designs are generally used to demonstrate causality, that is whether the independent variable (such as reading about a football hooligan) actually causes the effect upon the dependent variable (such as performing worse on a subsequent general knowledge test). To achieve this, three conditions need to be met:

1 Covariation. This simply means that as the independent variable changes, then so does the dependent variable. Thus, if we ask individuals to mentally rehearse a basketball shot, then their performance should change as a consequence if causality is to be demonstrated.

115

2   Time order. It is important to ensure that the independent variable (i.e. the cause) actually happens before the effect upon the dependent variable, for example that performance does not start to improve before the mental rehearsal.

3   Non-spuriousness. As I explained in Chapter 6, some relationships may be due to the existence of another variable. Thus, all variables need to be accounted for. In the case of shooting basketballs, it may be that practising the task has led to the improved performance.

Cross-sectional/survey designs

Cross-sectional or survey research designs are perhaps the most common design within the social sciences, especially within sport-related research. As the name suggests, this design takes a cross-sectional sample from the overall population, for example taking a sample from a telephone directory. Data are collected once from participants, most commonly through interviews or questionnaires. Relationships are then identified from this data, and causal relationships may be suggested, which can then be generalised back to the population. You may also see cross-sectional designs referred to as survey designs in some textbooks (sometimes the terms 'survey' and 'questionnaire' are used interchangeably which is incorrect, as a survey is a research design, rather than a method). An example of a cross-sectional design may be that of investigating gender differences in sport participation. The independent variable (gender) cannot be manipulated by the researcher, thus an experimental research design is inappropriate. A cross-sectional design therefore has to be used. A cross-section of the population is sampled and relationships assessed by statistical analysis; for example, the findings may be cross-tabulated. It may therefore be suggested, for example, that female athletes prefer team sports, whereas males demonstrate much less of a preference for these. The strengths of such a research design are that it is convenient to the researcher with limited resources. Obtaining a cross-sectional sample is often easier than obtaining an experimental sample, attrition rates will be lower, and random samples may be taken from the population to allow the findings to be generalised to the wider population.

One recent example of a cross-sectional study was that of Cronin *et al.* (2013), who were interested in the availability and use of defibrillators in amateur sports clubs in Ireland following a number of high-profile cases of sudden cardiac arrest (SCA) in sport. Rather than sampling the population of every hurling, football and rugby club within Ireland, they took a cross-section of clubs, totalling 171 in total. This allowed them to generalise their findings about the number of clubs that had a defibrillator, the various barriers encountered by those that did not, and the extent to which clubs had used the equipment in an emergency situation. They were thus able to confirm the widespread availability of defibrillators in sports clubs in Ireland.

Time series designs

A time series design involves measuring the dependent variable over an extended period both before and after the effect of the independent variable, or the measurement of a single variable a number of times across a specified period, to assess trends in data. This can be over a relatively long period of time, for example the study of Jakobsen *et al.* (2013), who were interested in the impact of hosting the Olympics or a major football tournament on foreign direct investment (FDI). To do this, they explored levels of FDI over a forty year period involving measurements of FDI a number of times before and after hosting an event, allowing them to determine that hosting a football tournament seems to have a small positive impact upon FDI in the years preceding a football tournament, whereas the Olympics has no effect at all. Alternatively, a time series design can involve a much shorter period of time, such as the study of Lloyd *et al.* (2013) who explored the impact of sporting events on alcohol intoxication cases in Australia, demonstrating that increased cases of intoxication could be identified the day preceding sporting events such as the Melbourne Cup and the Australian Football League Grand Final, perhaps reflecting the drinking culture associated with these events.

Longitudinal designs

A longitudinal study is one that uses the same sample group and measures particular variables over an extended period of time. For example, you may wish to examine the behaviour of employees of a sports organisation after a change in managerial policy to assess the effects of such a change, or you may wish to track the sport-related skills of a cohort of students throughout their education. You would take a measure of behaviour at X1 (beginning of the study), X2 (after six months), X3 (after 12 months) and so on. The period of time involved could range from just a few weeks to several years. Chen *et al.* (2014a), for example, were interested in how destination image (DI) changed among sport tourists in the months following their participation in a marathon event at that destination. Through undertaking a longitudinal study collecting data two weeks, 10 months and 20 months after the event, they were able to identify that cognitive DI, that is the beliefs and knowledge about a destination, remained unchanged over a 20-month period, affective DI (related to the emotions generated about the destination) significantly declined in the first 10 months, but then rebounded in the following 10 months, while conative DI (behavioural aspects, such as an intention to revisit) showed a continuous decline over the 20 months.

Longitudinal research needs to be approached with caution. It can take more time and resources than cross-sectional research, and there is always the issue of attrition, or dropout from participants. One alternative, although not totally desirable, is to approximate a longitudinal study using a cross-sectional research design. This is done by asking the sample to recall past attitudes and behaviours, describe their present attitudes and behaviours, and predict their future attitudes and behaviours. This is obviously a questionable research design, but it may prove useful where issues of time constraints and attrition are important. Another alternative to the traditional longitudinal approach is to choose groups at different stages in their development. For example, you may be interested in how attitudes towards competitive sport are developed during adolescence. Rather than take measurements with a single cohort over an extended period of time, a sample could be selected from different age ranges at the same time, and these could be compared, which would essentially be a cross-sectional research design.

PROSPECTIVE STUDY

You may come across the term prospective study when reading about longitudinal or time series research. This means that the subjects of the study are first identified and then are followed over time as opposed to a retrospective study, in which subjects are identified after any intervention or treatment has occurred. Data is thus collected and analysed at the time any event takes place. Retrospective studies often follow a cross-sectional design. Prospective studies are stronger in terms of their reliability and validity, but require a much greater time investment on the part of the researcher.

Case study research

Case study research involves the intensive study of a specific case; a case refers to a specific instance. For example, you could undertake case study research on:

- An organisation.
- A sports team.
- A school.
- An individual.

The use of case study research is based upon the argument that understanding human activity requires analysis of both its development over time, and the environment and context within which the activity occurs. Case study designs are used to gain this holistic understanding of a set of issues, and how they relate to a particular group, organisation, sports team, or even a single individual. These issues are often researched using a variety of methods, over an extended period of time.

Gall *et al.* (1996) note four characteristics of case study research:

1 Phenomena are studied through focusing on specific cases.
2 Each case is studied in depth.
3 Phenomena are studied in their natural context.

4   Case study research takes the perspective of those within the case, rather than the researcher's perspective.

You may consider the use of a case study design in three instances according to Yin (2008):

1   Your theory suggests particular outcomes in a particular context. Thus, you would need to choose a case that provided such an appropriate context.
2   To be able to describe and explain a unique or rare situation.
3   To describe and explain a case that has yet to be studied in any detail.

A CASE STUDY OF AN INDIVIDUAL ATHLETE

The positivist dominance of early sport research focused very much on identifying larger sample sizes, the findings from which could be generalised back to the broader population under investigation. The case study approach seeks to identify patterns of behaviour, and phenomena within a particular context, and thus seeks depth, rather than breadth, meaning that small sample sizes, even to the extent of a sample size of one, are appropriate. Sparkes (2000) was interested in the experiences of elite athletes whose career had been prematurely terminated by injury or illness. To do this, he undertook a biographical study of a single athlete, using the symbolic inter-actionist approach of interpretative biography. This approach involved 'The studied use and collection of life documents that describe turning points in an individual's life' (Denzin 1989, p.69 cited in Sparkes 2000, p.16), studying the individual in depth from a variety of disciplinary perspectives, involving extended contact with the participant. Through extended interactive interviews, Sparkes was able to collect extensive data about the subject, allowing him to conclude that the subject's strong athletic identity actually acted as an 'Achilles heel' in terms of reactions to injury. Thus, although not directly generalisable to the wider population, the findings were able to suggest that by understanding this 'Achilles heel', health care and physical activity professionals would be better able to deal with athletic injury or illness, enhancing the recovery and experiences of the athlete.

The case study of a single athlete was able to provide such findings as it allowed the researcher a sense of the 'complete' experiences of the athlete, a depth of study often only available with the case study method. Had a larger sample been taken, then it would have been entirely possible that some of the depth, and thus understanding, would have been lost to the researcher.

There has been a growing acceptance of the use of smaller sample sizes over recent years, with a number of high quality studies utilising small numbers of participants. Anyone thinking that a sample size of one is too small for any meaningful research should read Barker's *et al.* (2011) text on single-case research in sport psychology, or many of the increasing number of excellent case studies being published in a varied range of disciplines.

Grounded theory designs

Grounded theory is strongly associated with the inductive approach to research (see Chapter 2), but has its own specific procedures of sampling and analysis. Rather than enter the research field or setting with any pre-determined theories or ideas, the researcher will usually have no more than a generalised idea of the intended outcomes of the research. Theory is still an important part of the research, but is developed from the initial data collection, rather than testing pre-determined hypotheses. These theories can then be tested, and the theory modified. More data can then be collected, and the theory continually modified through a combination of inductive and deductive approaches. This ensures that the theory is grounded within the data. While this approach has its undoubted strengths, it can be time consuming, and the continual process of data collection and analysis can mean it is often beyond the scope of many research projects. It can also be a risky strategy for student research. Grounded theory is also often misunderstood or conflated with inductive research, especially in terms of how difficult it is to carry out, especially with its use of specific techniques, such as constant comparison and theoretical sampling (Jones *et al.* 2013).

Action research

Action research is research that involves the researcher actively participating within a group or organisation to solve a problem or improve a process through a continual cycle of research and reflection. In some ways, this can be seen as analogous to the researcher carrying a series of experiments. The aim of action research is to bring about change, and for that change to be based on empirical evidence, for example the research of Rovio *et al.* (2012) who explored team building processes in Ice Hockey, choosing action research because of its abilities to 'enable opportunities for continuous planning, acting, and reflecting on the data-collection processes, feedback generated discussion, and problem solving' (p.587), making it an ideal design with which to approach the longitudinal nature of team building.

Ethnography

Ethnographic research is becoming increasingly accepted as a research design in social research into sport. I will deal with ethnography in some depth in Chapter 11, but will briefly outline the main concepts here. Essentially, ethnography involves the in-depth study of a group or community through immersion into the culture of that group, often for an extended period of time, using multiple methods of data collection. The aim is to understand the behaviour or culture of that group by seeing it through the perspective of members of the group themselves. This involves the researcher becoming part of the group under investigation. Data collection is much more flexible, and data are collected as and when appropriate from available sources.

Autoethnography

Autoethnography is an approach where the researcher focuses upon their own experiences, and connects those experiences with the wider context within which those experiences are enacted. Essentially the researcher becomes the primary participant and source of data. Autoethnography may lie on a continuum from the descriptive autobiography to the more analytical (and preferable) account that attempts to make sense of the experiences of the researcher in light of their connection to the wider social context. One excellent example that sport students will find of particular interest is that of Butterworth and Turner (2014) who have

122

presented an interesting account of the first author's progression from being an undergraduate sport studies student, to working within an elite performance analysis environment, and how stepping out of his 'comfort zone' allowed accelerated personal development. This is augmented by further autoethnographic data from the second author, explaining how the student's own progression related to his own educational philosophies and background as a lecturer on the programme. Despite the emergence of a number of high-quality autoethnographies, there remains some resistance to its use, and it is often accused of simply being a self-indulgent account, lacking interest to the wider academic community. As with any research design, done badly, an autoethnography can demonstrate a number of weaknesses. On the other hand, however, it can also provide a different and innovative way of examining sport. It is not, as may wrongly be perceived, an easy option, and can be a difficult task. As Edwards and Skinner (2009, p.190) suggest:

Researchers must be adept at identifying pertinent details, introspection, descriptive and compelling writing, and confronting things about themselves that may be less than flattering.

Anderson (2006) identifies five features of an autoethnography, these being:

1   The researcher is a 'complete member' of the social world being investigated, either through opportunistic means, such as having innate knowledge of the group through day-to-day involvement, or being thrown into a group through chance circumstances, or covet means, such as developing a research interest first, and subsequently joining the group as a means of data collection.
2   Analytic reflexivity, or the ability of the researcher to be able to locate themselves within the research situation, their effects upon it, and the subsequent impacts upon the analysis.
3   The researcher should be visible and active within the reporting of the research, and be seen as part of, rather than hidden from the analysis.
4   Although the self is the primary source of data, dialogue with others in the group is important to develop knowledge.
5   A requirement to an 'analytical agenda', that is the research should not simply report experiences, but attempt to analyse through reference to, refinement of, or development of theory.

Writing the autoethnography differs from other forms of academic writing, with a strong autobiographical element. As such, autoethnography requires the researcher to present themselves to an audience, and you need to be comfortable with this if this is an approach you are considering.

AUTOETHNOGRAPHY: EXPERIENCES OF ANOREXIA, EXCESSIVE EXERCISING AND PSYCHOSIS

Brendan Stone (2009), in a frank and honest paper, presented his experiences of anorexia, excessive exercising and psychosis as a teenager. His autoethnography involved an interaction between his 'current' self, that is the researcher whose role is to remember, describe and interpret, and his 'historical self', that is the subject of the research, which, in effect, has shaped the current self. Stone's autoethnographic approach was justified by the subject matter, something that is difficult to research at any time, noting (p.68) that:

> to experience trauma or madness is to traverse a realm which reason and narrative cannot adequately describe. I have long thought that the conventions governing traditional academic discourse could have been designed to exclude the unsettling truths of those who have known that strange country.

The interpretation of the historical self by the current self allowed Stone to identify insightful findings about his past, findings of which he was previously unaware, to link his anorexia and excessive exercise to the repression of traumatic memory, which are described within the paper.

There is no hierarchy of research design, in that certain research designs cannot be said to be better than others. The research design is, effectively, the link between the research question and the data collected to answer that question. Thus, the overall choice of design should be coherent with the aim of the research. Although the research design will normally be chosen once the question has been identified, you can also use a preferred research design to help guide you towards a question. Thus, you might be interested in experimental design, intrigued by the nature of an autoethnography, or be a member of a sports team, and thus be in a position to carry out ethnographic research. You can then use your preferred research design to aid you in developing your question. As long as the final link between your research question and research design is coherent, then the order in which you make your decision isn't that important.

Sampling issues

Once you have decided what information you need, and the design with which to collect data to yield this information, you need to identify from where the data is to be collected. In most cases, the population under investigation will be too large to collect data from each member. Thus a sample must be taken. A sample refers to a subset of a specific population. The population refers to everyone who shares those characteristics defined by the researcher as relevant to the investigation; thus, for a study on anxiety among professional male tennis players, your population would be all male tennis players. For quantitative research the purpose of sampling is, in most cases, to gain information about the overall population by selecting a smaller number of individual cases from the population. The responses of the sample, if it has external validity, can then be applied to the overall population. An example of this would be if you were identifying the most common reasons why NBA basketball fans attended their first game. It would be impossible to question every NBA fan. Thus, a smaller number of fans who are representative of the population, are chosen. If, from this sample, it was determined that 50 per cent were taken to the game by their fathers, then it can be suggested that this is likely (within certain limits) to be the case for the entire population of NBA fans.

For qualitative research, sampling is less about identifying a representative group from which to collect data, and more about identifying a group that is of relevance, for example selecting a sample that demonstrates a certain theory or model particularly well, or simply to investigate a single group that is of particular interest to the researcher. In such cases, the results cannot be generalised to the overall population, and so you should aim to generalise to theory, that is your findings could be used to develop, refine, or simply confirm an existing theory, which could then be applied to different samples. Alternatively, qualitative researchers talk about the idea of transferability, or the extent to which findings could apply to other similar samples within similar settings. Thus, qualitative research involves non-probability sampling, as certain members of the population are much more likely to be chosen than others based on certain factors or characteristics.

Selecting a sample

The first stage in selecting a sample is to define your population. The population consists of every individual case that possesses the characteristic that is of interest to the researcher. Thus, in the above case, the population may be defined as everyone that has attended an NBA game in the current season. Populations can be varied in size and location, and often you may have to delimit your population, or define your sample more narrowly. Thus you may have to define your population as fans of a particular basketball team. The disadvantage of this, of course, is that you may also – although not necessarily – lose generalisability, that is the extent to which findings from your chosen team could be applied to the other teams in the NBA.

The second stage is to determine your sampling method. In most cases, your aim is to produce a sample that is representative of the population. A high-profile piece of research carried out for a number of years was the FA Carling Premiership survey. These surveys were designed to investigate the profiles, attitudes and behaviour of fans of teams in the English Premiership. Given the size of the population, a smaller sample obviously had to be taken. One serious criticism of the FA Carling Premiership surveys was that a number of questionnaires were distributed in match-day programmes. The achieved sample, that is the sample that completed and returned their questionnaires, was likely, in this case, to be unrepresentative of the population. The sample would, very possibly, under-represent less affluent fans who may not be able to afford the match-day programme, less well-educated fans, who may not want to read the programme, and also younger fans, whose parents would perhaps be more likely to buy the programme and complete the questionnaire themselves, in all likelihood leading to misleading data regarding the composition of the crowd. In this example, it seems unlikely that the results from the sample could have been generalised to the population with confidence. This demonstrates the importance of appropriate sampling, and it is worth spending some time considering your sampling method.

A number of sampling techniques can be used. The most common associated with quantitative research are:

1 Random sampling.
2 Stratified random sampling.
3 Cluster sampling.
4 Systematic sampling.

1 Random sampling. A random sample is where every member of the population has an equal probability of being selected. This is considered the best technique to obtain a representative sample, and produce findings that will be generalisable to the overall population. The first stage is to define your population. The next stage is to ensure that each member of this population has an equal chance of being selected. The easiest way to do this, if you know your entire population, is simply to place the names of all the population in a container, and pick names until the desired sample size has been achieved. Alternatively, each name can be assigned a number, and a random number table (available in most statistical textbooks and some research methods textbooks), or computer software can be used to select the sample. In many cases, provided you have a suitably focused question, then a random sample is possible. If you have a broad question however, then it is unlikely that you will be able to undertake a simple random sample, and one of the methods below will be required.

2 Stratified random sampling. If there are certain subgroups within the population, for example based on age, sex and so on, then it may be necessary to ensure that they are adequately represented in the final sample. In this case, the population is divided into subgroups. Random samples are then taken from within these groups. Thus, you may divide your population into 'male' and 'female', and randomly select 50 per cent of your sample from the list of your male participants, and the remaining 50 per cent from the list of your female participants. This will ensure your initial sample reflects the appropriate subgroups that are present within the population.

3   Cluster sampling. Cluster sampling is where groups are randomly selected, rather than individuals. Thus, if the researcher was interested in the attitudes towards intimidatory behaviour in little league baseball, then rather than select a random sample from the population of little league baseball players, a number of teams could be selected at random, and all players within those teams questioned. It is important to select a number of clusters to ensure generalisability with this method. Chen *et al.* (2014b) used this method when exploring physical activity in older people living alone within China. They randomly selected two towns, and subsequently four communities from within those towns. They were then able to approach all individuals meeting their criteria from those communities.

4   Systematic sampling. Sampling using this method involves selecting every *K*th case, for example taking every fourth name from a list, or every seventh person to enter a sports facility, for example Dixon *et al.*'s (2013) approach to measuring the economic impact of sport tourists attending university baseball, where they approached, after a random start, every fifth person entering the stadium. Systematic sampling is best recommended when the list from which the names are taken is randomly ordered, otherwise some bias is likely to occur.

There is a range of non-probability sampling methods, which will be of interest to the qualitative researcher. In many ways, the term 'sample' is perhaps less appropriate here, and 'selection' more reflective of the process, as generalisability is not the prime concern of the qualitative researcher, with the focus more upon participants who can describe, explain and illuminate the phenomena being explored. The means by which the qualitative researcher can select their sample include the following:

1   Snowball sampling. You locate your initial participants, and these initial participants identify further potential participants themselves. Thus, you may find access to a 'gatekeeper', or influential member of your population. They can then introduce you to other participants, who themselves will be able to give you access to further participants. One potential advantage of this is that by being introduced by a known member of the population, you may be able to engender greater trust between researcher and subject, with subsequent improvement in the quality of your data.

2   Theoretical sampling. You identify cases that demonstrate a particu-
    lar theory particularly well, or allow you to develop a theory. You
    may be interested in the explaining the influence of the influx of for-
    eign expertise upon the managerial culture of sports organisations,
    for example. You would therefore sample those from organisations
    that had experienced such expertise. As you develop your ideas, you
    then continue to select cases which help you further inform, refine
    and develop your emerging theory.

3   Purposive sampling. You choose your participants because they
    possess certain characteristics or traits. You may be interested in
    exploring how people's experience of forced retirement from sport
    compared with those who had a planned retirement. Your sample
    would need to include those from both groups.

4   Maximum variation sampling. You choose the full range of experiences,
    demographics and so on to capture the full range of the subject being
    explored. Jowett and Frost's (2007) study of the impact of race and eth-
    nicity on the coach athlete relationship in football sampled 12 male
    black football players from different levels of professional football, play-
    ing in different positions, from a variety of racial/ethnic backgrounds,
    and being both first generation and second generation British.

5   Typical case sampling. Your sample is chosen on the basis that they
    are 'typical' of a particular theory. For example, you may wish to assess
    the impact of changing legislation affecting those using sports stadia
    with reference to a particular stadium that you consider 'typical'. The
    findings can then be generalised to those using other 'typical' stadia.

6   Extreme cases. You choose cases that are extreme cases of a theory.
    An example of this would be an investigation into the personality
    characteristics of elite athletes. You may wish to sample Olympic
    medal winners as extreme cases (remember that this is a hypotheti-
    cal example ... in reality your chances of getting access to such a
    sample is minimal at best!).

7   Opportunistic sampling. You select samples as they arise, taking
    advantage of unexpected opportunities. For example, you may be
    introduced to a particular key informant at an unexpected time.

8   Convenience sampling. The sample is chosen as it is convenient in
    terms of location, accessibility and so on. Try to avoid convenience
    samples as far as you can – it is always tempting to hand out ques-
    tionnaires to those you are in day-to-day contact with, or interview
    people that you know, but try to consider this as a last resort and
    always acknowledge the limitations if you have to choose this route.

9   Key informant technique. Individuals are chosen on the basis of specific knowledge that they possess, for example, they may have a particular role or responsibility within an organisation.

PURPOSIVE SAMPLING – EXPERIENCES OF INJURY AND RETURN TO SPORT

Podlog *et al.* (2013) were interested in the extent to which basic psychological needs theory could explain adolescent athletes' experiences of injury and return to sport. To do this, they interviewed 11 athletes using a purposive sample, with the criteria for selection being:

- Sport involvement as determined by membership on a regional sport academy squad or a state/national team).
- A current musculoskeletal injury requiring a minimum one-month absence from sport participation.
- They were undergoing physiotherapy treatment for the injury at the time.
- The intent to return to a similar level of pre-injury participation or higher.

This allowed four themes to emerge, these being:

- Injury stress (the range of stressors and strain responses reported across the recovery phases).
- Coping (the specific strategies used to maintain motivation and reduce uncertainty).
- Experiences with social support.
- Recovery outcomes (perceptions of a successful/unsuccessful recovery).

Mistakes made in selecting a sample

Your choice of sampling technique can be an important one for the success of your research project, so it is worth spending time considering your approach. Some of the common errors made in sampling – especially at undergraduate level – include:

- Selecting individuals who are convenient, or readily available, for example individuals that are already known to the researcher.

- Selecting individuals who volunteer to take part as well as those who are more randomly selected without reference to the potential differences between these.
- Introducing bias through selecting a non-random sample.
- Using a random sample when other sampling methods would be more appropriate.
- Not obtaining a large enough sample for the purposes of the project.

Determining the sample size

A frequently asked question is 'how big should my sample be?' Unfortunately there is no simple answer to this question, other than to say 'make sure it is big enough'! For the type of quantitative analysis typically collected as part of a quantitative study, you will need to balance the need for as large a sample size as possible with constraints based upon the issues of cost and time required for analysis. For basic descriptive statistical analysis of questionnaire data, I would argue that an absolute minimum sample size of 50 would normally be required, with a larger sample much more desirable, as this sample would only have limited statistical power. Even for a relatively small population, a sample of one hundred should be a minimum target, and given advances in things such as online survey software, this should be within the reach of most studies. For more detailed inferential statistics 30 subjects per group would again be a suggested absolute minimum, so a comparison between males and females would require an overall sample size of 60, but again this would have limited statistical power. The advice is to obtain the largest sample you can within the constraints mentioned above. A common error is to assume that the sample should be a certain percentage of the population, for example 10 per cent. In reality, there is no such relationship, and it is only the size of the sample that is important. If you are looking at a number of subgroups, then you will also need to ensure adequate representation of each of these groups. For example, you may want to compare your findings above by gender. If your response is equally divided in terms of gender, then 50 responses will give you a sample size of 25 for each, which will not be enough to give you a sufficient degree of confidence in your findings. Thus, the more subgroups you intend to involve in your analysis, the larger the sample has to be.

For experimental designs, then there is always the trade-off between sample size and the simple pragmatics of undertaking your experiment, particularly at undergraduate level. You will find that time and resource issues have implications for how much data you can collect. This will vary among projects, but you must ensure that you maintain the integrity of the experimental design, rather than look for short cuts in the design to allow you to increase the sample. At undergraduate level, a well-designed experiment that has fewer subjects is always preferable to a poorly designed study with more subjects.

Sample sizes for qualitative research are much lower, and will depend on many different factors. The key with qualitative data is not the size of the sample, but the depth and quality of the data. Thus, sample sizes will range from one upwards. A study with too little data will be a weak one, but, counter intuitively perhaps, too much data can also be detrimental to a qualitative study where time and resources are limited. Too much data may result in weaker analysis, and you should bear this in mind. Six rich, detailed informative interviews that are well analysed are always preferable to 12 less detailed interviews that have had limited analysis. You need to consider first the question of the nature of the sample, in that a homogeneous group will require a smaller sample than a group containing a high degree of variation. Second, you will be guided by the issue of 'saturation', that is when you are collecting data but, in essence, not learning anything new (which is actually quite difficult to achieve in many cases). Finally, you need to consider the nature of the study, with narrative and phenomenological studies (see Chapter 9) requiring smaller sample sizes than generic qualitative approaches. The question you need to ask is not that of 'have I collected data from enough people?', but that of 'have I collected enough data?'.

Case study sampling

There are a number of issues of sampling that are specific to case study or ethnographic research. Your choice of case should rarely be random, rather it is more likely to be purposive, that is chosen to illustrate a particular situation. Often it may be a choice of convenience or access;

for example, you may have access to a particular organisation or sports-related body. When you are undertaking such research, the questions that you need to consider are:

- How many cases are required? Am I looking to provide a detailed analysis of the factors affecting one particular case, or would I like to be able to compare two or more cases to be able to assess the relative importance of such variables?
- Am I looking for a typical case, with which the results I obtain can be generalised to other cases? If so, how will I identify what is 'typical'?
- Am I looking for an extreme or important case which will demonstrate a particular theory or model well?
- Am I likely to get access to my sample?

Non-response bias

It is extremely unlikely that you will get responses from your entire sample, especially if you are using methods such as a postal or online questionnaire. Respondents may not have sufficient time, motivation or expertise to respond, they may fill in the questionnaire incorrectly, or they may simply not be reachable. As a result, the data you eventually collect may not always be representative of your population. This is less important for qualitative studies, but for a quantitative study it is good practice to assess whether this is the case before you can generalise your findings, and this can be done in a number of ways:

- Initially you should examine the characteristics of the achieved sample to try to identify any features that may suggest non-response bias, such as looking at the age and gender profiles, as well as any other variables that you may feel are important. Using a computer package such as SPSS for Windows (see Chapter 13) you could always display the response for certain variables graphically to examine response patterns.
- If the information is available, compare the characteristics of your respondents with those of the population under investigation. Thus, for example, at the very simplest level you should be able to compare the gender distribution of your achieved sample with

that of the population. If the gender balance of your population is equal, yet either males or females are under-represented in your achieved sample, then your sample is likely to be biased in this respect.

- Send a follow-up letter to those who have not responded. If any further responses are obtained, then you can compare the characteristics of those who didn't initially respond with the original respondents to see if they differ in any way from your original respondents.

What methods should I use to collect data from my sample?

So far in this chapter, I have covered the issue of research design, whereby you consider the overall framework of your data collection. I have also covered the issue of sampling, that is from whom this data is collected. The final issue within this chapter is that of how such data is to be collected. Thus the choice of appropriate methods becomes the final consideration of this part of the research process. Methods are, simply, the techniques by which you collect your data. The key methods that you may encounter include:

- Questionnaires.
- Interviews.
- Observation.
- Participant observation.
- Content analysis.

The choice of method is obviously important to the success of your project. Chapters 8–11 of this text examine each of the methods in turn, so I will only provide a brief outline here.

By this stage of the research process, you should be able to identify your own epistemological stance, tending towards either the positivist or interpretative. You should also have an idea of the type of data you need to collect, this being qualitative, quantitative or a combination of the two. Finally, you should also have an idea of your likely sample in terms

134

of who you would like to collect data from, and the desired sample size for a quantitative study. You can now begin to approach the issue of choosing your methods. There is no one set way to do this; however, the following questions can guide your approach:

1   Am I looking to collect quantitative data? If so, then if those data can be directly observed, consider the use of observation as your data collection method (Chapter 10). If not, then consider the use of a questionnaire (Chapter 8). Alternatively, if you are intending to analyse texts, such as newspapers, blogs, television programmes, letters, speeches, etc. then use content analysis (Chapter 10) or undertake online research (Chapter 12).
2   Am I looking to collect qualitative data? If you are looking to explore the thoughts, feelings, emotions and perceptions of others, then consider the use of in-depth interviews (Chapter 9). If you are looking to explore your own subjective experiences, then use participant observation (Chapter 10).
3   Am I looking to carry out an in-depth investigation of a particular group or culture? Consider the use of an ethnographic approach (Chapter 11) or a 'netnographic' design (Chapter 12).
4   Am I looking to strengthen the validity of the findings through triangulation? If so, consider using more than one method. I outline the concept of triangulation below.

You should also consider your own personal skills and preferences in making your choice. If you are not happy talking to others, then interviewing may not be the method for you! Or, if you lack confidence in dealing with numbers, then consider alternatives to a strongly quantitative questionnaire, requiring detailed statistical analysis. The most important thing to ensure, however, is that your choice of method is appropriate to meet your research objectives.

Triangulation

While you are considering your research design, you may wish to consider the appropriateness of triangulation. Triangulation in its most common form refers to the use of multiple means of data collection to explore a single phenomenon. Consider the following example. You may be interested in how pupils on a physical education course react to a change in the nature of their course of study. You may collect data using a questionnaire, which suggests that pupils are not overly concerned provided they can comprehend the rationale behind the change. If you have designed and piloted your questionnaire carefully, you may have some degree of confidence in these findings. Now imagine that you have followed up this initial data collection by using an additional method, for example by interviewing a sample of pupils. These pupils also suggest they are not overly concerned, again provided the rationale behind the change is clear to them. Now, your confidence in the findings should be increased, as you have data from different methods which allows you to draw the same conclusions. This is the basis of triangulation, which refers simply to the use of more than a single source of data (although poorly thought out triangulation can also have the effect of increasing error rather than reducing it!). A number of types of triangulation can be identified:

- Data. This may refer to the use of different data sources, for example, interviews and questionnaires. Alternatively it may involve using different informants, such as interviews with pupils and teachers, or informants with the same sample, but at different times.
- Investigator. Different researchers may collect, and draw their own conclusions from the same data.
- Theoretical. The same situation may be examined using different theoretical viewpoints. Generally, this form of triangulation will be beyond the scope of most student research projects.

As I have said, it is possible for triangulation to increase the error in your conclusions. In our example, pupils may have felt that the data from the questionnaires may have been made available to their tutors, and not wishing to be seen to be causing trouble, may have responded positively towards changes in their course. They may have been even more concerned about this during their interview, and again respond positively towards the changes. The researcher, meanwhile, writes up the report under the impression that the data triangulation has strengthened the validity of their findings! Thus, you need to be cautious in triangulating your data, and identify any potential problems that may arise.

136

Combining quantitative and qualitative approaches

So far in this chapter I have suggested that your design will lead to the collection of either quantitative or qualitative data. In many cases this is advisable, for example in terms of the expertise required in both approaches, the extended time required to actually carry out the study, and the need to keep research focused. As I noted in Chapter 2, however, it can sometimes be appropriate to collect both types of data, and often this can enhance a piece of research in a number of ways.

As I have already mentioned, triangulation from using different data collection techniques can strengthen the validity of the research. The two types of data may complement each other; for example, quantitative data may describe a phenomenon well, and qualitative data may be appropriate to gain an understanding of the phenomenon. Quantitative data may throw up questions that are more suited to qualitative analysis, and vice versa. You need to be careful in identifying your purpose in mixing data. For example, will you be looking at the same phenomenon using different data collection methods, or will you use one approach to investigate findings that have emerged from an earlier stage of the study? In the second case it could be argued that you are not mixing approaches, but simply looking at two separate research questions.

Ethical considerations in research design

Whatever research design, sampling techniques and choice of methods you choose to adopt, you will also need to consider the ethical issues associated with the research, that is the question of whether your research design is socially and morally acceptable. Certain research designs (for example experimental designs) often raise important ethical questions that need to be addressed, and you should do this before commencing any data collection from your sample. This is an area where it is better to be safe than sorry, especially if the research involves sensitive or vulnerable groups, such as children. You should always allow your research proposal to be scrutinised by an ethics committee, and accept their decision if the research proposal is considered unethical in any way.

Voluntary participation, involuntary participation and informed consent

The obvious way to overcome ethical issues in terms of who participates may be that of asking for volunteers to take part. Unfortunately, a voluntary sample is unlikely to be representative, and your sample is likely to be more highly educated, more socially oriented, more interested or more knowledgeable of the subject matter than the population as a whole. If this is the case, then it is difficult if not impossible for you to generalise your findings to the population. The motives of those volunteering may also be questioned; for example a relatively common practice in sports-related research in the USA is to require students to participate in research projects for course credit. The results from these findings cannot be generalised to the wider population without some degree of caution, as they are likely to possess certain characteristics that differ from the overall population. Occasionally an involuntary sample may be adopted, where the subjects are unaware of their participation. This is generally acceptable if the researcher is making what is referred to as unobtrusive measures, for example taking a frequency count of the number of people using a particular sports facility. Obtrusive research, that is influencing their behaviour in some way, such as setting up a contrived situation and monitoring subjects' reactions to that situation, however, needs much more ethical consideration before proceeding.

The best approach to take is that of informed consent. The sample should be chosen using an appropriate sampling technique as described earlier in the chapter. Each participant in the research should then be informed as to the nature of the study, and the use of the data supplied before data is collected from them through the use of a participant information sheet, which will then allow them to sign a consent form. Informed consent, however, as McNamee *et al.* (2007) note, is much more than a mere 'box-ticking' exercise, and in many cases, the level of information actually provided to participants fails to meet the necessary standards, in terms of failing to provide detail of the exact requirements of the study, or omit key details which may mislead the participant, or be written in jargon or specialist terminology that participants may not fully under-stand. Thus it is essential that informed consent is not simply seen as a paper exercise, but that the participant is given, and understands, all the necessary detail to allow them to make a fully informed decision to participate or not. Berg and Latin (2008) refer to this as 'valid consent', which summarises the principle well. In terms of the decision not to participate, it is also important that no undue pressure is put upon par-ticipants that may make them feel obliged to take part. Direct coercion should not be used under any circumstance to ensure participation in any way, and even more subtle forms such as intense persuasion are to be avoided. Subjects must also be given the right to withdraw from the study at any time, and be made aware of this. If it is highly likely that informing the participants as to the exact nature of the study would bias or invalidate the results in some manner, then the participants should be informed of the purpose of the study after data collection.

THE PARTICIPANT INFORMATION SHEET

You should always provide a participant information sheet so that partici-pants are able to make a fully informed decision about their participation in the research. The information sheet should give a summary of the research project, clearly outlining the entire process in a clear and accessible manner.

The following list is not exhaustive but gives an idea of the main topics to be covered:

- Outline the nature and aims of the research
- Explain that participation is always voluntary and that participants can withdraw at any time Explain exactly what participation means in practice (how long participation takes, where it takes place and what it involves)
- Outline clearly the inclusion criteria, that is why they have been chosen
- Outline any risks, inconvenience or discomfort that could reasonably be expected to result from the study
- Describe the benefits for participants, and for the wider society as a whole
- Explain how privacy and confidentiality would be maintained
- What will happen at the end of the study, for example will it be pub-lished, written up as a dissertation and so on
- Provide full contact details of the researcher, and their institutional affiliation.

LANGUAGE AND LAYOUT

- Use clear, non-technical language.
- Use appropriate language for the target audience. For example, consider the different ways needed to communicate to primary school children as opposed to their teachers, or people with expertise in the area of study as opposed to people with no such expertise.
- Divide the text into paragraphs for ease of reading.
- Consider using sub-headings for clarity.
- Make sure the font is legible.
- Have someone else read through your information sheet before it is circulated.

Deception

The issue of deception is a complex one. The primary argument for deception is that if the subject is aware of the nature of the investigation, then this may affect the results. The argument against is that deception is basically unethical in society. Some deception may be acceptable, if there are no questionable outcomes to the subjects, or if the subjects are not harmed or affected in any way. Other deception is more questionable. For example, in a well-known study in a non-sport context, Rosenthal and Jacobsen (1968) informed teachers which children were likely to show better academic performances and which were not. Despite the fact that the two groups were actually chosen at random, those expected to do better actually did so, compared to those who were expected to fare worse. Such an experiment, it could be argued, may have had an extremely harmful effect on the subjects, both in the short and long term. In this instance, I can suggest no justification for the research, and would take the overall view that such deception is very rarely justified. I would again stress that, at the very least, if you feel that deception is warranted, you should ensure that you strongly justify your argument and an ethics committee at your university or organisation assesses your research proposal.

Confidentiality

All participants should be informed as to who will have access to research data. Ideally this should be as few people as possible, and only those that actually need access to such data (in many cases this may be only the researcher) and you must ensure that once data is collected, then no one will have access unless authorised to do so. A further recommendation is to ensure that individuals cannot be identified by using pseudonyms, or assigning numbers to individuals in the data set (but if you keep a key that allows real names to be linked to numbers, for example, then this must be stored in an entirely separate location). Again, precise detail needs to be considered, and McNamee *et al.* (2007) identify some key questions, including:

- Precisely how are the data being recorded?
- How and where are the data stored?
- Who has access to the data?
- How long are the data held for?

Assessing the ethics of your research

Carrying out research into social phenomena such as sport is difficult to do without coming across some ethical issues. Make sure you read the codes of conduct laid down by your specific discipline. For example, if you are interested in the psychology of sport, then you should familiarise yourself with the guidelines of the American Psychological Association (APA) or the British Psychological Society (BPS). Such codes generally include the following key requirements:

- Risks to participants are outweighed by the benefits of the research programme.
- Participation should be voluntary.
- Risks to participants are eliminated or minimised as far as possible, including psychological and social, as well as physical risks.
- All information should be treated as strictly confidential.
- The participants have the right to be informed of the purpose of the study.

- Participants may withdraw at any time.
- Participants should be debriefed after the research programme.

Using ethics to improve your research

It's important to remember that, in research, ethical considerations are an aspect of the research process that you must get right, without exception, as they ensure the safety and well-being of others. You should ensure that you gain ethical approval from the relevant committee at your institution before any research programme commences. You mustn't see getting such ethical approval, however, as a tick-box exercise or a barrier to be overcome. Ethics and methodology are closely related, and careful consideration of ethical issues can only ever improve the overall research design, and that's how you should approach research ethics. Although it is not the job of an ethics panel to comment on your research design as such, their advice can only ever strengthen your project and, equally important, ensure the well-being of those participants involved.

Summary

1   You should have a carefully considered approach to the collection of your data, in terms of who you will collect data from, when such data will be collected, and how such data will be collected. This is your research design.
2   I have identified nine research designs: experimental, cross-sectional, time series, longitudinal, case study, grounded theory, action research, ethnography and autoethnography.
3   Whatever research design you adopt, it is unlikely that you will be able to collect data from the entire population. Thus you will have to collect data from a smaller group within that population – your sample.

4   You will also have to choose the methods by which you are going to collect data from that sample. Those methods should be appropriate to the type of data required and characteristics of your participants.
5   It may be possible to increase the validity of your research by undertaking some form of triangulation. Triangulation means collecting data from more than one perspective; for example, it may involve collecting qualitative as well as quantitative data.
6   You will also need to consider the ethical issues involved in your research, and you should gain approval from the committee responsible for ethical issues at your institution before you collect data collection.

Activity

Look again at some of the pieces of research that you have already read. Can you answer the following questions about each article?

● What research design has been adopted for the research? Do you feel this is appropriate for the research in question? Can you identify any alternative research designs that may have been considered?
● What methods have been adopted in the study? Why?
● Can you identify any ethical issues that may have arisen? If so, have the authors addressed these issues?

1   Can you clearly identify and justify the research design you are using?
2   Have you considered any alternative designs?
3   What type of sample are you going to choose? Why?
4   Have you considered using triangulation as a technique to enhance the validity of your research?
5   What are the ethical issues involved with your research project?
6   How will you ensure that your research project will not breach any guidelines?
7   Have you ensured that your research has been assessed by the appropriate ethics committee?

Further reading

The ethics of any study are of paramount importance, so I would strongly recommend reading:

McNamee, M., Olivier, S. and Wainwright, P. (2007) *Research Ethics in Exercise, Health and Sports Sciences*, London: Routledge.

8

Collecting data I: the questionnaire survey

This chapter will:

- Discuss the use of questionnaires as a method of data collection, including a brief introduction to internet-based questionnaires.
- Introduce some of the advantages and disadvantages of using questionnaires in your research project.
- Outline some of the issues of questionnaire design and administration.

Introduction

So far, I have largely dealt with the background to your research project in terms of reading and assessing the literature, clarifying the role of theory, developing the conceptual framework and deciding upon a research design. The next stage in most cases is to collect primary data to test your hypothesis, or answer your research question. The next few chapters deal with issues of data collection, beginning in this chapter with an examination of the use of questionnaires in sports research.

Defined simply, a questionnaire is a standardised set of questions to gain information from a subject. They are often associated with quantitative research designs, when relatively simple measurements are required from a large sample group (although you can collect qualitative data using questionnaires, it is not desirable in most cases and other methods are generally more appropriate to collect anything other than a very limited amount of qualitative data). Questionnaires generally fall into one of four categories:

1   Postal questionnaire. The questionnaire is given or posted to the participant, who completes it in his or her own time. The participant then posts the completed questionnaire back to the researcher.
2   Online questionnaire. Respondents are able to complete the questionnaire electronically, and the researcher downloads results.
3   Telephone questionnaire. The researcher questions the participant over the telephone and the researcher fills in the responses.
4   Face-to-face questionnaire. The researcher and participant are in the same location, and the researcher asks the questions 'face-to-face', and fills in responses as they receive them, generally using a laptop or tablet.

Questionnaires can thus be designed for completion either by the researcher (interviewer completion) or by the subject (respondent or self-completion). Interviewer completion questionnaires are effectively the same as structured interviews, and the issues associated with this particular technique will be dealt with in the next chapter. This chapter will provide an overview of respondent completion surveys, the type of questionnaire that you are most likely to use.

146

When is the use of a questionnaire appropriate?

The first consideration that you must make is whether a questionnaire is actually an appropriate method to collect the data you need. Once you have developed and focused your research question, considered the relevant concepts and developed your conceptual framework (see Chapter 6), and determined your choice of research design (Chapter 7), you should be able to list your information needs, that is the information you require to answer your research question (including information needed to account for any moderating variables). Three questions can now be asked:

1   Can I get the information I need using data from a questionnaire?
2   Is a questionnaire the best or most appropriate method, or are other methods more appropriate to collect the data?
3   Are other methods excluded, for example interviews, because of time and cost restrictions?

Questionnaires are appropriate in a variety of contexts, where relatively simple, generally quantitative information is required from a large sample group. This data can then be summarised through the use of tables or charts, or analysed statistically to answer a research question. Research projects such as the FA Carling Premiership surveys (SNCCFR 1996–2000) are a good example of the use of postal questionnaires. The main aim of this research was to discover a wide range of relatively simple information about English soccer fans, for example measuring variables such as age, gender and spending upon football-related merchandise. Given the number of clubs in the Premiership (twenty in total) and combined attendances of many thousands, interviewing a sufficient number of fans was obviously impractical both in terms of time and cost. Simple observation would not have allowed the appropriate data to be collected. Questionnaires were, however, ideal to collect such a large volume of simple data. If more complex information had been required, however, questionnaires would have been unlikely to be able to yield such information, and other methods would have been more appropriate in such a case.

147

Advantages of using questionnaires

As you will learn over the next few chapters, each of the methods you may adopt as part of a research project has its own advantages and disadvantages. In most cases you will have to assess these when considering your choice of method. What you will ultimately need to do, however, is to be able to justify your eventual choice, utilise their advantages and minimise the potential disadvantages. The advantages of using a questionnaire include the following:

- Accessibility. The postal and especially the online questionnaire allows you to collect data from a geographically dispersed sample group at a much lower cost than interviewing a similar sample. Internet surveys, for example, allow you potential access to a global audience. In addition, as you don't need to be present to ask questions yourself, using questionnaires allows a larger sample to be investigated.
- Potential reduction in bias. With a well-designed questionnaire there is little opportunity to introduce bias into the results as may be the case with interviews, for example through the way you respond to an answer, or your body language (see Chapter 9), or simply your presence in observational studies. You should be aware, however, that badly designed questionnaires can lead to bias in your data, hence using a questionnaire does not automatically mean a reduction in bias.
- Anonymity. The presence of the researcher interested in certain sensitive issues (for example, player violence, the use of drugs, or cheating in sport) may inhibit the respondent. A questionnaire allows anonymity, and may therefore improve the validity of your responses in certain cases.
- Structured data. Questionnaires tend to provide highly structured quantitative data that is easily comparable, either between subject groups, or between the same group studied over an extended time period. Such data is generally straightforward to convert into tables and charts, and to analyse statistically.
- Increased time for respondents. Respondent-completed questionnaires allow the respondent to fill in the questionnaire at a convenient time if necessary, or to be able to go back to the questionnaire at a later time if they recall anything further.

148

Disadvantages of using questionnaires

- Potential problems over complex questions. The questions have to be clear enough for all participants to understand, as there will often be no opportunity for the respondent to seek clarification, especially in a postal or online questionnaire. If complex questions are required, then you may need to be present to explain them. Thus, to a large extent, you are restricted to relatively simple questions.
- No control over who completes the questionnaire. Unless you specify exactly who is to fill out the questionnaire, an inappropriate party may complete it. Even if you do specify that it has to be completed by a particular individual, it may be that the respondent delegates the task to somebody else without your knowledge.
- No opportunity to probe. Once the respondent has answered the question there is no opportunity to get him or her to expand upon or explain any of the points that may have been made.
- Potentially low response rates. Response rates from questionnaires are notoriously poor, and can range from as little as 5 per cent or so upwards. Low response rates may have a serious effect on the reliability and validity of the study. Potential means of improving your response rates are highlighted later in the chapter.

Using internet-based questionnaires

The internet, through tools such as Survey Monkey or Google Docs, is becoming a valuable tool for data collection, and offers the sport researcher a number of advantages over more traditional paper-based surveys. Wright (2005) has summarised these as follows:

- Greater access to certain populations – online surveys may allow you to identify and access certain groups more easily, for example you may be able to access fans of a particular sports team through accessing the team's forum or through social media sites. They also allow you to reach samples at a global rather than national level.
- This may allow larger sample sizes to be achieved. In the past couple of years, I have supervised a number of final year dissertations that

have, with relatively little effort, achieved sample sizes of well over 500 respondents.

- 'Cleaner' data – Lonsdale *et al.*'s (2006) study of New Zealand athletes determined that the group sent online questionnaires provided fewer missing values when compared with a control group that was assigned paper-based questionnaires.
- Time efficiency – as well as being quicker to send out, data is also quicker to analyse in that responses can be downloaded to a database or statistical package rather than having to be manually input.
- Cost – the costs of postage and printing are removed through use of online surveys, although needs to be weighed up against the costs involved when using certain online survey tools. Many sites allow a certain amount of free usage, but will involve a cost for things such as being able to access more than 100 respondents, or to download directly into software packages such as SPSS for Windows. This will generally be cheaper than the costs associated with postage however.

The design and use of internet-based questionnaires is, in most cases, relatively simple, and it is something that you will be able to pick up fairly quickly if you have basic IT skills. It is worth trying a number of different sites, there are advantages and disadvantages to whichever you will choose, so my advice is to test a couple of options before you go into 'live' data collection.

USING ONLINE QUESTIONNAIRES – WHO ARE THE SPORT GAMERS?

Stein *et al.* (2013) have noted how little is known about those who play sport video games such as *FIFA14* or *Madden NFL 11*. To fill this void in the literature, they decided to utilise an online survey to explore gamers playing habits, their experiences of games, and the links between their 'real' and virtual sporting experiences. Once the questionnaire had been designed and launched on a server, they recruited participants through posing information and a link to the survey on social media sites such as Twitter and Facebook, as well as related game blogs and web sites. Over a period of approximately 1 month, they were able to achieve a total of 1718 respondents. This allowed them to determine a range of information, such as gamers tending to be overwhelmingly young and male, and identifying strong links between their real life sporting activity and their virtual sporting activity.

There are, however potential disadvantages, and you shouldn't necessarily see the use of online surveys as a simple solution to overcoming issues of paper-based surveys. You need to consider:

- Sampling bias – online surveys will generally not involve random samples from the population under investigation. For example, not every fan of a sports team will post on a forum, and the sample may be skewed to younger, more committed fans. One option is to combine online and paper-based surveys, and to compare characteristics from each group of respondents.
- Potentially low response rates – increasing numbers of 'spam' emails may make it difficult to get respondents to open, let alone read the covering email. Lonsdale *et al.* (2006) have, however, indicated that online questionnaires may actually result in a higher response rate, so the evidence is equivocal.
- The offer of incentives to overcome low response rates may encourage individuals to fill in multiple responses to increase their chances of winning.
- Access issues – members of an online community may resent researchers getting in contact and respond by ignoring the message, moderators of the group may delete the message, or the researcher may encounter abusive responses, especially if they are seen as an outsider to that group.

COMBINING ONLINE AND PAPER SURVEYS – VISITOR SPENDING AT A SPORTING EVENT

Are the findings from a questionnaire survey administered during an event different from those administered after the event online? Case *et al.* (2013) explored this with reference to participant spending at a running event in the United States. Each approach has a number of advantages, such as the high response rates, and the ability to use randomised sampling techniques possible with on-site surveys, or the convenience of online surveys, as well as their ability to account for all spending, something that on-site surveys do not always capture. To explore the differences in the data provided, Case *et al.* obtained event-related expenditure from out-of-town participants prior to the race starting. Four days after the event, on online survey was emailed to all participants, with instructions that those who had already completed the survey at the event were to ignore the email.

They found that those who completed surveys at the event estimated higher spend than those who completed online surveys after the event, when, the authors suggested, they were able to look at specific detail, such as credit card statements to provide a more accurate account of their spending. The wider implications of the study are that online surveys after the event are better able to provide accurate factual information, such as event-related spending, and are thus preferable. However as the authors suggest, the method should match the purpose of the study, and for researching other aspects of the event, such as participant experiences, I would suggest that on-site methods would be preferable.

Designing the questionnaire

Once you have decided that it is an appropriate data collection technique, the second stage of questionnaire-based research is that of the initial design of the questionnaire. A good questionnaire is difficult to design, and takes considerably more time than is often anticipated. While a questionnaire that may seem to have some relevance towards the research objectives is relatively easy to put together, designing questions that actually fulfil all of the researcher's needs and is both reliable and valid is more time consuming. As Oppenheim (1992, p.7) notes:

> Too often, surveys are carried out on the basis of insufficient design and planning or on the basis of no design at all. 'Fact-gathering' can be an exciting and tempting activity to which a questionnaire opens a quick and seemingly easy avenue; the weaknesses in the design are frequently not recognised until the results have to be interpreted – if then!

Three questions need to be asked at the beginning of the design stage. These are:

1 What information do I need to answer my research question?
2 What questions can I ask that will provide me with data that will, when analysed, give me such information?

152

3   How am I going to analyse the data that I get from such questions to give me the answer to my research question?

Thus, before designing the questionnaire, it is important that your information needs have been clearly identified. As a rule of thumb, you should try to keep the questionnaire as short as possible, yet ensure that it will provide all of the necessary data. Do not be tempted to include questions that are not required, even if you consider them to be interesting! You should be able to justify the inclusion of each question, and identify how that question will help answer your research question. You also need to think ahead in terms of how you intend to analyse your data, which will influence you in the type of data that you decide to collect (for example will you need your responses to provide you with ordinal or ratio data?). In terms of the data that you need, you should be guided by the aim and objectives of the research, the literature review and your conceptual framework, which should be related. If the research objectives are detailed and specific enough, then these should provide a clear starting point.

There are a number of different question formats that you can adopt when designing your questionnaire. The most common formats are described below.

Closed/pre-coded questions

The respondent is asked to choose one or more responses from a series of choices pre-determined by the researcher, for example:

Q.1 How many competitive matches have you played so far this season? (please tick one box)
0–5 ❑   6–10 ❑   11–15 ❑   16–20 ❑

If the question involves relatively simple information, and you know all of the available responses beforehand, such as a question on the sex of the respondent, then use a closed question. This will provide you with the information in its simplest format, which will be easy to analyse, and provide easily structured data. Such questions are also easier for respondents, and take less time than other question formats to complete.

153

Open questions

Sometimes it is not possible to anticipate all of the answers you are going to receive, or you may anticipate a wide variety of different answers. Here you will need the respondent to write their answer with no prompting. For example:

Q.2 What, in your opinion, are the attributes of a good sports coach?
....
....
....
....

You can use open questions within a questionnaire to obtain limited amounts of qualitative data, although you need to be careful, as partici-pants are unlikely to be willing to write down lengthy answers to your questions! Open questions can be harder to analyse, as the respondent can give a wider range of answers. The answers to any open questions will need to be coded for qualitative analysis, or converted into numbers if you are going to quantitatively analyse your data (see Chapters 13 and 14 for an overview of data analysis).

Often, you will have the choice between using open and closed ques-tions. Rather than make an arbitrary choice, you should think about the purpose of your questionnaire. The following guidelines may be of use. Use closed questions if:

- You require quantitative data.
- You have a clear idea of all of the likely responses.
- Responses are likely to be simple.
- It is important for respondents to answer using a pre-determined set of responses.

Use open questions if:

- You require qualitative data.
- You are unsure of the likely responses.
- Responses are likely to be complex.
- The respondent's own words are important.

154

An alternative approach is combine open and closed questions, so that a number of responses are provided but the respondent has the opportunity to respond in an alternative manner if none of the responses are appropriate, or to elaborate on a particular response. For example:

Q.3 Who was the most important influence on you in your decision to take up your chosen sport? (please tick one box)

Father ☐
Mother ☐
Brother ☐
Sister ☐
Teacher ☐
Other ☐ (please state) . . . .

Using scales

Occasionally you may need to measure a concept using a scale. A scale is a series of questions designed to gain a single measure of a concept, such as an attitude towards or opinion on something. Thus, several questions will contribute to an overall score. A number of different scaling techniques exist.

Likert scales

These are generally used to assess attitudes. A Likert scale allows the respondent to indicate the extent to which they agree with a certain statement. At its simplest level, such a scale may provide a statement and the respondent may be asked whether they agree or disagree. Often, however, a respondent will be unhappy about being forced into such an either/or choice. Likert scales can be used to measure the extent to which participants agree or disagree with a particular statement, and are useful for questions where there may be no clear responses, such as 'yes' or 'no'. Responses can be scored, for example, if there is a five point scale (respondents have the option of ticking one of five possible responses) then a response that ticks the first box scores one, a response that ticks the next box scores two, and so on, thus providing ordinal data.

Q.4 Do you agree that sponsorship of major sporting events is an effective marketing strategy for major corporations?

Yes, very much so ☐ ☐ ☐ ☐ ☐ No, not at all.

Semantic differential

This format measures the respondent's reaction to a specified concept using a scale with contrasting adjectives at each end. For example:

Q.5 Just before I start a football game I feel:

| Relaxed | ❑ ❑ ❑ ❑ ❑ | Anxious |
| Optimistic | ❑ ❑ ❑ ❑ ❑ | Pessimistic |

The responses are scored in the same way as for a Likert scale. Semantic differential scales are also useful to assess respondents' attitudes towards a particular phenomenon without forcing them into an extreme choice. You should ensure that the two adjectives are related, however. For example, you couldn't use 'anxious' and 'confident', as respondents may score highly on both.

Using existing scales

Inexperienced researchers often feel that to add to the originality of their research, they should always develop their own questions or scales, and that the use of somebody else's questionnaire lays them open to

156

the charge of plagiarism. In reality, you are, in almost every case, better off using existing questions and scales, especially if they have been designed to measure the same concepts that you are interested in (provided, of course, that you fully acknowledge the source of the original questionnaire!). These will already have been assessed in terms of their reliability and validity, and using existing questions allows you to compare your findings with those of others much more easily. Valid and reliable scales are difficult and time consuming to develop and even apparently straightforward concepts may be difficult to measure using a scale. Sport is a complex social phenomenon, and the concepts within it are rarely one-dimensional, that is they cannot be measured using a single question. Scales therefore have to measure the multidimensionality of concepts, and developing such scales can often be a task that is time consuming even to experienced researchers. Thus, when searching the literature, you should be prepared to look for information not only about the relevant concepts and ideas, but also about how such concepts and ideas have been measured in the past.

Ranking questions

Ranking questions ask the respondent to place responses in order of importance. These are appropriate when you want respondents to consider the relative merits of particular items.

Q.6 Please rank the following sports in order of preference 1 to 3, with 1 signifying the sport you like most, and 3 signifying the sport you like least:

Field hockey   ❑
Basketball   ❑
Tennis   ❑

Ensure that you don't have too many choices to rank with this type of question. Asking respondents to rank ten items in order is an extremely difficult task.

List questions

These questions allow the respondent to indicate several responses to one question. For example:

157

Q.7 Which of the following companies have sponsored sports events to your knowledge in the last twelve months? (please tick as appropriate)

General Motors ❑   Ford ❑   Gillette ❑   Coca-Cola ❑

One of the issues that you need to be aware of with questions such as this is that when you come to enter this data in SPSS, you will have to treat each response as a separate question, so instead of analysing Q.7 as a single question, you will have to analyse each sponsor separately, and whether the response was 'yes' or 'no'.

Filter questions

It is important that you don't alienate potential respondents by asking them to read through and respond to large numbers of irrelevant questions. Filter questions can be used where appropriate to prevent this. Often some of your questions will be inapplicable to certain respondents. Rather than forcing respondents to read each question and decide whether or not it is relevant, questions which are not applicable can be filtered out using the following format:

Q.8 Have you paid to attend a live sports event in the past seven days?
No ❑ please go to question 9.
Yes ❑

If YES: what event(s) did you pay to watch? . . . .

. . . .

Using filter questions can minimise the time taken to complete the questionnaire, and reduce the potential frustration that respondents may feel when reading through a number of questions that don't apply to them. This can be a useful way of helping to increase your response rates.

Ordering the questionnaire

Once you have designed the specific questions, it is then important to consider their sequence within the questionnaire. There is no set order, but you should consider the following points:

- Try to begin the questionnaire with a few straightforward, closed questions requiring factual answers if at all possible. It is important to get the respondent to actually start completing the questionnaire. Once the first few questions have been completed, it is much more likely that the respondent will persevere.
- You should therefore avoid putting complex questions, questions requiring detailed thought, or questions requiring lengthy responses at the beginning of the questionnaire.
- Group questions on a similar theme together, and avoid jumping from topic to topic.
- The location of personal, or what might be perceived as potentially threatening questions needs to be carefully considered. Some authors suggest that they are placed at the end of the questionnaire, however others argue that this may give the impression of them being 'hidden away', and that it is better to be open, and include them at the beginning. You need to firstly think about whether such questions are actually needed, and make a judgement using your own competence as a researcher.

Designing internet surveys

There are two broad means by which you can collect survey data online. The first (and preferable) is to undertake an internet survey, which involves the questionnaire being hosted online, using specialist survey software such as Survey Monkey, or a tool such as Google Docs. An alternative is to undertake an email survey, which involves including the survey in the body of the email, or as an attachment. Including the survey within the body of the email does restrict the design and layout of the questionnaire, and the use of an attachment does involve greater effort on behalf of the respondent, with a subsequent risk in terms of response rates. You also lose many of the benefits of a hosted questionnaire, such as the option to download data directly to your analysis software.

The process of undertaking an internet survey differs slightly from that of paper based survey. The stages are as follows:

1   Initial design of the questionnaire.
2   Piloting of the questionnaire. This can be done, at this stage, using a paper-based copy of the questionnaire. This stage is key to ensuring that the nature and wording of the questions are appropriate, clear and so on.
3   Create the questionnaire electronically, using a package such as Google Docs or Survey Monkey.
4   Pilot the online survey. As well as testing the wording, this stage is to test the experience of completing the survey, the clarity of instructions, ease of navigation and so on.
5   Invite potential respondents to complete the survey, for example through emailing the relevant URL to your population.
6   Monitor the progress of data collection, sending reminders if appropriate.
7   Close the survey, and download data for analysis.

Poynter (2010) provides useful guidance in terms of designing an online survey:

- Ensure a welcoming first page that includes the necessary information (see designing the covering letter in Chapter 7), and a last page that thanks the respondent for taking part, as well as providing any relevant informant about how the data will be used, any incentives, and allowing the respondent to make any comments, through including an open question. Use a multi-page design, where no scrolling is necessary, rather than including all questions on a single page where the respondent has to scroll down.
- Put related questions together on the same page. Otherwise, one question per page is acceptable.
- If a single question is too long to be displayed on the screen without scrolling (e.g. there are a large number of potential responses), then tell the respondent that scrolling is necessary to read the entire question.
- Consider having a brief section at the top of each page or section where the questions are set in context, and any useful information can be given, for example a line such as 'the following questions are designed to examine your attitudes towards the cost of televised sport. For each question, please read the statement carefully, and indicate your level of agreement with that statement'.

- Provide an indicator of progress. Some packages will allow a graphical indication of how much progress has been made, if this isn't available, then a simple text based indication, such as 'page 3 of 4' is helpful.

In addition, you should also ensure the following:

- Respondents should be able to move back and forwards between sections.
- Don't overuse graphics, and ensure that colours and fonts should be appropriate and allow the content to be easily read.
- Make error messages both as precise and friendly as possibly.
- Avoid too many forced questions if possible. A forced question is one that has to be answered before progressing to the next one. Too many may encourage the respondent to fill in an arbitrary response simply to move on, or to abort the survey.
- Put personal questions at the beginning, rather than the end of the survey. Andrews *et al.* (2003) note that attrition rates are higher when such questions are placed at the end of the survey.

Enhancing the online survey experience

Whatever the data collection method, one of your responsibilities as researcher is to ensure that the experience is a positive one for the respondent, and this is certainly true for an internet survey. Poynter (2010) outlines a range of issues to improve the survey experience for an online participant. Two important aspects are:

1 Being 'better with people', so making it clear to respondents why they have been asked, and why their help is important. It is also important to be honest about how long the survey will take to complete, and ensuring all instructions are politely worded.
2 Improving the survey itself. You should thus ensure that the survey is as short as possible while collecting all of the required data. Questions should make sense, and have no mistakes (this should, of course, be picked up during the piloting).

161

Problems in questionnaire design

Unlike many other forms of data collection, questionnaire surveys, whether paper, telephone or online, generally only allow the researcher a 'one-off' chance at research. If the questionnaire is badly designed, then it is unlikely that you will get another chance to collect the data, due either to time restrictions, or the difficulties in finding further participants. Therefore, you should be aware of some of the potential errors in designing a questionnaire.

Ambiguous/complex wording

Keep the questions as simple as possible. Questions that may seem clear to the researcher may not be clear to the respondent, especially if the sample group is likely to be diverse. You should also avoid using technical, or 'academic' language. The questions should be understandable to the lowest level of education or understanding that the sample may encompass. For example, if you are collecting data from a broad cross-section of the population, then your questionnaire must be understandable to children. Otherwise, you are likely to under-represent this group in your achieved sample, leading to non-response bias.

Incorrectly pre-coding closed questions

An easy mistake to make is to incorrectly identify the pre-determined responses that you provide for your respondents. An example of this would be the following question:

Q.9 How many times a week do you train?

Never ❑
1–2 times ❑
2–3 times a week ❑
More than 3 times ❑

Those respondents who train twice a week could fill in more than one box, leading to problems of reliability and validity. Alternatively you may omit possible responses, so that none of the available responses are appropriate to the respondent.

162

Leading questions

Questions such as 'Do you agree that potentially dangerous performance enhancing drugs should be banned?' should be avoided, as respondents may feel pressured to agree with such statements. Try not to influence respondents in any way by your question wording.

Double-barrelled questions

Avoid asking for respondents' views on two separate issues in the same question. Questions such as 'Do you agree that rugby is a dangerous sport and should be banned?' asks two different questions, yet only allows for a single answer. Ensure that each question measures a single concept.

Vague questions

Questions such as 'Do you regularly take part in physical activity?' may be interpreted in different ways by respondents. Some may interpret 'regularly' as meaning once a week, for others it may mean once a year. Both interpretations are valid in their own way. In the same way that you have to be able to clearly define each concept in your conceptual framework, as outlined in Chapter 6, you should be able to clearly define the concepts in each question, and ensure that your understanding of those concepts is the same as the person completing the question. If necessary, define any terms.

Threatening questions

It is often difficult to obtain valid information if the respondent is likely to feel threatened at all. When undertaking research into violence in sport, or the use of performance enhancing drugs, for example, the respondent may well under-report, or even deny such activity. The researcher must first identify any threatening questions, and second, carefully word these questions to reduce bias. Try to word such questions in a neutral manner. If you are asking such questions, then you should clearly highlight the confidential nature of the data to potential respondents.

Incorrectly operationalising concepts

If the concept has not been suitably operationalised, then it will be impossible to collect valid data. An example may be that you have operationalised commitment to playing for a particular amateur sports team in terms of how many times a respondent plays a season. It may be that an individual is extremely committed, yet can only play irregularly, perhaps due to work or family commitments. In such an instance, the data obtained would lack validity.

Questions being subject to a positivity bias

Matlin and Gawron (1979) described something called the Pollyanna effect, or the tendency for people to tend to agree with positive statements about themselves. Thus, asking people to agree or disagree with questions such as 'I am generally an honest person' are less likely to receive responses that disagree. This is also related to the Forer effect, which is an effect whereby individuals are also likely to rate vague and generalised statements as highly accurate for them individually. Thus, questions such as 'you are someone who enjoys taking part in sport and physical activity on a regular basis' are likely to produce high ratings in terms of agreement.

Not including a 'don't know' or 'not applicable' option

There may be questions where respondents simply do not know, can't give, or don't want to give an answer. Ensure that they have the option not to respond.

Piloting the questionnaire

No matter how well designed you think your questionnaire is, it is vital that it is piloted beforehand. A pilot survey refers to a small-scale administration of the survey prior to the main administration. The pilot survey performs a number of important functions, including:

- To check that the wording of the questionnaire is clear, unambiguous and understandable to the intended sample.
- To check that the sequence of the questionnaire is clear and logical to respondents.

164

- To assess the likely completion time of the questionnaire.
- To check the administration of the questionnaire, from its initial distribution to receiving the completed questionnaire.
- To allow you a 'dry run' at analysing the data collected from the questionnaire.

The last point is one that is often overlooked. It is worth inputting your preliminary data from the pilot questionnaires into whatever package you are going to use for analysis (see Chapter 13), and using this data to try to answer your question to ensure that the data you collect is suitable for your purposes.

Your pilot survey should be carried out in conditions as close as possible to the main survey, and with as similar a sample group as possible. Thus, if your questionnaire is going to be administered to a sample that includes children, then the pilot sample should also include children. The results of the pilot should be closely monitored. Once changes have been made, then the survey must be re-piloted and the need for any further changes assessed. You should then continue to pilot your questionnaire until you are completely happy with its design, even if it takes a number of attempts.

MEASURING THE ECONOMIC IMPACT OF VISITORS TO SPORTS TOURNAMENTS AND SPECIAL EVENTS

UK Sport (1999) provided a set of guidelines for those conducting research into the economic impact of major sporting events. These studies are generally done through visitor surveys, and the additional expenditure generated within a city as a consequence of hosting an event can partially be evaluated through self-completion questionnaires. Through examining the design of their questionnaire, we can develop an idea of how questionnaires should be designed to achieve their research objectives. It is important that a questionnaire of this type is kept as short as possible to maximise response rates. Thus, as with any good questionnaire, each question has a particular purpose related to the objectives of the research.

The objectives of the research were as follows:

- Objective 1. To quantify the proportions of respondents who live in the host city and those who are from outside the host city.
- Objective 2. To determine the catchment area of the event by local, regional, national and international responses.

Economic impacts refer only to expenditure made by out-of-town visitors. Thus a question is required to differentiate between local and non-local respondents. This question also allows researchers to identify the proportion of out-of-town visitors to the event, as well as enabling the catchment area of an event to be identified.

Q.1 Where do you live? (Please specify town or city) . . ..

Note that an open question is used, as it is not possible to list all potential responses. It is important to specify the level of detail, by ensuring respondents specify the town or city, otherwise unhelpful answers such as 'England' may be returned. At this point, those who live within the host city can be identified, and the data collection terminated.

■   Objective 3. To group respondent types by their role in the event, for example, media, spectators, competitors, officials, etc.

Different groups will show different characteristics, therefore it is important to have knowledge of which group the respondent belongs to.

Q.2 Which of the following are you?

Athlete   ❏   Coach   ❏
Official   ❏   Media   ❏
Spectator   ❏   Other   ❏

In this instance, all the appropriate responses are known, thus a closed question is appropriate. This allows easy analysis of responses, as well as being easier and quicker for the respondent.

■   Objective 4. To identify the basic characteristics of respondents.

Certain characteristics – such as gender – are easily observed. Other characteristics, such as the size of the group of which the respondent was a part, are included on the questionnaire. Note the use of a filter question to minimise the need to answer irrelevant questions:

Q.3 Are you attending the athletics alone?   Yes ❏   No ❏

If YES please go to question 4a.

If NO: How many other adults (over 16) are there in your party today?   ❏

If NO: How many other children (under 16) are there in your party today? ❏

166

- Objective 5. To quantify the number of people from outside the host city staying overnight in the host city and from this subsample to quantify how many are staying in commercially provided accommodation. Accommodation is by far the largest expenditure item, and those staying overnight are likely to spend more elsewhere. Thus, it is important to quantify such individuals. By using two questions, the location where respondents are staying, the type of accommodation utilised, and the proportion of day to overnight visitors could be ascertained:

Q.4a In which town/city are you staying tonight? . . . .

Q.4b Is this

At home ❑   With friends/relatives ❑   A guest house ❑

A hotel ❑   A camp site ❑   Other ❑

If OTHER, please specify . . . .

Note the importance of allowing respondents an alternative option if none of the given options are appropriate.

- Objective 6. To quantify how many nights those staying in commercial accommodation will spend in the city and how much per night such accommodation is costing. The revenue from visitors staying in commercial accommodation is, as we noted, the largest source of economic revenue. To calculate this revenue, two questions are again needed:

Q.5a How many nights are you staying in town/city X? . . . .

If you are not staying overnight in town/city X go to question 6.

Q.5b If you are staying overnight in town/city X: How much are you spending on accommodation per night?. . . . .

Simple analysis thus allows the number of commercial bed-nights (number of visitors X number of nights stayed) and revenue (commercial bed-nights X average cost per bed-night) to be calculated.

- Objective 7. To quantify the amount spent per day on six standard categories of expenditure.

For such a study, it is also important to quantify the amount spent on other products and services by all respondents (not just overnight visitors).

It is important that only expenditure made in the host town or city is included, and thus the question is designed to reflect this:

Q.6 How much will you spend in town/city X TODAY on the following?

Food and drink ❑   Programmes/merchandise ❑   Entertainment ❑
Shopping/souvenirs ❑   Travel ❑   Other (parking, petrol, etc.) ❑

- ▪ Objective 8. To quantify how much in total people have budgeted to spend in a host city and on how many other people this expenditure will be made. People may combine an event with another activity, such as a mini-break or business, for example.

To identify additional expenditure that would not otherwise be picked up, a question is included to quantify the total amount individuals have budgeted to spend in the host city. The final part of this question asks how many other people this expenditure is being made for. Response to this question enables any amount of expenditure already identified to be put on a per capita basis.

Q.7 How much have you budgeted to spend in TOTAL during your stay in town/city X?

Total expenditure . . . .

Does this include expenditure on others   Yes ❑   No ❑

If YES: how many others is this expenditure for? . . . .

- ▪ Objective 9. To establish the proportion of people whose main reason for being in the host city is the event under investigation. It may be that, in certain instances, those attending the event are not in the host town or city specifically for that event. Thus, any economic impacts from such visitors cannot be attributed to the sporting event itself. A question is needed to identify such individuals:

Q.8 Is event Y the main reason for your being in town/city X today?

Yes ❑   No ❑

- ▪ Objective 10. To determine if any respondents are combining their visit to the host city with a holiday. For some, an event may lead to a deci-sion to take a break, or a holiday. For example, the World Cup may lead to supporters spending an extended period of time in the host nation.

168

For such individuals, their economic impact is clearly greater than on the day or days of the event. Thus, it is important to have some data about these people:

Q.9 Are you combining your visit to event 'Y' with a holiday? Yes ❑ No ❑

If YES: Where are you going? . . . .

For how long? . . . .

Can you provide us with a rough estimate of your total budget for this part of your trip? £ . . . .

The results of this question allow the wider economic impacts of an event to be assessed. For some events (such as the World Cup, Olympic and Commonwealth Games, etc.) such extended impacts are significant, and an important consequence of hosting them.

Increasing your response rate

As well as the design of the questionnaire itself, you need to be thinking about its administration, that is how it will be given to potential respondents, how it will be returned, and how you will ensure that as many are returned as possible. It is important to maximise the response rate for both academic and pragmatic reasons. A low response rate leads to the question of whether there are any particular groups that have not responded and why, what are the effects of the non-response on the findings, and whether there is bias in the data as a consequence. If children, for example, have not completed the questionnaire because it was too complex, then how can an accurate overview of the entire population be made? Taking a more pragmatic view, especially from the point of view of those undertaking student dissertations, low response rates can be expensive if you have to send out a considerably higher number of postal questionnaires than you originally anticipated (especially if you remember that each questionnaire will involve not only the postage costs involved in sending it to the recipient, but also the cost of the pre-paid reply envelope).

Ethically, it is important to remember that you cannot coerce participants to complete a questionnaire – it has to be done voluntarily. You can take steps to persuade them gently, however, but without putting undue pressure on them. Frankfort-Nachimas and Nachimas (1996) have identified a number of techniques that may be adopted to increase response rates. You should not focus on only one or two of these techniques, however – all of them should be considered.

- Follow-up – a gentle reminder at an appropriate time, for example after two weeks, will encourage non-respondents. Make sure the tone of the follow up is appropriate, and not coercive.
- Inducement – an incentive, provided it is one that is valued, can be helpful.
- Sponsorship – support from an organisation or individual of which respondents are aware may be helpful.
- Method of return – the easier the method of return, the higher the response rate. Online surveys are advantageous here.
- Format – the layout must be totally professional and user friendly.
- A population that is interested in or familiar with the subject will result in a higher response rate, as is one that feels that the survey may be of some use.

The covering letter

You should always include a covering letter or accompanying email with any questionnaire that includes the information required in your participation information sheet (Chapter 7). As well as fulfilling your ethical requirements to provide your participants with information about the study, it is extremely important as one method of maximising the response rate. It should be separate to the main survey (i.e. as a separate letter, never as a few lines at the top of a questionnaire, or as an introductory email followed up with a separate email linking to the questionnaire).

If you are carrying out a telephone or face-to-face survey, you should also cover the same points as would be included in your covering letter.

This can be done using a 'script' that has been prepared in place of the covering letter. Covering letters should also be piloted, to ensure that you have not been ambiguous, or said anything that lacks clarity or relevance to your sample.

Administering the questionnaire at sporting events

Although having an appropriately designed questionnaire is important, it is not simply a case of distributing questionnaires wherever and whenever possible. If you have access to details about your population, then it is generally straightforward to provide them with the questionnaire. In some cases, however, you will need to distribute your questionnaire during a sporting event (provided you have appropriate permission). The following process is suggested by the Sport Industry Research Centre (SIRC).

Preplanning

Each potential respondent group must be considered, so that a strategy can be implemented for optimum data capture. Thus, the following issues need to be assessed:

- How many of each respondent group will there be?
- When will they be arriving?
- Where will they be staying?
- How will it be possible to get convenient access to them?
- Are there any unique circumstances relevant to any group which may have an effect on the research?

You will also need to consider how the questionnaires will be given to potential respondents, and how many assistants you will need to undertake this task.

Collection

You then need to consider whether questionnaires will be left with the sample, to be returned at a later date through the post, or whether they will be completed face-to-face. Postal questionnaires (distributed either at the event or through lists of attendees where available) are considered cost effective, and allow participants to complete the questions in their own time. However, response rates may be low, and two or more follow-up letters may be required to achieve a desired response rate. An alternative is to hand participants the questionnaire and wait with them while they complete it. This can be problematic, as during the event spectators are unlikely to have the time or inclination to complete a questionnaire, and this method is also much more resource intensive. Unless you have a team of helpers, it is unlikely you will be able to collect sufficient data unless you are prepared to spend a considerable time within the field. One possible answer to this is to use the approach of Pol and Pak (1994), and obtain names and addresses during the event, which can then be used after the event has finished.

Following up non-respondents

After the final date for questionnaire returns has passed, you will need to contact those who have not returned their questionnaires. This is usually done by sending a follow-up letter or email, and a copy of the original questionnaire or reminder of the link to the questionnaire, as well as a pre-paid envelope in which to return the questionnaire if appropriate. Do not send the original covering letter, as this was obviously unsuccessful in eliciting a response first time round! Instead, one approach is to suggest that the failure to return a completed questionnaire was an oversight on the participant's part, rather than a straight refusal. Stress the importance of the study, and how valuable the contribution that would be made by completing the questionnaire. You must ensure as before, however, that you do not coerce the respondent into completing the questionnaire in any way. Remember to include a further cut-off date as appropriate.

172

Summary

1   Questionnaires are generally an appropriate method to collect large amounts of relatively simple data.
2   The advantages of using questionnaires include the accessibility of your sample, reduced bias, anonymity, structured data and allowing time for respondents.
3   The disadvantages include the need for relatively simple questions, no control over the completion of the questionnaire, no opportunity to probe responses and relatively low response rates.
4   The design of the questionnaire is crucial. Careful design and piloting are required.
5   There are a number of means whereby you can improve your response rate. Of these means, following up non-respondents, inducements, sponsorship by an outside body and an appropriate covering letter seem to be the most effective.

Activity

1   You should use your research question developed in the suggested activity at the end of Chapter 4. Design a preliminary questionnaire suitable to obtain data to answer this research question, using a range of question formats.
2   Pilot this questionnaire to a sample of approximately five others. Get your sample to critically comment on the design of the questionnaire.
3   Redesign your questionnaire in light of the pilot study.
4   Produce a covering letter for the questionnaire. Again, pilot this to a small group, asking them to critically comment upon it, and redesign as necessary.
5   Explore one of the online survey tools, such as Survey Monkey or Google Docs. Create a short questionnaire to get the feel of designing an online survey. Email the link to the questionnaire to 4–5 people and, as above, get them to critically comment upon its design and layout.

173

If you are thinking of using a questionnaire, consider the following points:

- Can I justify using a questionnaire as the most appropriate method by which to collect my data? How?
- What type of questionnaire is most appropriate, for example would an online survey be preferable?
- What steps can I take to ensure the validity and reliability of the data that I collect using this method?
- What will be the effect of a low response rate on the reliability and validity of the data that I collect? How can I maximise my response rate?

Further reading

Oppenheim, A. (1992) *Questionnaire Design, Interviewing and Attitude Measurement*, London: Pinter.

9

Collecting data II: interviews

This chapter will:

- Discuss when interviews are an appropriate data collection tool.
- Introduce the different types of interview that you can undertake.
- Discuss some of the issues of interview design and administration.
- Introduce the concept of the focus group, or group interview.

Introduction

The interview can be contrasted with the structured nature of the questionnaire (Chapter 8) in both the type of data that is collected, and how it is collected. Whereas the questionnaire collects highly structured, generally quantitative data, and is often completed without the presence of the researcher, the researcher is a key element of the interview process, and his or her skills, attributes and interviewing technique are all an integral part of the success of this method in obtaining 'rich', qualitative data. The interview is undoubtedly the most common method by which qualitative data is collected in sport research. Culver *et al.* (2003), for example, have noted that in their review of sport psychology research, the interview was by far the most common method to collect qualitative data in that particular discipline.

When is interviewing appropriate?

Interviewing is often associated with the collection of qualitative data, that is, the 'why' and 'how' of a phenomenon, from the respondent's perspective. Interviews can collect data concerned with concepts that are difficult or inappropriate to measure, tend to allow respondents much more freedom in terms of their answers, and tend to explore questions of 'why' and 'how' rather than the 'how many' and 'when'. Interviews tend to provide much richer data than, for example, a questionnaire survey, where respondents are generally limited to short and relatively simple responses by the format of the questionnaire, or lack the motivation to provide long, written answers. Whereas questionnaires are appropriate for collecting limited data from a large sample group, interviews are better at gaining richer data from smaller sample groups. As well as its effectiveness in collecting qualitative data, Veal (2006) notes three further situations where interviews tend to be used:

1 Where there is only a low population, making the quantitative approach of the questionnaire inappropriate.

176

2   Where the information is expected to vary considerably among respondents, and such information is likely to be complex and thus difficult to measure using other methods.
3   Where the research is exploratory, and interviews may be used to identify information that could be used to refine and develop further investigation.

As always, the key questions are those of 'what information is needed?' and 'will this method provide such information?' If rich, qualitative data are required, or you are looking for explanation, rather than description, then interviews are likely to be an appropriate method. If relatively simple data are required, then it is likely that questionnaire surveys will be a much more efficient method.

The different types of interview

Interviews can generally be classified under five categories: the structured interview, the semi-structured interview, the unstructured interview, the narrative interview, and the focus group (or group interview).

- The structured interview. This is essentially a questionnaire where the questions are read out by the researcher, who also notes the responses. This has the advantage over a respondent completion questionnaire that the respondent can seek clarification over questions that may be unclear or ambiguous.
- The semi-structured interview. This approach uses a standard set of questions, or schedule. However, the researcher adopts a flexible approach to data collection, and can alter the sequence of questions or probe for more information with subsidiary questions.
- The unstructured interview. Here the researcher has a general idea of the topics to be covered, but the respondent tends to lead the direction of the interview. Further questions are developed by the researcher as the interview progresses. This allows the respondent to provide information from his or her own perspective, and to develop areas that are important to them, rather than being led by the interview schedule. Phenomenological interviews (see later in the chapter) tend to be unstructured.

- The narrative interview. This is an approach whereby the interviewee allows the participant time to describe and develop a story, and relive their experiences, and life histories, and how they see or make sense of things that have happened to them with very little involvement from the interviewee. The story emerges almost entirely from the participant. Although there are guidelines and areas to cover within a narrative interview (see below), the researcher takes less of a role guiding the narrative interview than would be the case with an unstructured interview.
- The focus group. Essentially this is an interview involving a group, often consisting of between four and eight participants, rather than one-on-one interaction, and interaction between members of the group is an important element in obtaining data. Focus groups tend towards being semi-structured in nature.

Advantages of interviews

There are a number of methods that can be utilised within qualitative research, however interviews have a number of advantages that make them appropriate in certain situations. As with any other methods, the important thing is to take advantage of the strengths of the methods while minimising any potential limitations.

- Interviews enable participants to talk about their own experiences in their own words, and allow them to elaborate on any areas of particular interest or importance.
- The interview can be more insightful than other methods. As Yin (1994, p.80) notes, the interview 'provides perceived causal inferences' from the actor's, rather than the researcher's point of view. This allows the respondent to become more of an 'informant', providing data from their own perspective, which is often desirable, especially within inductive research.
- Interviews allow unexpected data to emerge. Unstructured or semi-structured interviews allow the emergence of important themes that may not emerge from a more structured format. This enables the subjects to reveal insights into their attitudes and behaviour that may

178

not readily be apparent to the researcher from their prior awareness of the phenomenon. Questionnaires are restricted to a series of questions developed by the researcher, and respondents are limited to these questions, with the occasional final question along the lines of 'if you have any further comments, please write these below', which can be less than ideal in persuading participants to introduce new areas of information.

- A face-to-face interview allows you to assess the participant's body language, facial expressions, tone of voice, etc. which may be useful in some cases.
- By using interviews, the researcher can introduce him or herself to the subject and establish trust and rapport, especially if any information is considered confidential, or sensitive.
- Interviews allow you to investigate target groups that may be less able to complete surveys (such as the less well educated, or older or younger respondents for example).
- Interviews may allow the researcher to develop a sense of time and history, rather than providing a series of 'static' responses, which may be the outcome of a survey. They allow the responses to be put into context, rather than providing a 'snapshot' picture.

Disadvantages of interviews

As well as the undoubted strengths of interviewing as a data collection method, it does have a number of potential weaknesses that need to be considered before you carry out any interviews:

- Interviews require more resources than questionnaires. They may be expensive both in terms of time and travelling, and as a consequence the resulting sample may be small and unrepresentative of the wider population, especially if your budget is limited.
- It is possible that you may add bias as a result of your – often unconscious – verbal and non-verbal reactions, for example through nodding at certain responses, which may encourage the informant to answer in the manner that he or she thinks you want. It may be the case that the participant thinks that they have to provide the 'right' answers, rather than their own views, which may

be exacerbated by you nodding or shaking your head after each response.

- The interviewee may become dominant and lead the interview in unwanted directions. The researcher must be prepared to guide the interviewee back to the interview schedule.
- Analysis of the data may be difficult. The analysis of questionnaire data is often relatively straightforward, and requires little or no interpretation on the part of the researcher. Analysis of qualitative interview data may be more difficult, especially where there may be ambiguity. As Fontana and Frey (1998, p.47) suggest: 'Asking questions and getting answers is a much harder task than it may seem at first. The spoken word always has a residue of ambiguity, no matter how carefully we word the questions and report or code the answers.'
- As with all self-report measures, the quality of the data is dependent upon the responses of the interviewee. Interviewees are subject to problems of recall, misperception and incorrect knowledge.

Thus, as with all methods, the strengths of the interview need to be consolidated, and the weaknesses eradicated as far as possible. The use of appropriate probes, neutral body language and validation of your interpretation of the data by others (more on these points later) can be used to minimise such bias.

Designing the interview guide

Designing the interview largely follows the same process as designing a questionnaire, that is you need to identify what information is required, and how you will get that information using an interview. The two key differences are that first, your interview guide is likely to be much less prescriptive that a questionnaire, and may simply include a list of bullet points regarding topics that you are looking to cover (or even less, if undertaking an unstructured or narrative interview), and second, once you have determined the structure of your questionnaire, you are generally unable to alter it, whereas you may be able to continually develop and refine your interview guide to some extent between, or even during

180

interviews. A few points to note when constructing your initial interview guide are as follows:

- Introduce the purpose and structure of the interview beforehand. In much the same way that a covering letter for a questionnaire provides the respondent with important information, your introduction should also 'set the scene', and you may find it useful to apply the guidelines about participant information sheets in Chapter 7 to your introduction to the interviewee.
- Group questions about the same concept together, and try to avoid jumping back and forwards between topics. Keep the interviewee on your side, one way to ensure you don't do this is to have an illogical structure to your interview.
- Begin with one or more 'easy' questions that will put the respondent at ease, and encourage them to begin talking comfortably. This question need not be directly relevant to the research – it is more important at this stage to gain the co-operation and trust of the interviewee. Don't spend too long on background questions though, as they may be busy and have limited time, and you do not want them to have to end the interview before you have elicited all of the required information.
- Ensure that the questions are clearly worded, unambiguous and understandable to the interviewee. Make sure too that the relevance of each question is clear. If the relevance is not apparent, or if the interviewee seems unclear, then take time to explain the purpose of the question.
- Ask personal, or potentially threatening questions (if necessary to the research) towards the end of the interview, once you have had a chance to develop trust between interviewer and interviewee. Again, make it clear as to why such questions are being asked.

Once a preliminary interview schedule has been developed, then it is important to pilot it, in much the same way as you would do with a questionnaire. As well as testing the questions, piloting an interview provides a further important function. It will provide a useful run through for the interviewer, and may increase confidence when it comes to the actual interviews, especially for the inexperienced researcher. You will find your first interview difficult, so a pilot will be helpful to you.

USING INTERVIEWS TO EXAMINE SPORT AND BELONGING AMONG NORWEGIAN MUSLIM WOMEN

Walseth (2007) wanted to explore the commonly held belief that sport creates and enhances a sense of belonging to a community by collecting data from a number of young immigrant Norwegian Muslim women. To do this, she decided upon a life history approach, an approach which aims to get the respondent to provide a rich, detailed narrative of their life in their own words, in chronological order. The requirement for rich, detailed data from a life history normally (although not always) makes asking respondents to write this detail impractical, thus making one-on-one interviews the logical choice. Second, the need for respondents to be able to focus on areas they, rather than the researcher, considered important is more suited to such a method. The interviews consisted of three parts. The first covered descriptive data, such as family background. The second involved respondents being asked to describe their lives as a book, where their life story was divided into different chapters. The final part allowed the researcher to ask about areas of interest that did not emerge in part two, focusing on sport and physical activity.

The findings from the interviews demonstrated that for some Norwegian Muslim women, sport acted as a source of social support, and allowed reciprocal friendships to develop, and in cases led participants to feel part of a wider, 'imagined' community. Second, sport was a place of 'refuge' for some, whereby it provided an avenue to escape from the trials of everyday life. Third, sport provided a means for positive identity confirmation and image building. For some, however, sport contributed to feelings of exclusion, especially where barriers were perceived between respondents and others within the sport.

Carrying out the interview

It is important for you to project professionalism, enthusiasm and confidence to the interviewee. Both appearance and demeanour are important in projecting these. As well as being appropriately dressed, you should ensure that you appear knowledgeable about the subject under discussion, and can discuss this confidently. Thus, it is not a good idea to rush into interviews before you have become proficient in your field of study. The location of the interview is important. It needs to take place where the interviewee is comfortable answering questions, such as their own home or office. The location should be relatively private so that there will be no bias from the presence of others (ensure that the interview cannot be overheard, as this can be extremely off-putting to the participant). Finally, the interview should take place in a location free from high levels of background noise, especially if the interview is being recorded.

The skills required by an interviewer are more than those of simply being able to talk to others. Always remember that the overall objective of the interview is to gather rich, detailed data to answer your research question. To achieve this, Hannabus (1996) suggests the following techniques:

- Establish rapport – this should start from when you first contact your interviewee.
- Keep the discussion going. Short periods of silence may actually be beneficial, in that the interviewee may be persuaded to provide further data, but try to avoid periods of lengthy silence. Know when not to interrupt and let silences work for you, but be prepared to step in with a comment or further questions if appropriate.
- Avoid asking questions which can be answered with simply a 'yes' or a 'no'.
- Avoid jargon and abstractions with which the interviewee is unlikely to be familiar.
- Avoid double negatives and loaded expressions.
- Be non-judgmental in your reactions to the interviewee's responses, and avoid reacting in any way that may influence further data collection.
- Remember to keep focusing on your research objectives, and try not to stray from them.

In addition, Fontana and Frey (1998) provide some useful guidelines that may seem obvious, but are often overlooked by researchers. These include:

- Never deviate from the introduction, sequence of questions (if it is a structured interview) or question wording unless you feel that you will be able to obtain better data from the interviewee.

- Never let another person interrupt, or offer their own views on the question.
- Never suggest an answer, or show agreement or disagreement with a response. Your own views should not be apparent to the interviewee.

PROBING

One key advantage of the interview as a research method is that of your opportunity to probe. For many interviews, the most important questions that you can use are not the initial questions from your interview guide, but the questions you use to follow up the initial responses, such as:

- 'Why do you think that is?'
- 'Can you tell me more about that?'
- 'Can you give me an example of that?'
- 'How did this make you feel?'
- 'What happened next?'

These are examples of probes. A probe is where the researcher can gain additional information from the respondent through using particular techniques. Two types of probe can be used:

- Clarification probes. These allow you to clarify any point that was not clear, or open to misunderstanding by the interviewee, or to clarify your understanding of a point made by the interviewee.
- Elaboration probes. These are used to elicit a more in-depth response about a particular point related to the interview. For example using phrases such as 'why is that?', 'could you expand on that?' or 'could you tell me more about that?' will often enhance the richness and quality of your data. You may be interested in the reasons why people purchase sports equipment. Their initial response may be something along the lines of 'I like the appearance'. You would then ask something along the lines of 'what is it about the appearance you like?', and then follow up with a further probe, such as 'why is that important to you?' This method allows you to collect a lot of rich detail from relatively few questions.

Interview skills do need to be practised. Although they may be relatively easy to achieve in an informal or social setting, the artificial nature of an interview makes them harder to attain, and it is likely that you will feel

184

after your first few interviews that perhaps things didn't go quite as well as they could. Don't worry – your technique will improve as you persevere. If you have videoed your initial interviews, then it can often be a good idea to observe your own interviewing technique. Otherwise, you may be able to gain feedback from interviewees, and develop your technique accordingly.

Phenomenological interviews

Phenomenology is both a philosophical and methodological concept which focuses upon people's experiences and perceptions of the subjective world within which they exist, or their 'life-world', collecting data normally through one-to-one interviews. The aim of phenomenology is to describe a phenomenon as it manifests itself to the person experiencing it using first-person accounts to arrive at an understanding of both the meaning and essence of experience (Jones *et al.* 2013). Phenomenology may be descriptive, or interpretive. Whichever approach is adopted, the aims of the phenomenological interview remain similar, firstly to allow participants to express their own world as fully as possible, and to allow the essence of that life world to be captured, such as achieved by Brymer and Schweitzer's (2013) exploration of the 'search for freedom' in extreme sports, which utilised 15 phenomenological interviews to identify six elements of freedom. To develop this type of understanding, the phenomenological interview starts with a request for the interviewee to describe an experience as fully as they can. Rather than any other pre-determined questions, the researcher will then need to rely on relevant probes and prompts to elicit further information, which should be as open as possible. Thus, the phenomenological interview can be a difficult one for the novice researcher.

Narrative interviews

Narrative interviews are designed to elicit stories. These rich, detailed stories then allow us to understand how people make sense of, and interpret what has happened to them. A narrative has a number of elements, such as an overall plot or storyline, patterns of events, actors within the story, and a temporal element. The role of the narrative interview is to elicit these with the minimum interruption or participation of the researcher, and its important only ask questions as and when needed to develop the narrative. Thus, although you may have a list of potential questions, these should only be used sparingly, and the participant should be allowed the freedom to control the interview. Narrative interviews are particularly useful in identifying how individuals' relationships shape their lives, and reflecting their own personal experiences, and issues of identity, as demonstrated, for example, through Papathomas and Lavallee's (in press) narrative analysis of disordered eating in sport, or Knowles *et al.*'s (2014) narrative analysis of physical activity in adolescent girls.

Motivating the informant

The overall objective of the interview is to ensure that the respondent feels willing to provide the desired information, otherwise it is likely that the data will lack validity, especially if the interviewee feels pressurised into taking part, or just wants to get the interview finished as quickly as possible. Frankfort-Nachimas and Nachimas (1996) identify three factors that will help motivate the interviewee to co-operate with the researcher:

1 The respondent must feel that the interview will be enjoyable and satisfying. Three factors are important here. First the personal demeanour of the researcher must be such as to create a good impression. Second, the informant must be briefed as to the nature of the interview and how it is to be carried out, and given an indication of the likely length. Third, the location and timing of the interview are important, and it is advisable to let the respondent choose these as far as is practical.

2 The respondent needs to see the study as worthwhile. The respondent should feel that they are making a contribution to a worthwhile study. This can be done when individuals are initially approached to take part in the interview, as well as in the briefing beforehand.

3 Perceived barriers in the respondent's mind need to be overcome.

4 Trust needs to be developed. This can be done by explaining who you are and why you are doing the study, as well as how the respondent came to be chosen, and by ensuring the confidential nature of the research.

186

A further factor is also important here, this being the credibility of the interviewer. You also need to project your competence and credibility to be undertaking such research, and demonstrate an awareness of the key issues related to your interview. You will need to demonstrate a level of knowledge about the subject area yourself, but also demonstrate a willingness to learn from the interviewee.

Asking sensitive questions

You may, at some stage in the interview, need to ask questions that the interviewee may perceive as sensitive, or even potentially threatening in some way. It is often tempting simply to play safe and not ask these questions; however, it may be that such sensitive information is important to your research. If you do have to ask sensitive questions, you should ensure that you follow a number of guidelines:

- Ensure that the respondent is aware of the confidentiality of the data.
- Be careful in your use of language when you first approach the interviewee for help. Avoid phrases such as 'I want to investigate ...', which may imply that you are looking to uncover something underhand, and use neutral language, such as 'I am hoping to explore ...' instead.
- Don't ask sensitive questions at the beginning of the interview. Wait until you have established trust and rapport with the interviewee.
- Try not to ask such questions in any way that could be construed as 'loaded'. This is one area where piloting of the interview can be extremely useful.
- Ensure that it is clear to the respondent, if at all possible, why you are asking the question. If the respondent can see the face validity of the question, then they are more likely to give you a response.
- If you are seriously worried about asking a particular question or series of questions, then acknowledge this to the interviewee.
- Do not coerce the respondent into giving an answer. They are entitled not to answer any questions, and cannot be forced to do so.

Using visual methods within interviews

When designing your interview, you don't need to focus purely on verbal questions. There are other techniques to elicit information, and these are often referred to as 'visual methods' (you can also embed these within questionnaires, but information using these methods is generally elicited through interviews). One example of this is photo-elicitation. This is a method whereby images are introduced into the interview and used to stimulate discussion. These images may be produced by the researcher, or created by the interviewee themselves, but are used to develop deeper analysis and reflection, for example the research of Mills and Hoeber (2013) which used photo-elicitation to examine the perceptions of skaters towards various artefacts in a figure skating club through asking their interviewees to take 20–25 photos which were later discussed. The term 'photo voice' refers to the method whereby participants are given the means to record data themselves to reflect their own lives (generally through photographs or video), and present their own contexts or circumstances, rather than that of the researcher. These are, again, discussed within the interview. Such techniques are useful additions to the sport researcher, yet perhaps under-utilised, and certainly worth considering,

Recording the interview

Interviews must be recorded in some form – it is simply not possible to rely on recall alone. The choice is generally between that of written notes or audio/video recording. Sometimes the respondent will determine the choice of method, in that certain individuals may be uncomfortable with it (you must ask for their consent before recording). Taking written notes has two main advantages: first, it precludes potential problems created by using recording equipment, such as ensuring responses are audible, battery failure and so on. Second, if the researcher records only data that are relevant to the research question, then time may be saved in identifying and discarding irrelevant data. Writing notes can, however, result in a loss of rapport between interviewer and interviewee, and the interviewer's focus may be divided between the respondent and writing down notes. Recording the interview will allow more rapport to develop, which may result in more information being divulged from the respondent. This will, however, result in much more data to be analysed, and a great deal of irrelevant material to be identified and discarded. As you are likely to have only one chance to undertake each interview, I would suggest that the best option is to record it (with the interviewee's permission), as well as making limited notes.

HOW TO BECOME A GOOD INTERVIEWER

Some years ago, Baker (1994) noted five basic rules that you should follow for every interview. These are still as valid now as 20 years ago, and are as follows:

1   Understand the interview. You need to know the purpose of the interview, and also clearly understand the concepts under investigation.
2   Be committed to completing the interview. There may be the temptation to complete the interview in the shortest possible time, or to end the interview early. You should be committed at every interview to spend sufficient time to gather enough data (although the participant must be able to withdraw at any time).
3   Practise the interview. In the same way that a questionnaire survey is piloted, or pre-tested, an interview must be rehearsed beforehand.
4   Minimise the effects of your personal characteristics. Factors such as your age, dress, demeanour and so on may all affect the responses given. Depending on the nature of the interview, you should minimise these through appropriate dress, language and so on.
5   Use common sense. Be prepared to use common sense if things seem to be going wrong, or problems arise. Take each situation as it comes, and be prepared to exit the interview if things do go wrong.

Maximising the quality of the interview

As I have already noted, the concepts of validity and reliability relate less to qualitative methods such as interviews and focus groups. If you are using these as criteria to assess your approach, however, then reliability can be enhanced through a standardised interview schedule, maintaining a consistent interviewing environment, and recording with the interviewees' permission, which should then be transcribed within as short a time as possible by the researcher. Validity is harder to ensure, given that transcriptions are a tool for interpreting the interview, rather than an analysis in themselves. The key is to achieve those criteria by which qualitative research is more appropriately assessed, such as plausibility, truthfulness and credibility. A number of problems need to be considered at the outset. These are:

- Will the informant interpret the question correctly? This will be more of an issue with younger or less educated participants.
- Are informants able to verbalise their thoughts, to say what they actually feel? That is, are they able to accurately convey their feelings and experiences through their own command of language? Responses need to be critically questioned by the researcher. The researcher's own experience through participant observation will be important in this respect in being able to tacitly assess responses.
- Is the informant giving a response that is applicable only to that moment in time, or are his or her views more long term? Although their behaviours may be relatively stable, responses may be affected by events or occurrences at the time of the interview.
- Will the informant's own values affect the response? That is, will people provide information based upon what they think is the correct response, rather than their own attitudes?

Dean and Whyte (1978) have noted that the interviewer needs to take into account four major factors prior to the interview. These are:

- Does the informant have any motives that may influence his or her responses? This may be the case if the informant stands to benefit in any way from a particular response. Thus the researcher should stress the confidential, or 'blind' nature of the interview.
- Are there any 'bars to spontaneity'? That is, are there any instances where the informant hesitates to mention things that will show him or her in a negative light?
- Will the informant attempt to please the interviewer?
- Are there any idiosyncratic features that may affect a response? An example of this potential effect may be a particular news story related to a sporting event on a particular day that will have a short-term effect on the respondents' attitudes.

190

All of these considerations need to be accounted for before each interview. Two suggestions are made by Dean and Whyte (1978) to maximise the quality of the data obtained. First it is important to ensure that the subject is aware of the confidentiality of the interview. Second, it is generally a good idea to structure the interview so that a range of questions may be asked on any areas that may cause concern in terms of validity, thus using a form of 'within-interview triangulation'. The interviewer cannot always assume a relationship between responses and actual behaviour. This framework will allow a more reasoned evaluation as to what is reality, and what is distortion.

Gender and race can be important issues when collecting interview data. Watson and Scraton (2001) discuss both of these issues, demonstrating that the researcher must be aware that their own personal characteristics may have implications in terms of the data obtained. Will a white female collect the same data as a black male in a certain context, for example? They stress the need for reflexivity throughout the research process, and it is an issue that you should consider. As well as the personal characteristics, the ability of the researcher should also be critically questioned. Before undertaking interviews, the question of whether the interviewer has the appropriate skills and experience to undertake the interview needs to be evaluated. This is rarely done, and, as Biddle *et al.* (2001) note, it is rare for this issue to be addressed, even in research published within international journals.

Telephone and online interviews

Not all interviewing is carried out face-to-face, and telephone or online interviewing can be an appropriate method in some cases. Telephone interviews maintain many of the characteristics of face-to-face interviews, with the obvious exception of not being able to see each other and assess body language. Online interviews will vary, depending upon whether they are synchronous (taking place in real time), such as via Skype, or asynchronous, such as through email, where the researcher may wait some time for a response, and to be able to ask further questions, thus taking more time. Synchronous methods will need some form of data capture, which will involve specialist software such as IMCapture. Whichever form is chosen, there are both advantages and disadvantages. Cost is greatly reduced, especially if the participants are

191

geographically dispersed, and in certain cases one of these methods may be the only feasible option. Second, some individuals may prefer to be contacted by telephone or email, rather than by the interviewer in person. Finally, they may be appropriate if face-to-face interviewing would involve access to restricted or potentially dangerous locations. There are disadvantages with these methods, however. It may be more difficult to develop a rapport, and trust from the participant. Second, it is not possible to observe non-verbal reactions to questions. Third, for telephone interviews it can be difficult to record interviews without specialist equipment. Finally, online interviews through email or similar means will generally result in shorter, less detailed responses.

Interviews and sample size

The issue of sample (or 'selection') size in the collection of qualitative data is a common area of confusion. As I noted in Chapter 7, unlike quantitative analysis, where there is often a requirement for the largest possible sample size, that represents the overall population, qualitative research has different requirements. Quantitative methods such as questionnaire surveys tend to obtain relatively shallow information from a large sample. The purpose of qualitative research is to generate 'rich' data, from a small sample group, with many published studies interviewing fewer than six participants. It has been argued that a large sample group in qualitative research may actually be detrimental. Kvale (1996, p.103) suggests, with reference to qualitative research, that

> many research projects, would have profited from having fewer interviews in the study, and from taking more time to prepare the interviews and analyse them. Perhaps, as a defensive overreaction, some qualitative interview studies appear to be designed on a quantitative presupposition of 'the more interviews, the more scientific'.

As a qualitative researcher, the issue of sample size is not one that you should determine at the beginning of a study. Instead, you should aim to achieve what is referred to as 'saturation'. This refers to the stage in the fieldwork where any further data collection will not provide any different information from that you already have, that is you are not learning anything new. This point can be difficult to determine, however. If you undertake, for example, three or four interviews consecutively where no additional data are obtained, then this would be a good indication that saturation has occurred. Occasionally you may find that saturation does not occur, and in certain instances other considerations such as time or cost may be more important factors. If you do not reach saturation in your data collection, then the advice is to complete as much data collection as possible within your constraints.

**QUALITY RATHER THAN QUANTITY
IN INTERVIEW SAMPLING**

Andrew Sparkes (2000) was interested to find out the 'complex ways in which a strong athletic identity can act as an Achilles heel in terms of both shaping an individual's reactions to a disruptive life event, and the consequences of these reactions for personal long-term development' (p.15), that is how an elite sports person would react to the ending of their athletic career. The objective was not to generalise the findings to a wider population – rather to gain an understanding of the processes by which the athlete coped with the termination of their athletic identity. In this instance a purposive, rather than a random sample was chosen, consisting of a single subject – Rachel. Through examining Rachel's reactions to the end of her sporting career, Sparkes was able to explain some of the issues, which could then be generalised to other athletes. By having a small ($n = 1$), non-random sample, Sparkes was able to discover a great deal of information, and demonstrated that, in qualitative research, it is the amount of data that is important, rather than the amount of subjects.

The key informant interview

You may be able to identify one or more key informants, who will be able to supply you with specialist knowledge, based upon their position or relevant experience. Often, the key informant interview can complement data collected from other sources. For example, you may be researching the impact of a change in policy upon sport participation, and you may be able to collect data from the individual responsible for such a change. This, while not answering the question itself, will be able to provide you with useful background information, as well as developing your own knowledge of the subject matter. Be careful to assess their perspective on the issue, so that any particular views can be taken into account. An employee of a sports organisation, for example, is unlikely to provide an opinion that may go against the organisation's policies, or show that organisation in a bad light.

KEY INFORMANT INTERVIEWS:
THE RESPONSE OF PLANNING AND TRANSPORT
PROFESSIONALS TO PUBLIC HEALTH GUIDANCE

There have been a number of government policies in the UK aimed at promoting physical activity. One of the key stakeholder groups is that of planning and transport professionals, who have a potentially significant role in promoting physical activity on a day-to-day basis. Allender *et al.* (2009) wanted to find out the perceptions of these professionals to government guidance. To do so, they chose a key informant technique, whereby respondents were chosen on the basis of having appropriate knowledge and involvement within urban and transport planning and/or issues related to physical activity. Thus, key informants included:

- Transport planners
- Urban planners
- Architects
- Designers and managers of public open spaces
- School sports partnerships staff
- Primary school head teachers.

Focus groups based on these key informants identified that evidence-based guidance would be a powerful driver of future planning practice; however, such guidance might well be 'lost' within the huge volume of other guidance provided. It was also concluded that evidence-based guidance would simply confirm what was already being done.

Focus groups

Focus groups are similar in many ways to interviews, with the key difference being that a small group of people, rather than a single respondent, is used. Members of the group are able to interact with each other, with the interaction leading to a greater depth of discussion, in that ideas can be generated and discussed between group members, allowing for 'richer' information to be gathered than if participants were asked individually. The interviewer will take on the role of facilitator, and will stimulate discussion while keeping it relevant to the topic being investigated. Focus groups are often used when the information collected would be richer than that from an interview. An example of this would be research into youth groups, where young people may be unwilling to talk to a researcher on their own, but would be happy to discuss things as part of a group of other young people.

A focus group can consist of between three and 12 people (although three is undesirable, and 12 is often too many – you should really aim between four and eight, so that everyone has a chance to make some sort of significant contribution), who have not met beforehand if possible. It is important to ensure that everyone within the group contributes, and the discussion is not dominated by one or two individuals. Your role is to channel the discussion in much the same way that you would with a semi-structured interview, to ensure that the discussion is relevant, and all participants have the opportunity to contribute. This can be a difficult task, and as a consequence it is unlikely that you will be able to make any notes during the discussion. Thus you should ensure that you record the focus group, and also use a colleague to make notes of the most salient points. It is preferable to video record focus groups rather than record sound only, as this will allow you to identify which data came from which participant much more easily.

Although focus groups are a valuable means of collecting information, they can require much more in the way of organisation and resources than other methods. Successfully running a focus group is difficult to do, and you will often need to carry out a number of them before you feel totally confident, especially if the group needs a lot of guidance. Therefore you should think carefully about the use of focus groups as a method. If you do decide to use focus groups, then much of the guidance given above on interviewing applies.

**IDENTIFYING THE OUTCOMES OF OUTDOOR
AND ADVENTUROUS ACTIVITIES THROUGH
FOCUS GROUPS**

The benefits of outdoor and adventurous activities (OAA) have been discussed by a number of authors, two of whom (Dismore and Bailey, 2005) wanted to explore their impact upon children, and how this affected subsequent learning in school. An interpretative qualitative methodology was adopted, given the view that it was important to place the child at the centre of the analysis, and allow them to create and report their own accounts of their experiences, from their own perspective.

Interviews would have been a possible data collection method, but focus groups were chosen as they were seen to elicit contributions from those who otherwise may have felt, first that they would not want to be interviewed on their own (the children were aged between nine and ten years old), and second those that felt that they had nothing to say would be encouraged to contribute within a group discussion, especially if ideas could be generated by others within the group. This allowed the authors to make tentative suggestions about the benefits of OAA in terms of positive intellectual, affective and social development. The focus group method in this context allowed much richer data from a wider sample than had interviews been used.

Focus groups and difficult to research populations

Focus groups can be particularly useful to collect data from groups that may otherwise be unwilling to provide it. Children, for example, may be uncomfortable discussing issues with an adult interviewer. However, they may well be more willing to discuss those issues with other children as part of a focus group guided by the researcher. You should be careful as to the quality of the data you collect in some circumstances, as participants may be tempted to provide false data to make an impression upon others in the group, so do be aware of this.

196

Summary

- Interviews can be an appropriate method to collect qualitative data.
- They are especially useful when the information to be collected is varied or complex, or the study is exploratory.
- Three general types of interview can be used – the structured, semi-structured and the unstructured.
- Data collected from interviews can be rich and varied, especially if the interviewer is skilled at using 'probes' to elicit such information.
- Undertaking an interview is a skilled task, and one that should not be approached lightly. The quality of the data can often be dependent upon the skill of the interviewer.

Activity

You should gain interviewing experience by undertaking an interview with a colleague on a sports-related topic of your choice. Try to ensure that you use a range of questions, and practise your use of probes to maximise the information obtained. You should also carry out a focus group, again on a topic that you decide. You should try to ensure that data is obtained from all members of the group, and that the group is not dominated by certain individuals.

In both cases, obtain feedback from those involved. Try to assess your strengths and weaknesses as an interviewer and focus group facilitator, and identify how your performance could be improved.

If you are using interviews as a data collection tool, then consider the following points:

- Think about the design of your interview schedule. How are you going to ensure the quality of the data that you collect?
- Are there any personal characteristics that may affect the quality of data that you collect? If so, how will you deal with this issue?
- Can you justify your choice of the sampling method that you used to obtain your interviewees?

Further reading

Brinkmann, S. and Kvale, S. (2014) *Interviews: Learning the Craft of Qualitative Research Interviewing*, London: Sage.

King, N. and Horrocks, C. (2010) *Interviews in Qualitative Research*, London: Sage.

Kvale, S. (2007) *Doing Interviews*, London: Sage.

Weiss, R. (1995) *Learning from Strangers: The Art and Method of Qualitative Interview Studies*, New York: Simon and Schuster.

10 Collecting data III: unobtrusive methods – observation and content analysis

This chapter will:

- Introduce two forms of unobtrusive method – observation and content analysis.
- Introduce some of the advantages and disadvantages of using unobtrusive methods in your research project.
- Outline the procedure by which each of the methods described can be carried out.
- Briefly outline the various sources of data that may be used for a content analysis.

Introduction

The questionnaire survey and interview methods I discussed in Chapters 8 and 9 still dominate the research literature in sport, in terms of both peer-reviewed studies, and undergraduate and postgraduate dissertations. Kellehear's (1993) views of over 20 years ago are still valid when he suggests that this is due to the fact that these are the obvious methods by which to elicit information from others. As he says (p.1):

> There is today, in social science circles, a simple and persistent belief that knowledge about people is available simply by asking. We ask people about themselves, and they tell us.

Although there has been steady growth in the use of alternative ways of collecting data, the dominance of such methods is slightly disappointing, although perhaps understandable, especially in terms of student dissertations, where it is perhaps more tempting to stick with a 'safe' approach. Over recent years, however, there has been increasing use of other methods, especially those that can be referred to as unobtrusive methods (sometimes referred to as non-reactive measures). Unobtrusive methods are those which do not have any effect upon the social environment under investigation, and require no interaction between subject and researcher that may otherwise influence the data collected. This chapter introduces two forms of unobtrusive method, observation and content analysis, and outlines their potential use in sports-related research.

Advantages of unobtrusive methods

As I noted above, there may be a tendency to focus on interviews and questionnaires as a 'safe' approach; however, unobtrusive methods have a number of advantages that can, in certain cases, be beneficial to the research.

- Unobtrusive measures do not involve the researcher disturbing the environment to the same extent as other methods. Because the methods are unobtrusive, participants are less likely to react to them, and alter their behaviours. As a consequence, they are often repeatable, and the researcher can revisit the research site to collect additional data.

200

- Unobtrusive measures may therefore be stronger in measuring actual behaviour, which is not always the same as reported behaviour. Interviews, focus groups and questionnaire surveys are always prone to the possibility that respondents will provide false or incorrect data. Thus it could be argued that the validity and reliability of such approaches may be potentially greater in some instances.
- Access to certain data may often be easier. For some unobtrusive measures, such as certain observational data collection, permission will not always be required, and for methods such as content analysis, access to data will be significantly easier.

Disadvantages of unobtrusive methods

As with any approach, there will always be limitations with using unobtrusive methods, and these need also to be acknowledged by the researcher.

- As the researcher is not interacting with the participants in the same way, then it may be difficult to understand or explain the phenomenon under investigation. While it may be relatively straightforward to describe what is happening, it may be more difficult to gain a clear understanding of why it is happening.
- In the same way that interview responses can be distorted to present a particular image or viewpoint, data collected by unobtrusive measures can also be subject to distortion, especially if the subjects are aware of the research.
- For unobtrusive methods such as observation, data collection may be difficult without the use of specialist photographic or video recording equipment.

Observation and participant observation

Observation remains, arguably, the most neglected research technique in sport, yet it has a number of advantages, and can be an excellent method to choose, whether as a single method, or as part of a multi-method study, and is an essential method in ethnographic research (Chapter 11). Questionnaires and interviews rely on self-reporting by participants in research. This may lead to bias from respondents who may wish to present particular information about themselves, which may not always be accurate, or from those who cannot accurately recall or verbalise events. An alternative is to observe behaviour. Observation is often classified as being on a continuum between non-participant and participant observation. Non-participant observation is the simplest form, and is where the researcher will observe the phenomenon 'from outside' with no engagement with either the activity or the subjects. An example of this would be observing the behaviour of sport fans during a game. This could be done using various techniques, for example video, photography, or simply watching and recording the data on a laptop or tablet. The other end of the continuum is that of participant observation, where the researcher actually takes a full part in the phenomenon being studied. An example could be where the researcher is investigating issues of customer care at a stadium, and becomes a fan, taking a full part in the activities, such as buying a ticket, accessing refreshments, watching the game and so on. They would collect data about their own experience as a fan, to try to gain an 'insider's' understanding. Data in this instance would be recorded by the researcher in the form of field notes, whereby the researcher's experiences would be recorded. This is not, technically, an unobtrusive method, as the researcher may have some effect upon the social environment, although it could be argued that this impact should be minimal, and that the researcher should not, as long as they are careful about their own conduct, alter the behaviour of others in any way.

When is observation appropriate?

Non-participant observation is, put simply, an appropriate method when the phenomenon under investigation can be directly observed. Thus, if you are interested in researching whether sports fans are more likely to wear clothing related to their team after they have won, as Cialdini *et al.* (1976) found, then observation is a suitable method. If, however, you want to identify why they are more likely to wear such clothing, then observation would be less suitable, as it would not be able to collect data to answer such a question. Non-participant observation, as a result, is generally, although not always, more suitable for descriptive rather than for explanatory research. A second justification for the use of observation would be when other methods are inappropriate. A good example of this would be investigating patterns of play in children's sports. Children themselves would almost certainly be unable to accurately describe how they play sport, therefore interviewing or using a questionnaire would be unreliable and lack validity. Observation would allow you to describe the children's play more accurately, especially – as an unobtrusive researcher – you would be less likely to influence their behaviour in any way. Observation can also be a useful method if researching contentious issues, such as violence or cheating in sport. Respondents may be unlikely to accurately report their own violent or aggressive behaviour, or may even over-report such behaviour in some cases. Unobtrusive observation would allow you to assess the validity of such claims made by participants. It is often used in combination with other methods, and such triangulation (see Chapter 7) will help strengthen the validity of your research. Observation can also be used in a non-triangulation manner with other methods. Take, for example, the case of the sports clothing described above. Observation would allow you to identify that individuals do wear their team's clothes more after they have won. Another method, such as in-depth interviews, may allow you to explain why they do so. Thus, such methods can be complementary.

CASE STUDY

THE USE OF OBSERVATIONAL METHODS TO EXPLORE COACH–ATHLETE INTERACTIONS

Turnnidge *et al.* (2014) were interested in the relationship between coach behaviour and the experiences of athletes with disabilities taking part in sport programmes alongside their siblings. One element of this research was to actually identify the behaviours demonstrated by coaches. The use of methods such as a self-completion questionnaire was clearly problematic, given the difficulty in coaches being able to accurately recall this information. Thus, they used systematic observation, using an approach called the Para-Coach Athlete Interaction Coding System (Para-CAICS). This system allows observers to identify the occurrence of a range of coach behaviours such as humour, positive reinforcement/ encouragement, technical instruction with modelling, and keeping control, and a range of athlete behaviours, such as helping others, positive responses, and general communication with the coach. These observations helped the research team to determine that a successful sport environment within this particular context was characterised by patterned and positive coach–athlete interactions that were focused on the athlete, rather than the disability.

Participant observation is appropriate when you are interested in uncovering some of the more subtle features of group behaviour, and trying to uncover meanings that are not directly observable. The researcher experiences, rather than observes, what is going on, and it is this experience that provides the data for the researcher.

PARTICIPATION OBSERVATION TO INVESTIGATE TEACHERS' PERCEPTIONS OF PHYSICAL EDUCATION

Kim and Taggart (2004) explored teachers' perceptions of physical education in an urban Korean primary school, a context where the authors describe the 'loss of the class', where teachers allowed pupils complete freedom, with little or no instruction provided, with difficulties in achieving pupil engagement with physical activity. One of the researchers had previously worked within a school teaching physical education, and this allowed them to undertake participant observation as a method to collect data, as well as take advantage of the close relationships that were formed with teachers, which, arguably, provided better data than that if the researcher had maintained a role as 'outsider'. This was reinforced by the researcher being able to help and support some of the other teachers in their roles, to form trust, and thus allow triangulation between her experiences, and those of the other teachers.

Advantages of observational methods

Participant and non-participant observation both have a number of advantages that make them well suited for data collection in certain circumstances. The advantages can be listed as follows:

- Directness. It is possible to record a phenomenon as and when it happens, rather than having to rely on an individual's recall of a particular event at another time.
- Takes place in a 'natural setting'. The researcher is able to observe the phenomenon in its natural setting ('in situ') rather than in the 'artificial' surroundings of an interview or while completing a questionnaire. This allows the researcher to observe the context in which such behaviour takes place, and – in the case of participant observation – to experience that context for themselves.

- The identification of behaviours not apparent to the subject. The individual may simply be unaware of how they behave in a particular situation, or believe that they act in an entirely different way. Observation will allow the researcher to identify the 'true' behaviour.
- The identification of behaviours that the subject may be unwilling to disclose. This is an issue when researching potentially sensitive subjects. Respondents may be unwilling to incriminate themselves in an interview or questionnaire. It may be possible to observe such behaviours, however.

Disadvantages of observational methods

Although observational techniques do have their advantages, there are also a number of potential disadvantages of which you need to be aware:

- Misunderstanding of the phenomenon. A drawback to observational methods is the likelihood that the researcher may simply misunderstand what they are seeing, especially if they are researching a subject in which they have little or no experience. This may be overcome to some extent through using observation in conjunction with other methods, such as interviewing, to ensure that the phenomenon has been correctly understood. As Gilhespy (2006) points out, it is not simply a case of looking and recording. Instead, what we look for and perceive as significant are influenced by our own values, and this must be recognised by the researcher.
- Difficulties in data recording. What to actually look for, and how to ensure that nothing of importance is missed are key issues in observational research. The use of technology, such as video recording, may prevent this to some extent, but this is often an unrealistic option for many researchers. An alternative is to have a number of researchers each recording the phenomenon, in which case inter-observer reliability becomes an issue (see Chapter 6) unless suitable training is given.
- The effect of the observer on the subjects. It is always possible that the researcher will affect the subjects' behaviour to such an extent that it may invalidate the entire research. The option of covert observation exists, where the subjects are unaware that they are being watched. However, this raises two issues: first the ethical question, that is

whether it is ethical to undertake research on a group without them being aware of the research, or without the option of not taking part in the research; and second the issue of how the researcher records their data without making the subjects aware that they are doing so.

Carrying out an observational study

As with any other means of data collection, it is important that you don't rush into the data gathering stage of the research without careful consideration of what data is required. It is often tempting to observe a sporting phenomenon and collect reams of data, only to find that such data are inadequate for the purposes of the research. Thus, you should carefully plan and pilot your data collection (especially if you are observing a one-off event). A number of planning stages can be identified:

1   Defining the variable(s) under investigation. The first stage is to identify the variable(s) to be observed. Are you interested in a particular behaviour, for example? Ensure you are clear about what exactly you are recording. If you are observing usage at a particular sports facility, then are you interested in quantitative measures such as the number of users, the breakdown between male and female users, etc.; or are you more interested in qualitative measures such as how they use the facility, their patterns of behaviour and so on? You should relate these issues back to your research objectives, that is determine what information is required to achieve these objectives, and what data is needed to provide such information, and identify the variables as appropriate.
2   Decide on your sample. Your sample should, ideally, be systematically chosen. Once you have decided upon your variables, you need to decide from which individual or group you will collect your data. As well as sampling particular individuals, behaviours and so on, you will also need to choose a sample of times. Sometimes you will be able to sample an entire event, such as a single sports match. Otherwise you will need to choose when you will make your observations.
3   Decide how the variables are to be recorded. Will you use video recording equipment or rely upon making notes with a pen and paper? Can you produce a pre-determined data sheet that simply needs to be filled in, or will you collect all data longhand?

206

4   Pilot your study. In exactly the same way that you would pre-test a questionnaire or interview schedule using a pilot study, then you should pre-test your observation, and identify any potential factors that may affect your data collection beforehand. This should be done in conditions that are as close to those of the actual data collection context as possible.

Recording data

Provided you have clearly identified the variables under investigation, the recording of quantitative data should be relatively straightforward. Generally it will involve the recording of information using a simple checklist, for example the checklist shown in Figure 10.1, which is taken from a study into basketball tactics and strategies.

It is difficult to record more than one variable at a time, so you should avoid recording large numbers of variables, unless you are using techniques such as video recording. If you do need to record more variables without the use of such technology, then you should either alternate between variables, that is record one variable for a specified period, and then another, or use multiple observers. If you use multiple observers, then you have to ensure reliability through careful training and briefing of all observers to ensure that they are measuring what you intend them to measure.

For each play made by the sampled individual, tick the relevant action								
Player no. 'X'								
Dribbled then shot	✓	✓	✓					
Dribbled then passed	✓	✓	✓	✓	✓			
Immediate shot	✓	✓	✓					
Immediate pass	✓	✓	✓	✓				
Lost possession	✓	✓						

Figure 10.1 Recording data using an observation checklist

Data can be recorded directly on a pre-produced recording sheet, dictated into a recording device, or recorded onto a laptop or tablet. The danger with the second option is that, in many sports contexts, the level of background noise will make the recording inaudible. If you choose the third option, then consider pragmatic issues such as battery life.

Qualitative observation records data using field notes. Field notes are a summary of the observations made by the researcher, and follow a less structured format. Field notes should be:

- Descriptive. They should include a description of the setting, the participants, and the relevant actions and behaviours, as well as any other features that may have relevance for the research.
- Detailed. The description should be as detailed as possible. It is not possible to be able to rely on memory to recall all of the important occurrences.
- Reflective. The field notes should also contain the researcher's account of the situation, and any information that may later help interpretation.

USING OBSERVATION WITH OTHER METHODS

Dennis and Carron (1999) were interested to find out whether the location of an ice hockey game had any influence on certain decisions of the coaches, in this case the extent to which they told their team to forecheck assertively (i.e. in a more attacking manner) or passively (more defensively). A questionnaire was distributed to coaches from the National Hockey League ($n = 23$) and the Ontario Hockey League ($n = 17$). The data from the questionnaires suggested that more assertive forechecking was carried out while playing at home, and against teams of lower ability. The authors noted, however, that questionnaires may be limited in collecting such data in that what the coaches reported may not reflect the teams' actual play. Dennis and Carron therefore used observation to collect data, videoing a random sample of games. The forechecking style was recorded for each game, and a random sample was analysed by a second observer to ensure reliability. Through the use of such observational methods, the data collected by the questionnaire were shown to be an accurate measure of the team's forechecking style, thus confirming the findings from the questionnaire survey.

Mistakes made in observational studies

There are a number of mistakes that are regularly seen within observational studies. You should ensure that these are not an issue within your research!

- Attempting to observe and record too many variables.
- Not evaluating the effect of the researcher on the subjects.
- Not taking a sample of times and/or locations.
- Making inadequate field notes and over-relying on recall.

Content analysis

Sport is now communicated through a huge variety of media, and to a varied range of consumers. As a result, content analysis is an excellent approach to develop an understanding of certain aspects of sport. Content analysis refers to the analysis of the content of communications. It involves the use of systematic procedures to describe the content of a text. This text can be written, audio or visual, for example a television programme, a newspaper, an internet site, various forms of social media, a sports autobiography or a radio broadcast. Content analysis generally involves the researcher determining the presence, meanings and relationships of certain words or concepts within the text. Almost any type of text can be analysed, either quantitatively (for example in terms of the number of times a particular word or phrase is used, or the percentage assigned to negative stories within tabloid newspapers), qualitatively (for example a qualitative analysis of the imagery associated with advertising a sport product), or both. Content analysis can prove to be a rewarding method, especially for those interested in how sport is communicated, and for looking more deeply into what can seem to be, at times, fairly ordinary messages about sport.

Stages in doing a content analysis

Once you have identified a research question, and chosen to undertake a content analysis, then the following steps are useful as a guide.

1 Identify the text to be used. The choice of text will, of course, be largely dependent upon your research objectives, and may actually emerge before the research question. Thus, you may be interested, for example, in how sport is presented through social media. You may then decide to undertake a qualitative content analysis of athlete Twitter accounts, and then develop a question.
2 Identify the data set to be used. If you have chosen a newspaper as your source text, for example, then which newspaper(s) is to be used, which editions, how many and so on. Be realistic in terms of your sample, and what you can realistically analyse without losing quality, especially within a qualitative analysis.
3 Collect the data as appropriate given your research objectives.
4 For a qualitative analysis, identify your categories, or codes into which the data will be placed. Codes can be taken from existing theory, or you may develop your own. Ensure that your codes are appropriate to fulfil your research objectives. Place each relevant statement/article/other data unit into the appropriate code. Analyse the resultant data (see Chapter 14 for an outline of qualitative analysis).
5 For a quantitative analysis, record the data as required using an appropriate framework, for example making a note of the number of times that certain words appear, the number of photographs showing a particular athlete, and so on.
6 This data can then be analysed using SPSS for Windows, for example (see Chapter 13).

Fishwick and Leach (1998) carried out a content analysis of BBC television commentaries of the 1994 Wimbledon Tennis Championships. They wanted to find out whether there was any gender bias within the commentaries, for example whether the male tennis players were perceived as powerful and important, whereas female players were seen as subordinate. The coding grid that they used is shown in Figure 10.2.

Men/women:		
Match:		
Round:		
Comments	*Male commentator*	*Female commentator*
• Positive		
Fitness/athleticism		
Play		
Misc.		
• Negative		
Fitness/athleticism		
Play		
Misc.		
• Victories		
• Defeats		
• First name calling		
• Emotions		
• Character flaws		
• Beauty and fashion		
• Patronising		

Figure 10.2 Sample coding grid for content analysis

GENDER AND ETHNICITY PORTRAYALS ON
ESPN'S *SPORTSCENTER*, 1999–2009

SportsCenter is ESPN's flagship sports programme, and as a result is a dominant force in sport broadcasting, influencing, for example, how people view female athletes, and athletes from ethnic minorities. Using a longitudinal research design, Jacob Turner (2013) examined representations of gender and ethnicity on the programme, to explore the extent to which hegemonic white masculinity was perpetuated, and to identify any changes over a 10-year period. To do this, 42 episodes were used as a sample, 21 from 1999 and 21 from 2009. A number of basic variables were recorded for each story aired, these being its length, the level of competition to which the story referred, and the specific sport. This was followed by an analysis of the type of story, such as human interest, score reportage or news update, whether the story was 'episodic' (without broader context being provided) or thematic (with broader context). This was followed by an analysis of the newsworthiness of the story, based on its prominence, singularity, timeliness, impact and controversy. Finally, the sex and ethnicity of those involved in the programme (athletes, reporters, hosts and so on) were recorded. Overall data were collected from 746 stories. This allowed Turner to determine that, over the 10-year period, coverage of women's sport actually dropped (although not significantly so), and women remained largely invisible. When women's sport was covered, it was generally covered in an episodic way, compared to coverage of male sport, which was more thematic, and the majority involved score reportage. Men's stories also lasted about twice as long as stories about women. In contrast, African–American athletes were generally over represented on the programme, whereas white people remained over represented in terms of positions of power, such as head coaches and owners. As Turner concluded, such results about the coverage of women's and ethnic sport, 'when taken together, point to the perpetuation of normative hegemonic white masculinity in mediated sports' (p.1). there are great opportunities to replicate and extend Turner's study in a range of different contexts, and this is an area with great research potential if you are interested in issues of power, and the method of content analysis.

As well as frequencies of occurrence, you can measure a number of other variables as part of a content analysis. You may wish to measure the prominence of a particular concept; for example, where does the concept appear? Does it appear early or later within a text? How much space in the text is devoted to the concept? In what context does the concept appear? What you choose to measure should, of course, be chosen to achieve your research objectives. Some sources available to you are described below:

Public records. These are generally produced by local or central government. Although records such as the census may seem to be objective sources of data, care still needs to be taken to assess such sources. The census, for example, may under-record certain groups in society. Other sources that may be of interest include summaries of information such as Social Trends or the Annual Abstract of Statistics.

The media. The media can be a useful source of data; however you should be aware of the following issues:

- The intended audience. You need to assess who the report was written for, and how the intended audience may influence the report.
- Accuracy. It is generally difficult to check the accuracy of newspaper reports. If you use one particular newspaper, it is useful to crosscheck reports with another as far as is practically possible.
- Distortion. The reporting of news follows a complex path, along which it is highly possible for distortion to take place. Occurrences may be distorted by witnesses, who misreport incidents, journalists, who try to make a story 'newsworthy', editors, and so on. Again, cross-checking is important here.

Social media. Various forms of social media (blogs, Twitter and so on) are potentially rich sources of data for sport-related research. Their immediacy, accessibility and interactivity provide valuable opportunities for the researcher. Social media sources may provide visual and audio, as well as written data, and their potential for providing a rich and varied understanding about sport should not be under estimated. Chapter 12 explores the issues surrounding such research in more depth.

Advertisements. Advertisements can provide extremely useful data, not only in terms of the words used, but also the imagery presented. Lucas (2000), for example, examined three television commercials produced by Nike demonstrating how Nike portrayed itself as being actively involved in the decision of women to participate in sport, yet at the same time could be seen to be constraining such participation by directing them towards certain types of sporting activity. In this research it was not just the words or the imagery, but a combination of the two that was analysed to allow the author to conclude that such advertising disempowers sportswomen by telling them the 'right' way to play sport. Company brochures may also provide a wealth of useful data.

Private papers/diaries/letters. These can be extremely difficult to obtain, and there may be ethical considerations in using such documents. In reality, private papers are generally only an option if you have clear and agreed access to such documents before the research commences – you should not commence a research project and hope to gain access to such papers. Diaries have the added advantage of recording information significant to the diarist at, or very close to, the time that events took place.

Autobiographies and biographies. Accounts of the lives of many well-known sportsmen and women are freely available. They can provide an insightful account of an individual's sporting experiences, and give an understanding into differing areas, although be careful, as most will be ghost written. Biographies tend to be less reliable, but they may still provide some useful information. As with analysing media reports, you need to take into account issues of audience, accuracy and distortion when assessing your sources.

Photographs, films and video. It is not just words that can be analysed. Pictures can provide a wealth of descriptive data, and may be used in a similar manner to non-participant observation.

You should be aware of a number of issues before you decide to undertake documentary or archive research. If you require permission to access official documents, the timescale may also be inappropriate – gaining permission to use government documents may take a number of months, therefore if you are constrained by time, you should reconsider your approach. You may also have to gain permission even to photocopy material. Retrieving the documents also takes time – often you will have to spend considerable time identifying and locating the appropriate source. On many occasions, what you think is appropriate will turn out to lack relevance for your research, hence such research can be extremely time consuming. I am not trying to deter you from documentary research, but it is important that you consider the potential pitfalls beforehand!

Mistakes made in content analysis

Again, you should be aware of some of the more common errors seen within content analyses. The main issues for you to be aware of are as follows:

- Not collecting a representative sample of texts. Consider your sampling method clearly, and ensure that it fulfils the objectives of your research.
- Not considering the validity of the data from the context of the text. Do not unquestioningly use data from sources such as newspapers without critically assessing the validity of such data.

Summary

1 Unobtrusive methods are those where the researcher does not interact with the subjects or environment under investigation. Such methods are advantageous in that they may be stronger in measuring actual, rather than reported, behaviour. They are also generally much easier to undertake.
2 The lack of interaction may make it difficult for the researcher to be able to clearly interpret the phenomenon being investigated.
3 The two main forms of unobtrusive investigation are those of observation and content analysis.
4 Observation can be used to collect qualitative and quantitative data from subjects in their natural environment.
5 Content analysis is used to collect data from texts, such as newspapers, television, photographs, and so on.

Activity

Observation

Identify a research question for which observational data is appropriate. Undertake a brief observational study, paying particular attention to the following points:

1 Sampling. What is the best location? Who or what will you observe?
2 Data collection and analysis. How will you record your data? How will you analyse the data you do collect? (You may want to read Chapters 13 and 14 before you do this.)
3 What other additional means could you use to strengthen the reliability and validity of your findings?

Content analysis

Choose a contemporary sporting issue. Identify two contrasting newspapers, and undertake a content analysis to determine differences in how the issue has been covered. You should pay particular attention to how you operationalise your variables, for example what exactly will you be trying to measure or identify within the text? How does this relate to your overall research objective?

ABOUT YOUR RESEARCH PROJECT

If you are using unobtrusive methods for your research project, consider the following points:

- If you have chosen one of the methods described in this chapter, then can you justify why the method you have chosen is the most appropriate one for your research project?
- Consider the issues of validity and reliability. How will you ensure that your observational or content analysis study is both reliable and valid? What are the threats to reliability and validity?

Further reading

Kellehear, A. (1993) *The Unobtrusive Researcher*, St Leonards, NSW: Allen and Unwin.

Neuendorf, K. (2001) *The Content Analysis Guidebook*, London: Sage.

Schreier, M. (2012) *Qualitative Content Analysis in Practice*, London: Sage.

11 Collecting data IV: ethnographic research in sport

This chapter will:

- Outline what is meant by an ethnographic approach to sports research.
- Describe the characteristics of an ethnographic approach.
- Describe the stages of undertaking a sport-related ethnography.
- Discuss some of the issues of writing up an ethnographic research project.

Introduction

*I once heard a distinguished anthropologist say something that I
have shamelessly plagiarised ever since. 'There are,' he declared,
'only two basic methods of social research. One is called 'asking
questions' and the other is called 'hanging out'.*

(Dingwall 1997, pp.52–3)

One of the consequences of the growing maturity of sports research
has been the use of an increasing number of different methods and
methodologies, often as a reaction to the historical dominance of positivist approaches. One such methodological approach that has become
increasingly popular is that of the sport ethnography. Defining the term
'ethnography', as Atkinson and Hammersley (1994) and Silk (2005) note,
is a difficult task, with many different types of ethnography and different authors providing differing definitions. However, this chapter will
examine the broad ethnographic approach.

Ethnographies are generally characterised by their focus on a particular
group, or subculture, and the inseparable relationship between individuals and their social context. They involve the collection and use
of extremely 'rich' data, and depth of information, often using several
data collection methods, most notably observation, participant observation and in-depth interviews with key informants, focusing not only on
what is said, and what is observed, but the approach may also explore
what is heard, smelt, touched or tasted; see for example Sparkes (2009).
Atkinson and Hammersley (1994, p.1) themselves suggest that:

*We see the term as referring primarily to a particular method or
set of methods. In its most characteristic form, it involves the
ethnographer participating, overtly or covertly, in people's daily
lives for an extended period of time, watching what happens,
listening to what is said, asking questions – in fact, collecting
whatever data are available to throw light on the issues that are
the focus of the research.*

Thus, ethnography investigates a group through collecting data over
a substantial period of time while being immersed within the day to
day activities of the group. Holt and Sparkes (2001) approach their

definition from a slightly different angle, and suggest that the defining feature of ethnography is its purpose. This purpose is the study of a group of people and their culture, where understanding of the group is obtained through examining behaviour from the group's, rather than the researcher's perspective. To achieve this, the researcher has to take on the role of 'insider', and spend an extended period of time within the group, during which time data is collected.

AN ETHNOGRAPHIC INVESTIGATION INTO BOXING SUBCULTURES

The aim of the researcher undertaking an ethnographic approach is that of immersion within the group. As Sugden (1996, p.201) remarks:

> It is only through total immersion that he or she can become sufficiently conversant with the formal and informal rules governing the webbing of the human interaction under investigation so that its innermost secrets can be revealed.

Sugden's own research into various boxing subcultures required him to become part of each subculture himself, so that the values, norms and behaviours otherwise hidden from the researcher could be uncovered (pp.2–3):

> The essence of good sociology is making sense of the mysterious. Here was a social universe which was buried deep within a subcultural envelope about which I knew next to nothing and about which there was virtually nothing written.

To 'make sense of the mysterious', Sugden became immersed within the group over an extended period of time (p.3):

> For the next two years I led a dual existence: in the semi-rural idyll of the University campus as John Sugden, the anonymous college postgraduate student; and in Hartford's ghetto and in the basement gym as 'Doctor John', the idiosyncratic English ethnographer and the boxing club's odd-job man.

By becoming part of the subculture – albeit not completely immersed as a boxer, but rather as observer – Sugden was able to uncover many of the otherwise hidden values held by the group. During one bout in Havana, for example, it was noted (p.162) that:

Despite the fact that there is a lot at stake and that the fights themselves are conducted with furious intensity, the young boxers show incredible self-discipline and emotional restraint. There is little overt sign of anger, even in the most bruising encounter. After the fight the two boxers hug one another, thank the referee and the opposite corner men and skip out of the ring without further ado.

Such a scene may prove difficult for the non-ethnographic researcher to understand, yet through immersion into the group, Sugden was able to explain (p.162) that Ajo (their coach):

tells me that while winning and losing have some significance, at this level he is more interested in combinations of technique and temperament, believing that if the balance between these can be established early in a fighter's career, then the victories will automatically follow later.

Thus, by a combination of immersion within the group for an extended period of time, and the use of different data collection methods while immersed, Sugden was able to both describe, and, more importantly, explain the behaviours of members of the particular boxing subculture by collecting data that would – in all likelihood – be unavailable to the non-ethnographer.

Characteristics of ethnography

Ethnographies generally have a number of common characteristics:

- They investigate human behaviour, and how such behaviour is related to the values and attitudes of the particular group under investigation. These 'cultural patterns' can then be used to explain the behaviour of members of the group.
- The ethnographer studies the group on its 'own ground', observing natural behaviours in a natural setting.
- The ethnographer will often use a range of methods to collect data.

- Often these methods will be flexible, and data are collected from whatever sources are available or appropriate at the time.
- The ethnographer is generally more interested in taking an holistic perspective than in focusing on individual aspects. It is the complex networks of interdependencies rather than isolated areas that are of interest to the ethnographer. Thus, it may be that the normal, mundane behaviours are more important than the extraordinary or unexpected behaviours.
- Ethnographies focus on the emic perspective. The emic perspective is that of taking the point of view of the people being studied, rather than the etic, or researcher's perspective.
- To gain understanding of the complex relationships within a culture, immersion is often necessary for a considerable period of time. Time is needed to gain access, to develop trust with those being studied, and to develop an understanding of what is actually going on within the group.

EMIC AND ETIC PERSPECTIVES

You will come across the terms 'emic' and 'etic'. Essentially, they are differing ways of examining something. An etic approach is one that takes the viewpoint of the researcher, and describes and interprets things from that 'outsider' perspective. An emic approach, on the other hand, seeks to understand and describe from the perspective of those being researched and produce an account that is meaningful to those being researched.

Undertaking a sport ethnography

A sports-related ethnography is a very flexible methodology, in that data collection is often unstructured, unplanned and even unexpected! Thus, unlike an experimental study for example, it is difficult to provide a precise framework with which to approach such an undertaking. The following provides a generalised series of stages for undertaking an ethnographic piece of sports research.

1   Identifying the problem

The researcher normally would not enter the field without having some sort of idea what the research problem is. Although a characteristic of these types of study is their inductive nature, that is where the theory emerges from, or is grounded in the data (see Chapter 2), some concept of the overall objective of the study has to exist so that the researcher will know what to observe in the field. What the researcher should not do, however, is impose a theoretical framework upon the research prior to data collection. As Holt and Sparkes (2001, p.242) suggest:

> An important requirement of ethnography is that researchers suspend a wide range of common-sense and theoretical knowledge in order to minimise the danger of taking on misleading pre-conceptions about the setting and the people in it. ... In researching settings that are more familiar, it can be much more difficult to suspend one's preconceptions, whether these derive from social science or from everyday knowledge. One reason for this is that one finds it so obvious. ... Therefore, while the ethnographic insider has the problem of making the strange seem familiar, the ethnographic insider has the task of making the familiar seem strange in order to maintain analytical distance.

This does not mean that the researcher cannot enter the field without an idea of the research question – this may well emerge from the initial time spent with the social world under exploration; however, this may take time.

2   Deciding upon an ethnographic approach

The next stage is to determine whether an ethnography is actually a suitable research design. If a rich understanding of a group or subculture is your objective, then an ethnography may be appropriate. If you require more descriptive data, or wish to assess a large population using statistical techniques, then other methods are more appropriate.

3   Considering your personal characteristics

Your own characteristics will be an important consideration. Your age, gender and even sporting experience or ability may all have a potential impact on your choice of ethnography. Look again at the case study in this chapter of Holt and Sparkes (2001). Could this ethnography have been carried out if one of the authors had not been a footballer himself? Could a female researcher have carried out the ethnography and collected the same data? In both cases, it seems unlikely that this would be the case. You may wish to allow your personal characteristics to dictate your choice of sample. For example if – such as with the Holt and Sparkes study – you are already a member of a group such as a football team, then consider using this opportunity to undertake an ethnographic study of your team. It is not always the case that your research question should determine the sample. In certain cases, the sample may determine the choice of research question!

4 Selecting the setting

As stage 3 suggested, although the setting is often chosen after the research question has been determined, it may also be the case that the setting is chosen first, maybe because it is familiar, or accessible to the researcher. The important issue is that the choice of the setting and the research question are compatible. Some settings, such as a sports organisation, may have clearly defined boundaries. Others, for example that encountered when undertaking an ethnographic study into a particular sporting community, have much less clearly defined boundaries. It is relatively easy for the researcher undertaking an ethnography into a sports organisation to identify the setting in terms of both the physical location and the members of the group being studied. In other cases this can be more problematic, and this needs to be considered so that the boundaries of the ethnography do not become too broad and unmanageable.

5 Considering the timeframe

Ethnographies are characterised by the researcher spending a considerable duration of time within the setting. Unlimited time and resources are not generally available, however, and the researcher needs to delimit the time spent on the study. The timeframe needs to be evaluated against the objectives of the study – will there be sufficient time for you to collect the data you need to achieve your research objectives?

6 Gaining entry to the setting

Gaining entry to the group from which you want to collect data is a key stage in ethnography. The method of entry has implications for the subsequent reliability and validity of data obtained, and thus must be approached with care. One method, as used by Giulianotti (1995; see also the case study 'An ethnography of sports fans' on page 229), is to find a 'gatekeeper', trusted by group members, who can then introduce you to other members. Other methods may be more fortuitous, such as Gallmeier (1988) who was able to use his father's position as sports editor of the local paper and associate of the owner of the local team to gain access to the otherwise inaccessible players of a professional ice hockey team. You need to consider how you enter the setting, and the information you provide to members when you do enter. As Grills (1998) suggests, your access to informants, and thus data, will be strongly influenced by how those in the group interpret your motives and interests as a researcher. Entry is a crucial stage in ethnography, and one you should consider at length. Ultimately, there is no one 'best practice' that we can recommend; it is dependent upon a number of variables related to the characteristics of the group, and you as a researcher.

7 Considering your sample

Sampling in this respect takes on a slightly different meaning from that we have already encountered. A group may have many members, many behaviours, values, artefacts and so on. The researcher – especially if constrained by a limited timeframe – simply cannot record all the potential data, and thus choices need to be made about what data to measure. In terms of who you should collect data from, Atkinson and Hammersley (1994) suggest two categories. First, there are those that you, in your initial fieldwork, identify as suitable informants. Second, there are those who volunteer themselves, or are volunteered by other members of the group. It is one of your roles, as ethnographer, to assess the most appropriate sample. Unlike methods such as questionnaire surveys, or in-depth interviews, the choice also needs to be made about what, as well as who to collect data from. The types of things you should be observing will vary, depending upon the research objective, but can include:

- The history and context of the setting. What background information will be useful to explain the data you collect? What is the history of the group? Are there any idiosyncratic features that may influence your observations? Do similar groups exist elsewhere?
- The physical environment. You should note the location and its appearance. You can also note the other physical factors, such as the smell, the noise and so on. You should aim to gather as much data as possible to allow the reader of your ethnography the sense of what it is actually like to be within that setting.

- Artefacts within the setting. Artefacts such as pictures, posters, décor and so on can all provide useful data in an ethnography. Where are they located? What is their purpose? Asking questions such as these can be extremely useful to the ethnographer.
- The people within the setting. Be descriptive – how many people are there, what do they look like, what are their characteristics?
- The relationships between people. How are people interacting? What norms and values are governing their behaviour? Does their behaviour seem to follow any patterns or rules? Why are they behaving in the way that they do?
- As well as listening to what people say, perhaps through interviewing them, observe what they do, and how they are doing it.

8   'Learning the ropes'

This refers to being able to fit in with the group, without arousing suspicion, standing out or antagonising those within the group in any way. As Gallmeier (1988) notes, there are no explicit guidelines for this; however, it is an 'absolute necessity' (p.220) to establish trust and rapport with those being investigated. This will enhance both the amount and the validity of the data that you collect. Without establishing such trust and rapport, you will find collecting useful data a difficult task indeed.

9   Collecting the data

A range of data collection methods is often employed, with observation and participant observation extensively used, as well as key informant interviews. Data are generally written in the form of field notes, although you may – with the participants' consent – wish to use tape recorders, cameras or even video recorders. If you rely on recording equipment, always back up against possible technological failures by making written notes as well. Detailed notes should be made using your field notes as soon as possible (preferably while you are in the field, unless circumstances dictate otherwise). At the beginning, don't restrict yourself in the data that you collect – quite often it is a case of collecting as much data as you can. As your analysis of the data proceeds, you can become more selective in what you record.

10   Analysing the data

Although we have put this stage as the final stage, data analysis in reality is a continual process and takes place during, rather than at the end of, the ethnography. Interpretation emerges from the data, and then further data can be collected to support or refute the interpretations. Thus, explanations can be continually developed, tested and refined.

AN ETHNOGRAPHIC STUDY OF SPORT OPPORTUNITIES IN A CANADIAN INNER CITY

Holt *et al.* (2013) wanted to examine the issues related to the provision of sporting opportunities to young men in a Canadian inner city. To do this, one member of the research team spent a total of 15 months undertaking participant observation within a range of sport programmes targeted at the homeless, or those living in subsidised housing. Throughout that time he was able to develop relationships with, and identify relevant gatekeepers, who were then able to introduce him to 12 youth workers involved in the delivery of such programmes. The process was emergent, in that the research team met regularly to discuss findings, and identify the future directions of the research as the data collection progressed. The interviews, combined with field notes taken during the participant observation (a total of 54 entries) led them to conclude that, at a personal level, sport allowed participants to overcome boredom, and provide an escape from day to day existence. Socially it allowed them to develop positive relationships with others. Such opportunities, however, were limited by structural constraints such as those relating to money, and the structure of the programmes offered.

Ethnographic methods

Although there are a number of methods traditionally associated with ethnography, it is not possible simply to say which methods should be used. The choice should, as always, be made in terms of which method, or methods will provide valid and reliable data to investigate the research problem. The following methods are the most commonly used within ethnographic research:

- Observation. Simply watching the group can provide a wealth of information, especially if you can observe different members of the group within their 'natural' environment. This is often an appropriate method during the early stages of an ethnography. As well as observation, think about things such as what you hear, what you can smell and so on, as these data may be extremely useful.

- Participant observation. In most cases, participant observation will be an essential element of ethnographic research, to try to gain an empathetic understanding of the group's behaviours that you may observe.
- Structured and unstructured interviews. You should consider the use of both forms. Structured interviews will allow you to collect pre-determined data, yet you should not limit yourself – you should allow new and important data to emerge from your informants through unstructured interviews.
- Life histories. Essentially this is the informant narrating his or her experiences to the ethnographer, so that a detailed picture of the culture or group can be developed. Life histories are an excellent method of understanding the group, and changes within the group. You should, however, be aware of the possibilities of forgetfulness, biased recall, exaggeration and so on.
- Unobtrusive methods. I have examined the use of unobtrusive methods in Chapter 10, and such methods can help enhance understanding of a group or culture as part of an ethnographic approach, for example through undertaking a content analysis of any documents or texts produced by members of the group, or analysing relevant blogs or social media.

You should also be flexible in how you collect your data, and be prepared to collect data at any time. Sands (2002) has noted how, as an ethnographer, he interviewed a sprinter almost immediately after a race. Sands recalls that: 'in that brief five minutes, what he told me was more succinct and from the heart than what I could have received in a two-hour interview' (p.67). As the quote from Sands suggests, you must, as an ethnographer, be prepared to be flexible, and grasp opportunities as they arise. Always carry a notebook with you when you are in the field, to take advantage of unexpected data collection opportunities.

Ethical issues in sport ethnography

By its very nature, specifically that of immersion within a group, the sports ethnographer will face a number of ethical issues about their role within the group. Palmer (2000) summarises a common ethnographic issue that she faced when researching La Société du Tour de France. The issue was that of gaining access – access was only available to accredited journalists, and not to researchers. Palmer was able to use her contacts with an Australian television network to obtain a press pass, and thus fraudulently gain access, raising key ethical issues regarding deception. As she notes, 'the researcher needs to be able to work with whatever is available' (p.371) and justified her approach on the grounds that the accounts she would have obtained otherwise would have been 'nothing short of fraudulent'. By posing as a journalist she gained access to situations where the influence of La Société was visible. Unfortunately, by posing as a journalist, she was unable to use many of the tools of ethnography, such as participant observation or detailed interviews, as to do so would have been inconsistent with her role as journalist. This is a good example of an ethnography where it is simply not possible to use the full range of ethnographic methods, and the researcher must weigh up the issues involved, and make the decision that would provide the best data. In this case, the justification was made on the basis of the validity of the data obtained.

ISSUES WITH ETHNOGRAPHIC RESEARCH: AN ETHNOGRAPHY OF SPORTS FANS

Giulianotti (1995) carried out participant observation with two groups of rival football hooligans in Scotland. Some of the issues that he faced were as follows:

- Gaining access. Gaining entry to these groups was difficult in that they were cautious of 'unsympathetic reporting', that is the possibility of condemnation by the researcher. Giulianotti struck a 'research bargain' to gain entry, by providing limited information on the opposing group to develop trust with the groups. Further entry was gained by the technique of 'snowballing', whereby one individual will provide access to another, who will then provide access to another and so on. This method is useful as trust can be further enhanced if an existing member of the group introduces the researcher.
- Risks while conducting research. Giulianotti encountered some initial hostility. However, the use of snowballing as a means of gaining access was instrumental in reducing risk – it is likely that a researcher obtaining an entrée to the group by other means would have been much more at risk. Giulianotti also notes that the researcher needs to be aware of the difference between threat and banter.
- Validity of data. Giulianotti's research posed a number of questions with regard to its validity. As he notes, each group were keen to portray themselves as the 'hardest' fans in Scotland, thus providing motivations for each group to over- or misrepresent their activities to the researcher.

Experiential ethnography

A relatively new term that has emerged within sport research is that of 'experiential ethnography'. Sands (2002) views this approach in terms of the researcher becoming a complete participant within the study. To do this, the researcher will have to go through a number of stages: learning about the group (anticipatory socialisation); becoming a member (recruitment); learning about the norms, values and behaviours of the group (socialisation); and finally acceptance as one of the group. Each of these stages, in itself, may provide understanding about the group. Experiential ethnography may allow the researcher to collect otherwise 'hidden' or inaccessible data. As Sands (2002, p.131) suggests:

> In my research with sprinters and football players, I experienced sensations and feelings through participation that would have lain outside the non-experiential ethnographer's boundaries of observation. In effect, my body's lived experience of performance and competition not only allowed me access to sensations of pain, elation, adrenaline rushes, and wild swings of emotion generated through cognitive appraisal of performance but also brought me closer to the cultural experiences of my team mates and other like athletes.

Thus, experiential ethnography would seem to have strengths in uncovering sports experiences. However, you must approach this methodology – as with any methodology – with some caution in terms of assessing its potential weaknesses as well as its strengths. It can be easy to simply become autobiographical in your write-up, with no real theoretical or explanatory framework within which to place your own experiences. Second, the danger of 'going native', or taking on the beliefs and values of the group may be an issue. Giulianotti (1995), for example, noted that each of the groups of football hooligans he investigated was keen to be presented as the 'hardest' in Scottish football. In the unlikely event of Giulianotti going native, then the value of his findings could have been questioned in terms of his own subjectivity, in perhaps selecting evidence to show that 'his group' was 'harder' than other groups. Perhaps the key for the researcher is to be 'objectively subjective' in being able to assess conflicts between his or her roles as participant and researcher.

230

Writing the ethnography

During your fieldwork, you may collect large amounts of data in the form of written field notes, taped interviews, photographs, videos, analyses of documents and so on. It is now that you need to make the move from viewing ethnography as a methodology to that of the written report. The process of producing a meaningful report – often restricted by time and word counts – can be, at the beginning, an extremely daunting task. Unfortunately, there is no set procedure that exists to guarantee success!

The first stage of reporting is that of making sense of the data. The best way to do this is through the process of coding. You should read Chapter 15, which deals with the issue of making sense of qualitative data. Through a systematic process of coding and analysis, you will soon begin to make some sort of sense of the data (you should, ideally, begin this process during the fieldwork). By being systematic in your coding, you can soon make the task seem less daunting than it initially appears.

Although there is no one correct way to present your findings in an ethnographic report, as a general guideline your write-up should include the following:

1 Statement and justification of the research problem.
2 Literature review, and its use in refining research questions and research design.
3 Detailed review of the study design, including a detailed description of the setting.
4 Presentation of the data.
5 Explanation of the findings.

Gall *et al.* (1996, p.607) provide a statement that should guide you in your writing-up: 'If an ethnography has been done well, readers of the final report should be able to understand the culture even though they may not have directly experienced it.'

Ethnography and student research

Although it is unlikely that those undertaking research as part of an undergraduate degree will have the time and resources to undertake a 'classical' ethnography, do not immediately rule it out as an approach. Even in relatively limited studies, an ethnographic approach can be fruitful for you. It is entirely possible for you as a researcher to become immersed into a group – although not to the same extent as the 'true' ethnographer – and to collect data using different methods to develop an understanding of the group in question, especially if you are already associated with the group in the first place, such as undertaking an ethnographic study of a sports team to which you belong. In such studies, it may be possible to collect a quantity of extremely rich and informative data. As always, consider your information needs, and identify the best approach to obtain data to supply such information.

Summary

1 Ethnography involves the study of a group, whereby the researcher becomes 'immersed' within the group's natural environment for an extended period of time.
2 Data collection is generally flexible and varied, being undertaken at whatever times are appropriate, often using a variety of methods.
3 The researcher needs to be aware of certain issues such as entry to the group, and their particular role within the group, as these may have implications for the validity of the findings.
4 Ethnography may be an appropriate research design in certain cases, but where time and resources are limited – for example in the case of a student research project – it needs to be carefully considered.

232

Activity

Locate a sport-related ethnography. Critically evaluate the ethnography, and try to determine why the ethnographic method was chosen, and how such an approach allowed the researcher to gain understanding of the group. Try to answer the following questions:

- Would the use of a different methodology have allowed the same understanding to be developed?
- What was the chosen setting? How and why was it chosen?
- How did the researcher gain access to the setting?
- What methods were used to collect data?
- What were the main conclusions of the study?
- Do you feel that you know what it would be like to be a member of that group from reading the paper?

ABOUT YOUR RESEARCH PROJECT

If you are undertaking an ethnography, consider the following points:

- Can you justify the use of an ethnographic approach? What will the ethnographic approach provide that other research designs will not?
- What is the justification for your choice of setting? Can you justify the choice in academic terms?
- How could your personal characteristics influence the data collection process? How will you take this into account when undertaking your research?

Further reading

Brewer, J. (2000) *Ethnography*, Buckingham: Open University Press.

Brownell, S. (2006) 'Sport Ethnography; A Personal Account', in Hobbs, D. and Wright, R. (eds) *The Sage Handbook of Field Research*, London: Sage, pp.243–54.

Hammersley, M. and Atkinson, P. (2007) *Ethnography: Principles in Practice*, London: Routledge.

Sands, R. (2002) *Sport Ethnography*, Champaign, IL: Human Kinetics.

Silk, M. (2005) 'Sporting Ethnography: Philosophy, Methodology and Reflection', in Andrews, D., Mason, D. and Silk, M. (eds) *Qualitative Methods in Sports Studies*, Oxford: Berg, pp.65–103.

Sparkes, A. (2002) *Telling Tales in Sport and Physical Activity*, Champaign, IL: Human Kinetics.

If you intend undertaking ethnographic research, it is also worth locating and reading as many ethnographic studies as you can, even if they do not relate directly to your own subject area, although there are an increasing number of high-quality ethnographies that have been published within sport journals over recent years.

234

12 Sport research and the internet

This chapter will:

- Discuss the sources of online data.
- Explain the process of undertaking netnographic research.
- Outline some of the key ethical issues specific to online research.

Introduction

Sport is now as much a digital phenomenon as a face-to-face one, and this rise in both the quantity and diversity of online sport provides a rich possibility for the sport researcher. To date, however, the use of online or 'netnographic' methods in sport research has yet to be fully exploited, and there is a wealth of opportunity for both the novice and experienced researcher alike. This chapter will outline some of the key issues surrounding online research in terms of the range of opportunities open to you, the process of undertaking online research, and the associated ethical issues that you will face as an online researcher. The chapter focuses more upon the 'naturally occurring' data that is present on the internet, and the use of the netnographic approach, rather than the use of the internet for conducting 'traditional' methods of data collection such as online surveys or asynchronous interviews, the principles of which are outlined in Chapters 8 and 9.

Sources of data

There is a wide variety of material on the internet that can be used to provide data. Some of the relevant sites, such as online newspapers, provide useful sources of data, and can be analysed in the same way as any text, through content analysis (see Chapter 10). As well as the analysis of texts, however, the internet provides a valuable research for researching people, through their use of, and involvement within various forms of social media. The term 'social media' refers to internet services where the content is generated and exchanged by the users themselves. There is a range of such media, with the common ones including:

- Blogs and microblogs such as Twitter.
- Social news networking sites such as Digg and Reddit.
- Content communities such as YouTube.
- Social networking sites such as Facebook.
- Specialist forums such as SportForum.net.

Each type is rich in a variety of material, such as text, photographs and videos, all of which can provide valuable data, which is continually being updated and is highly interactive. The data can be collected through various levels of researcher immersion within the chosen site. In its most basic form, this could simply be through a content analysis of data from various sites, such as an analysis of athlete maltreatment through Twitter (Kavanagh and Jones 2014), or an analysis of fan tweets following a team scandal (Brown and Billings 2013). At the other end of the continuum, this could involve the researcher immersing him or herself within an online community to develop a rich, descriptive and explanatory account of online behaviour in the form of a 'netnography' such as Kerrigan *et al.*'s (2014) study of the role of mobile music technologies to enhance the running experience.

A CONTENT ANALYSIS OF FAN REACTIONS TO ALCOHOL-RELATED PLAYER TRANSGRESSIONS

Smith *et al.* (2014) were interested in how sport fans reacted to reports of alcohol-related player transgressions within the Australian National Rugby League and the Australian Football League. To do this, they undertook a content analysis, studying 11 different fan forums, including specialist forums for each league, general sport discussion forums, and several newspaper sites. This allowed them to collect over 7000 pieces of archival data in the form of fan comments. This allowed them to conclude that the club or league's response to the transgression was more concerning to fans than the actual transgression itself, and the tension between needing to protect a club's image and brand equity and the social and moral expectations of players was problematic, with the key desire of fans to be that of parity across cases.

Undertaking a 'netnography'

The term 'netnography' (Kozinets 2010) applies the principles of traditional ethnography (Chapter 10) and applies them to online activity, with the same outcome, that of developing an understanding of a group or community through an approach that is naturalistic, immersive and through the flexible use of a variety of methods. Kozinets outlines a number of steps to undertaking a netnography.

1 Defining your research question. As I noted in Chapter 7, there has to be a clear and coherent link between research question and research design. Is a netnographic design an appropriate one for your study? Can you justify its use, or would alternative designs be better to answer the question. You also need to assess whether there is an adequate online presence, for some groups or communities, online interaction and engagement may be sparse.

2 Identifying your site. Which community are you going to choose? As Kozinets (2010) outlines, your site needs to be relevant, active, interactive, substantial, heterogeneous (that is have a variety of different participants) and data-rich. Take time to get to know the community before you attempt to gain entry, however.

3 Considering ethics. You must get ethical clearance before the research starts.

4 Gaining entry. How are you going to enter the online culture? Are you going to lurk anonymously, in which case your ethical stance will need to be justified, or become part of the community? If the latter, then how will you introduce yourself, and provide full details about your study so that informed consent may be provided by all of your participants? How will members react to an outsider entering their social world, and how will you react with the negative reactions that may result? How will you ensure that you are not seen as 'intruder' into a private world? How will you allow participants to get further information about the project, and its aims and objectives? You shouldn't overload participants with information at the very beginning, and make sure that only the essential information is provided, but also make it clear where further information can be located.

5 Collecting data. Collect data as soon as you begin to gain entry, and from all sources, such as emails, postings, blog entries, videos and so on. Remember that social media sites are ephemeral; site and links change often. URLs disappear, content changes, and pictures are removed. Also keep your field notes up to date on a regular basis, making notes of everything that happens. Data may be:

- Archival data – existing data that the researcher has had no role in creating or prompting. This can be downloaded through a variety of ways, ranging from manual searching to the use of more advanced data mining software, such as the use of Radian 6 to extract data from social media sites.

- Elicited data. Created through interaction with group members, for example through posting a comment on a blog, and recording the subsequent comments and reactions of group members.
- Field note data – your own records of the research, and your own reflections of the group, their behaviours and interactions, and your own place as a member of the group. Field notes are used not to record data, but to write down your thoughts on why things are happening, and to record your own experiences and reflections on the process. You can also record the key decisions you made during data collection, and the critical incidents encountered as netnographer.

6   Data analysis. As with any qualitative research, data analysis can be done manually or through appropriate software. One thing to be aware of, however, is that the potential volume of data that might be easily obtained from larger, more active sites, may well make manual analysis difficult, if not impossible. Don't fall into the trap of collecting an unmanageable volume of data, as this will only impact negatively upon the quality of your analysis.

7   Exit from the group. One further aspect that Kozinets tends to overlook is that of how you exit the community. The nature of netnography means that it is all too easy to exit too quickly, and to suddenly 'disappear' without any comment or acknowledgement. You need to ensure that your exit from the group is appropriate, and that any promises made, such as to share the key conclusions from your netnography, are kept. This is important not only for your own responsibilities as a researcher, but also to ensure that any future approaches by others wishing to undertake research are met positively.

Netnographic methods

A variety of methods are available to the netnographer. One characteristic of the netnographic approach is that of the eclectic, flexible approach to data collection, and the opportunity to collect a variety of data using various methods is a strength in allowing a rich, descriptive and analytical picture of the online community to be presented. Hooley *et al.* (2012) have outlined some of the methods that you might consider, which include:

- Participant observation – become involved in the community, take part in the activities, post articles and so on. Think about your experiences, and the rituals and behaviours that you notice.
- Interviews and focus groups – these can provide rich data beyond that of analysing the content of the sites, and allow rich descriptions and explanations to emerge.
- Online surveys – these can be useful to collect quantitative data.
- Examination of documents and written and visual culture online.

The key, however, is to immerse yourself within the community, and use whatever sources are appropriate to your research.

A NETNOGRAPHY OF THE POLITICS OF CANOEING IN ENGLAND AND WALES

Gilchrist and Ravenscroft (2011) explored the political tensions that emerged as a consequence of the dominance of the property rights of the owners of the waterways over the freedom of those canoeists wishing to use them. Using an extended period of immersion within a paddling forum, where they were able to detect a wide range of participants, they were able to virtually observe a wide range of discussions and debates among members, ranging in date from 2002 to 2011. This allowed them to present a rich, analytical picture of the community, and thus identify that their approach as 'roving bandit' was less likely to be successful in gaining rights than if they adopted the role of 'settled ruler'.

Assessing your data

The use of online data adds an additional set of questions to the researcher who is interested in assessing the quality of the data they obtain. The key issue is that of anonymity of your sources of data. Online, people have the opportunity to present themselves as something they are not, provide false information, and behave in ways that they would not be able to, or want to do in day to day life. Don't be put off by this – in reality, any method is open to such issues, and what you need to do, instead, is to try to assess the quality of the data that you do obtain. You may, for example, be undertaking a netnographic study of a fan community, and obtain a lot of data from a fan who is clearly unhappy with the team management. They might be a concerned fan, or they might be a 'troll', trying to inflame other fans. In this case you can have a look at things like when he or she joined the community, how many posts they have made, whether they have posted about other matters, seem knowledgeable about the team and so on. Otherwise, the criteria with which you assess your data are the same as those with which you would asses any other piece of qualitative research, such as trustworthiness, credibility and so on (see Chapter 7). The more immersed you get within the online community, the easier you will find assessing your data becomes.

The ethics of online research

Social media research provides a number of ethical challenges and dilemmas, to which there is often no clear-cut answer, especially within the areas of informed consent and maintaining anonymity. The differing models of online research do have differing ethical concerns, and it is important that the nature of the research, whether it is a simple content analysis of archival data, or a more interactive netnographic approach involving interaction between researcher and participants guides your ethical considerations. The ethical issues that go beyond those discussed in Chapter 7 are as follows.

Public versus private data and issues of informed consent

As I noted in Chapter 7, gaining informed consent is an essential aspect of any research project; however, the challenges of achieving this with internet research don't always make this possible, and there are debates as to whether it is always necessary. The area that seems most clear is that of data posted on closed sites, that is those that require some form of registration or logging in to access. Here, it is essential that informed consent is obtained. Archival data that are posted in 'public spaces' without any need for registration or logging on, however, could, it is argued, be seen as being in the public domain, and thus available to the researcher. The critical issue is that participants may have had no expectation that their comments or posting would be read by those outside of the online community when they were originally made. Kozinets (2010), however, clarifies the dilemma faced by the researcher when he argues that 'if the researcher does not record the identity of the communicators and if the researcher can legally and easily gain access to these communications or archives' (p.142), then their analysis should not come under traditional models of human-subject research. If in doubt, however, you should respect the expectations of the subject in terms of their privacy.

Elicited data, on the other hand, do follow a human-subject model of research, and here it is important that informed consent is obtained. This could be done via email or other written communication. The issue remains, however, of who is providing the consent, and the anonymity afforded by the internet does mean that the comprehension, competency or the age of the person providing consent cannot be ascertained with complete confidence. If there are doubts about the individual's ability to provide informed consent (for example you are unsure of their age), then you may well be better advised to undertake an alternative approach whereby the information can be ascertained. As with all ethical issues, if doubts remain, then you need to reconsider your approach.

Anonymity

Anonymity presents a number of challenges. Even if participant names or user names are omitted, then a Google search will quickly identify users either through a search of their user name or, if you report quotes verbatim within the research report. You may also find, however, that some users may wish to be identified or given credit within the report, for example the creator of a blog may want to be given recognition. I would advise you to treat online pseudonyms as real names, and in the same way that you would not report real names within a research project, then you should assign alternative pseudonyms to the names adopted by online participants.

ETHICAL CONSIDERATIONS FOR THE ONLINE RESEARCHER

Eysenbach and Till (2001) provide an outline of the ethical considerations that you need to be making before starting your online research. These are as follows:

- Intrusiveness – Discuss to what degree the research conducted would be considered 'intrusive' by members of the community.
- Perceived privacy – Discuss (preferably in consultation with members of the community) the level of perceived privacy of the community (Is it a closed group requiring registration for example?).
- Vulnerability – Discuss how vulnerable the community is: for example, a forum for those experiencing sport gambling issues is more vulnerable than those discussing training techniques.
- Potential harm – As a result of the above considerations, discuss whether the intrusion of the researcher or publication of results has the potential to harm individuals or the community as a whole.
- Informed consent – Discuss whether informed consent is required or can be waived (if it is required how will it be obtained?).
- Confidentiality – How can the anonymity of participants be protected?
- Intellectual property rights – In some cases, participants may seek not anonymity, but publicity, so that use of postings without attribution may not be appropriate.

The lack of clarity overall in terms of online ethics means that there is rarely a simple answer. The essential requirement for you, as a researcher, is to ensure that you fully consider all of the ethical issues associated with your project, and to ensure that you have full institutional ethical clearance before you start the research process.

Summary

1   There are a variety of online data sources available for you to use in your research.
2   The use of online sources of data may range from a simple content analysis, to a more immersed, in-depth netnography.

3 There are, however, a number of specific ethical issues of which you need to be aware before undertaking any online research.

Activity

Think about the online communities of which you are a member. Do any of them provide potential research opportunities, and if so, in what way? What sort of data would you collect from such communities?

ABOUT YOUR RESEARCH PROJECT

- Consider whether the use of an online research design would be appropriate for your study. If you were to undertake research into an online community, how would you negotiate access? Identify your strategy for entering the field.
- Identify the key ethical issues you would face, and how these issues would be addressed for this piece of research.

Further reading

Hooley, T., Marriott, J. and Wellens, J. (2012) *What is Online Research*, London: Bloomsbury.

Kozinets, R. (2010) *Netnography: Doing Ethnographic Research Online*, Los Angeles: Sage.

Poynter, R. (2010) *The Handbook of Online and Social Media Research*, Chichester: Wiley.

13 Analysing data I: quantitative data analysis

This chapter will:

- Describe how to prepare your quantitative data for analysis.
- Introduce SPSS for Windows as a data analysis software package, and briefly run through its use.
- Introduce some of the different statistical tests that you may wish to use to analyse your data.

Introduction

Quantitative data will not provide you with the answer to your research questions. The data need to be interpreted, and they need to be organised and analysed so that they may be meaningfully used to answer your research questions. This is the process of quantitative analysis. It is often at this stage that panic – especially among non-statisticians – may set in. From your reading of the related literature, you may already have encountered terms such as 'multiple regression analysis', 'repeated measures ANOVA', 'factor analysis', and so on, and found them difficult to comprehend, let alone to interpret. The field of statistics is a large and complicated one, and a book of this type can only provide you with a broad overview. We would strongly recommend that, if your research involves detailed statistical procedures, you should read one of the many available specialist texts such as Field's (2013) excellent *Discovering Statistics Using SPPS* or Vincent's (2005) *Statistics in Kinesiology*.

Statistical analysis can be broadly separated into two forms: descriptive and inferential. Descriptive statistics organise your data, for example in terms of producing frequency counts of participation in sport, or calculating the average points scored per game by a particular team. Inferential statistics allow you to infer relationships or differences that exist between two or more variables, such as calculating a correlation between experience and ability at a particular sporting task, or gender differences in sport preferences, and to draw conclusions about the overall population under investigation from your sample. In terms of your own use of statistics, you will have to ask the following questions:

- What exactly do I need to find out from these data to answer my research question?
- What statistical test will give me this information?
- What do the results from this statistical test mean?

There are a couple of points to note at this stage. The first, and one that I will repeat later, is that statistics in themselves have no meaning in themselves. They are simply tools with which to help you make sense of the data. Thus, simply to report the results of a statistical test is only the first stage. The importance lies in how such statistics are interpreted, and how that interpretation is related to your research objectives. The second point is that statistics can only interpret the data that you have collected, and if such data lack reliability, validity or relevance, then no amount of statistical testing can rescue those data.

The use of computer software in quantitative analysis

A number of computer packages are available to assist you with quantitative data analysis. The most commonly used package is Statistical Package for the Social Sciences (SPSS) for Windows, and it is worth learning to use this. It is relatively simple to pick up the basics of the programme, and a lot of the functions are intuitive if you have used other Windows software before. SPSS for Windows allows large data sets to be used, it has a wide range of statistical tests available, and it can produce professional-looking graphs and tables. It is a standard package used globally, and knowledge of SPSS is a valuable skill to have. There are other alternatives you could consider, for example Minitab, R or spreadsheets such as Microsoft Excel. You should remember, however, that it is not the case that certain software will produce 'better' results (the results produced should be the same whether you use SPSS for Windows, Minitab, Excel, or calculate them by hand). Your research project will not be assessed on what package you used to analyse your data, but rather on your interpretation of the statistical results. Throughout this chapter, I will assume that you will be using SPSS for Windows to analyse your data, and will provide guidance on carrying out the tests using this package. The underlying statistical principles of what follows, however, will apply whatever method you choose.

Data preparation

The first stage in analysing your data is to prepare the data for input into SPSS (or other appropriate statistical package). There are four steps that you need to undertake before the process of analysis begins.

1 Coding data

Coding refers to translating the responses that you receive into common categories, each of which can be assigned a numerical value, allowing subsequent statistical analysis. Coding can be relatively straightforward; for example, a question on age worded 'how old are you?' is already numerical in format (thus providing a ratio variable – see Chapter 6 for a reminder of the different types of data) and does not need to be coded. Non-numerical responses should be assigned numerical values; for example, responses to a question on gender could be coded so that answers of 'male' are coded as 1, and 'female' coded as 2 (thus providing a nominal variable). Open questions are slightly more problematic. Here, each response should be grouped together (coded) by the researcher. For example, responses to the question 'What is your favourite sport?' could be as follows:

- tennis
- hockey
- soccer
- basketball
- association football.

Each group would then be assigned a numerical value. Tennis would be coded 1, hockey 2 and so on. Soccer and association football would have the same numerical value as, although different responses were given, conceptually they are the same response and they would thus be coded together. Thus, each response is converted into a number. Occasionally you may encounter difficulties in deciding whether to code differing responses together or separately. The answer to this is dependent upon whether they are conceptually similar in terms of your research question. If in doubt, code the responses differently, as you can always combine different codes together as one afterwards, which is a lot easier than separating one code into two!

Responses from the other types of questions I have discussed should be relatively straightforward in terms of converting responses to numerical values. If you are using scales, then each potential response is allocated a number. Have a look at the following question, for example:

I take a positive attitude towards myself as a sportsman or woman

Never	*Seldom*	*Sometimes*	*Often*	*Almost always*
❑	❑	❑	❑	❑

Each response can be allocated a logical numerical value. Thus a response of 'never' is coded as 1, 'seldom' as 2, 'sometimes' as 3 and so on. Therefore, in the above example, the response would be coded as 4. Occasionally a question may be 'reversed', that is asked in the opposite way, for example, the question above may be asked as 'I take a negative attitude towards myself as a sportsman or woman'. The scoring for this would also be reversed, thus 'never' is scored 5, 'seldom' as 4 and so on. You may also need to add up the scores from all of the items in a scale, and include that score.

2   Inputting data

The numbers produced from step one should then be input into whatever software package you choose. Depending on the package used, you may have to set up your data entry sheet beforehand. I will run through data entry in SPSS for Windows later in the chapter.

3   Checking data

Once data entry has been completed, then a careful check should be made for accuracy. It is easy to make inputting errors, for example inputting making a double keystroke by accident and entering '11' rather than '1'. The data set should be checked beforehand as far as possible to minimise the effect of such errors, and any unusual or unexpected results that occur after the analysis (such as having three different response sets for a question on gender!) should also be checked in case of mistakes in data entry.

4   Dealing with missing values

The general practice is that questions that have not been answered should be assigned a value (for example '99' or '999') in the data set. This will allow you to distinguish between actual missing values and those that have been inadvertently omitted. You can inform SPSS for Windows that you have used a particular response for missing values so that your analysis will not be affected.

Using SPSS for Windows

The following section will give you a brief guide to the use of SPSS for Windows, which we would recommend for your quantitative data analysis. It is, once you have picked up the basics, a user-friendly package, and allows you to undertake any statistical test that you will realistically need. It will also provide you with high quality tables, charts and graphs which can be imported into your word processing package. You should ensure that you use the tutorial provided with SPSS as this will be extremely helpful. Another good way to learn about SPSS is to practise using hypothetical data sets, either those made up by yourself, or those that accompany some of the SPSS textbooks. You may also want to have a look at Ntoumanis (2009) for an overview of the use of SPSS for Windows.

There are four basic steps to analysing data using SPSS. These are:

1 Inputting your prepared data into the data editor.
2 Selecting an appropriate test, graph, chart and so on from the menus.
3 Selecting the variable(s) for analysis.
4 Interpretation of the results from the output file.

Upon opening the programme, you will encounter a window that asks you whether you wish to open an existing file, or create one of your own. For the first time, you should create a new file, and give it a name that summarises the contents (i.e. 'sport participation study' as opposed to 'data'). You will be faced with a screen that resembles a spreadsheet. This is the data view. This is where the data are to be entered, and is essentially a grid that displays all of the responses for all of the participants. Each of the grey boxes running along the top of the screen (containing the letters VAR) refers to a different variable. Each of the boxes down the left hand side, numbered from 1 onwards, refers to a participant. Thus, you are able to include each variable response for each participant on this screen.

Before entering data, you need to set up your variables. If you go towards the bottom of the screen, you will see that you are in the data view window. By clicking on variable view (next to data view), you will bring up a different screen. On this screen, each row represents a different variable. The grey boxes along the top represent some of the characteristics of the variable. The most important ones are as follows:

- Name. This refers to the name you assign the variable. Try to make this as simple yet as meaningful as possible, so name your variables 'age', 'score', 'weight' and so on, rather than 'question 1', 'variable 1', etc.

- Type of variable. This allows you to specify whether your data are in numeric form, date form, currency and so on.
- Label. This allows you to give a more detailed label to your data, for example your variable may be titled 'score' and your label may be 'what was the participant's score on the basketball shooting task'. This label will then be attached to whatever output you produce, such as graphs or tables so ensure that spelling of all terms is correct here.
- Values. Here, you can enter detail about the codes that you have used for each variable. By clicking on the small grey box within the cell under labels, a small window will open. Under label you should enter the codes you have used, and what those codes refer to under value label. For example, if you coded males as 1 and females as 2, you should enter '1' for value, and 'male' for value label, then click add. Repeat the action, except entering '2' for value, and 'female' for value code. Once you have done this, your output will automatically include the labels such as 'male' and 'female', rather than just '1' or '2'.
- Missing. This will allow you to identify which values are missing, for example, you may wish to enter '99' for missing values. You can enter up to three codes for missing values, so you can distinguish between reasons for their omission. For example '99' could be entered for those questions that were not applicable, and '999' could be entered if the participant failed to respond. When you define your missing values, make sure that they are unlikely to coincide with an actual value, for example, defining '99' as a missing value for the variable of 'age' may, although it is extremely unlikely, lead to respondents who are 99 years old being categorised as missing.
- Measure. This is where you define the level at which the data was measured, in terms of whether it is nominal, ordinal, or 'scale' data (scale data includes both interval and ratio data here).

You are now in a position to enter or download your data. Return to the data view window, and enter your data carefully, trying to avoid any errors, which may affect your analysis. Remember to enter missing values. Once you have entered all of your data, you are ready to undertake statistical analysis.

Analysing data using SPSS for Windows

There are several steps that you need to follow when analysing your data. These are:

1 Decide what you need to find out. List your requirements beforehand. What do you need to know? What variables do you need to compare? Only test what you have to; if one test meets your objectives then only carry out that one test. Don't trawl through the data trying to identify as many ways of exploring the data as you can if they are not required. Such post-hoc analysis seeking out as many significant results as possible is bad research practice and needs to be avoided.

2 Choose the appropriate test. Decide the appropriate statistical test to use to give you that data. Then, using the menus across the top of the screen, select analyse, and choose your test accordingly. There are a range of available options, including the production of tables as well as descriptive and inferential statistics. Also, identify whether your tests are to be one-tailed or two-tailed in advance.

3 Select the variables to be tested. Once you have selected your test, you will be asked which variables are to be tested. Highlight the appropriate variables in the box in the left of the small window (the dialogue box) that appears when you choose your test. Move them across to the appropriate sections, for example into the independent variable box. You may also need to select which groups to compare, for example the independent-sample t-test asks you to enter your grouping variable. Simply enter the codes for the two groups you want to compare, e.g. '1' for males and '2' for females.

4 Decide upon the level of statistical significance to be used. You must decide whether you are going to consider your results significant (see p-value, page 259) at 0.1, 0.05, or 0.01. This needs to be done in advance of the analysis, rather than afterwards, and normally, the level of 0.05 is chosen.

5 Interpreting the output. SPSS will produce an output window where the results are presented. Depending upon the test used, various information will be presented. The information that will be of most interest to you will be the level of significance. SPSS for Windows will state the level of significance, and if this is below the threshold

252

that you have set in the previous stage (such as $p = 0.05$) then you can reject your null hypothesis (more on this later).

6   Producing tabular/graphical output. This follows the same procedure as analysing your data. Tables will generally be produced in the output window, or there is an option to create basic and custom tables in the analyse menu. To create graphs, rather than select analyse, you should select graphs, and follow the instructions as above. Graphs can be copied and pasted directly into a word-processed document, and you can link the chart with the data file, so that if you update your data file, you can also update your chart in the document.

Methods of analysis

This section will present an overview of some of the commonly used methods of statistical analysis. As we have said, descriptive statistics are those which organise and summarise numerical data. Inferential statistics allow inferences to be made about the wider population from your sample by analysing the associations or differences between two or more variables.

Descriptive statistics

Measures of central tendency

A measure of central tendency is a value that describes a particular characteristic of a set of scores. The most commonly used measures are those of mean, mode and median. The mean is the average score of all observations of a variable. You may, for example, be interested in the attendances of a particular sports team. Rather than select one attendance figure (which may be misleading), a better approach would be to average out the attendance figures over a period of time, for example a single season. The mean is calculated by the following:

Mean = sum of scores/number of observations

Thus, for the example above, the average attendance would be the entire sum of attendances over the period of time, divided by the number of matches. Thus, three matches, with attendances of 481, 375 and 425 would result in an average attendance of the three attendances (481 + 375 + 425) divided by the number of occurrences (3), providing an average attendance of 427.

Sometimes, you may come across grouped data, as shown below:

Points scored	Frequency
0–2	3
3–5	5
6–8	6
9–11	1

In this instance, the mean is calculated by multiplying the midpoint (halfway between the upper and lower score) by the frequency, and then dividing by the total number of observations.

Points scored	Midpoint	Frequency	Midpoint frequency
0–2	1	3	3
3–5	4	5	20
6–8	7	6	42
9–11	10	1	10
Total		15	75

Thus, the mean points score is 75/15 which is 5 points.

254

A second measure of central tendency is the mode. You may be interested to find out the most common age for individuals to drop out from competitive sports. In this type of research, a modal score can often be more useful than a mean score. The mode refers to the category with the largest number of observations. Thus, the mode for the above example of grouped data would be 6–8, as that was observed six times, more than any other category. Finally, the median is the point that divides the observations, once ordered, into two equal parts. If the weekly hours spent training for a sport were measured as 2, 2, 4, 5, 6, 10, 10, 11, 15 then the median would be 6, as there are four values above this value and four below. A median split can be used to split one group into two subgroups for the purposes of comparison. It may be that the researcher is interested in the relationship between the time spent training and self-efficacy while competing. In this case, a median split could be used to divide the group into 'low' trainers (those scoring below the median) and 'high' trainers (those scoring above the median).

Measures of dispersion

Measures of dispersion indicate the spread of the data around the mean or other measure of central tendency. The most commonly reported measure is the standard deviation. The standard deviation (SD) measures the extent to which scores deviate from the mean. Thus, two samples may have identical means, but differing standard deviations. The researcher is then aware that the measures from the sample with the larger standard deviation are likely to deviate from the mean score to a greater extent, that is they will be more spread out. A further, although less commonly used measure of dispersion, is that of the range. The range is simply the difference between the lowest and highest score in the distribution.

Relational measures

Rate. Rates can be useful in comparing different populations. For example you may want to find out differences in sports participation between two countries with significantly different populations. Rather than simply provide figures as to overall participation (which would effectively be meaningless), a rate would provide a more useful comparison. A rate measures the frequency with which a value occurs compared to the maximum frequency with which it could occur. The calculation is simple:

Rate = number of actual occurrences/number of possible occurrences

The rate of regular participation in sport in the UK may be 0.15 (that is 15 people from every 100 participants) whereas the rate in the USA may be 0.18 (or 18 in every 100).

Ratio. You may be interested as to the proportion of different groups undertaking a particular activity. A ratio describes the numerical relationship of parts of a group to each other; for example, it could describe the numbers of males compared to females in a sports crowd. It is calculated using the following formula:

Ratio = number of members of subgroup one/number of members of subgroup two.

If there were 32,000 males and 24,000 females watching a sporting event, then the ratio would be 32,000/24,000, which is 1.3 males for every female.

Percentage. A percentage (%) compares a subgroup to the total group, for example, using the above scenario, the percentage of male fans in the entire crowd. This is calculated by:

% of subgroup = (number of members of subgroup/number of members of entire group) × 100.

So the percentage of male fans is (32,000/56,000) × 100, or 57.1 per cent. You may also wish to use percentages to ascertain levels of performance. For example, one individual may score 17 points out of 20, compared to another who scored 11 points out of 15. Because both scores were from different totals, it is not possible to compare them directly. One way to compare them is to convert them into percentages. Player one scored 17 out of 20, which equals 85 per cent. Player two scored 11 out of 15, which equals 73 per cent. The percentages can then be compared rather than the raw scores.

Presenting descriptive statistics

Descriptive statistics are generally presented in the form of tables and graphs. Tables should be included where the information is appropriate to the research question (you should not include every single result unless it is relevant). Tables should include percentages as well as raw scores – this allows easier comparison between groups of different sizes (you should also include the raw scores, and an indication of the total number of responses). You must also label each table accordingly. The format of your table should be similar to that presented in Table 13.1.

Table 13.1 Age of respondents

Age category	Per cent	n
0–10	18.1	17
11–20	26.6	25
21–30	29.8	28
31–40	14.9	14
41–50	6.4	6
Over 50	4.3	4
	100	94

Cross-tabulation simply involves producing a table with the responses from the dependent variable across the top, and the responses from the independent variable down the side, as demonstrated in Table 13.2.

Table 13.2 Gender comparison of sport preference

	Prefer contact sport (%)	Prefer non-contact sport (%)
Male	79	21
Female	22	78

USING SPSS TO CREATE TABLES

1 Select analyse from the menu.
2 Select custom tables.
3 Select either basic or general tables.
4 Select the appropriate variable(s). Move those variables into the central box.
5 Click OK. SPSS will produce the table in a separate output window.

Bar charts may be useful to present data visually. They consist of a 'bar' for each response (either horizontal or vertical), the length of which represents the size of response. A scale is placed along the side or bottom of the chart to indicate the size of response. You should always tabulate your results, and only use graphical means when it actually illustrates a point (so, for example, a response of 50 per cent male and 50 female would not merit any graphical output, but a response of 10 per cent male and 90 per cent female would be worth considering). Do be careful not to make charts over-elaborate, and be careful with the over use of bright colours or complex patterns.

Inferential statistics

The measures discussed above investigate single variables, such as team scores, hours spent training in a week and so on. Much explanatory research, however, is interested in the relationship or differences between two or more variables. This is the realm of inferential statistics. Inferential statistics assess the association between independent and dependent variables (you should go back to Chapter 6 if you are not clear about these terms). These may be bivariate (measuring the effect of a single independent variable upon a single dependent variable) or multivariate (involving more than two variables). Within this chapter, the focus will be on bivariate tests. There are two categories of inferential test:

1 Parametric tests. These tests use interval or ratio data (see Chapter 6 for a reminder). Parametric tests assume that the data is drawn from a normally distributed population (i.e. the data is not skewed) and have the same variance (or spread) on the variables being measured.
2 Non-parametric tests. These are used with ordinal or nominal data, and do not make any assumptions about the characteristics of the sample in terms of its distribution.

Inferential statistics require you to test a hypothesis, or more accurately, a null hypothesis. A null hypothesis suggests that there is no relationship between your variables. Thus, you are assuming no association, and it is the role of the test to contradict this hypothesis. Assume the null hypothesis is true until the evidence suggests otherwise.

258

Interpreting your results

Inferential statistics do not tell us whether there is a relationship between two or more variables. Instead, they calculate the likelihood of whether an apparent relationship or difference between two or more groups is down to chance or not. You could measure the heights of female basketball players from the UK and The Netherlands. If the difference in average heights was 15 cm, then you would probably see that as a significant difference. What, however, if the difference was 10 cm, 5 cm or 1 cm? At what stage can we say that there is actually a significant difference between the two groups? Fortunately, this uncertainty is largely removed through the statistics that are produced when we test such differences.

Inferential statistics provide a 'p-value'. The smaller the p-value, the less likely the result was due to chance, suggesting that there is an actual relationship between the variables. A p-value of 0.10 indicates that in 90 cases out of a 100, the result was due to an actual association, rather than chance findings. Thus, there is a 10 per cent chance of rejecting the null hypothesis when it is true. The probability of this being the case is indicated by the p-value. For example, $p < 0.1$ indicates a likelihood of incorrectly rejecting a true null hypothesis one time in 10, whereas $p < 0.01$ suggests that this would be the case less than once in a 100 times. A value of 0.05 is the generally accepted level of significance in sports studies, thus a p-value of 0.05 or less strongly suggests that you have a relationship that is not due to chance. If you have a larger p-value, then you could not really be confident enough that the results do show an actual difference or relationship.

p-VALUE

You may be interested in the difference between male and female ability at a sporting task. You want to know whether that difference in ability is due to the independent variable (gender in this case). Measuring the mean scores from each sample (male and female) will not be enough on its own to conclude that the wider populations have different means. It is possible that the populations have the same ability and that the difference you measured is simply a coincidence or chance finding. You cannot be sure if the difference you measured is representative of the wider populations, or if it is just a one-off result.

259

All you can do is calculate the probability that it is indeed representative. This probability is the *p*-value. The *p*-value ranges from zero to one. If the *p*-value is small (for example, 0.05 or below), you may conclude that the difference between sample means is unlikely to be a coincidence.

Instead, you'll conclude that the populations have different means, and that there is an effect related to the independent variable. If the *p*-value is higher (> 0.1), then it is very possible that your findings were, indeed, coincidence, and that no true difference exists between the groups.

It is important that you decide the level of significance before you undertake the statistical test. Although common practice, it is not good research to await the outcome of the test before deciding upon a significance level! You should also report your *p*-value in your results. In the past, precise values were not presented (due to the method of working out statistical significance, researchers reported the probability levels as either less than one in 10 ($p < 0.1$), less than one in 20 ($p < 0.05$), or less than one in 100 ($p < 0.01$). Nowadays, packages such as SPSS for Windows allow you to report the exact *p*-value, and this is generally accepted as good practice.

A significant test statistic, however, as Field (2013) points out, is not necessarily a conclusive finding, and in many ways still needs to be treated with caution. It does suggest an effect of the independent variable upon the dependent variable, for example, but it doesn't tell us the size of that effect. Indeed, even small effects can be statistically significant. We can also never be entirely certain that we can reject the null hypothesis, as there will always be differences between mean scores, even if they are very small. Thus, results still need to be carefully interpreted.

SIGNIFICANT AND NON-SIGNIFICANT RESULTS

You will often find that your results are not statistically significant, which might seem disappointing, however it is important to realise that the aim of quantitative research is not actually to find significant results. The whole point of your statistical analysis is to provide empirical data to answer a research question or test a null hypothesis, and if that evidence suggests no significance, then this is equally as valid as identifying a strong significant value. The reasons for the non-significant findings will provide you with some valuable material for when you come to discuss your results. So do not be discouraged by results that are not significant. They are not 'wrong' as such.

Tests of association

Tests of association refer to those tests that measure whether two or more variables are related, that is as the independent variable changes, then the dependent variable alters accordingly. Thus, you may be interested to examine whether there is a relationship between participation in sport and income. You are seeking to assess whether the two variables of participation and income are associated. There are a number of tests that you may consider using.

Correlation

Correlations investigate the relationship between two variables consisting of interval or ratio data, for example the relationship between advertising spend and subsequent sales of a particular sports product. A correlation can indicate:

- Whether there is a relationship between the two variables.
- The direction of the relationship (i.e. whether it is positive or negative).
- The strength or magnitude of the relationship.

A positive correlation exists where higher scores on one variable correspond with high scores on another; for example, performance may increase as self-efficacy increases. A negative correlation is where higher scores on one variable correspond with lower scores on another; for example, performance in a complex sporting task may decrease with increasing levels of anxiety. The size of a correlation will range from −1.00 to +1.00. A score of −1.00 represents a correlation that is a perfect negative correlation, that is as the score on one variable decreases, then the score on the other variable increases. A score of 0.00 represents variables that are not correlated, or have no relationship with each other, and a correlation of +1.00 represents a perfect positive correlation, that is the variables increase or decrease together.

While correlations are useful to identify relationships, they are unable to determine causality, that is the extent to which variable X causes variable Y. This is because it is often unclear whether it is actually X causing Y; for example, does increasing anxiety lead to a reduction in performance, or does *Y* cause *X*? Could it be that decreasing performance leads to increasing anxiety? A further possibility is that they are interrelated. Finally, there may be an unidentified variable that is leading to an increase in both *X* and *Y*. Thus you should be extremely cautious in assuming causal relationships from correlations. If you do, you have to be clear that you have correctly interpreted the independent and the dependent variables.

CORRELATIONS USING SPSS

1 Select analyse from the menu.
2 Select correlate from the options.
3 Decide the type of correlation you would like to undertake (normally, but not only, a bivariate correlation).
4 Move the variables you want to analyse into the appropriate box.
5 Decide what type of correlation you need to use, for example a Pearson's or Spearman's correlation, and whether the test is to be one-tailed or two-tailed.
6 Click on OK, and the correlations will be produced.

The result will be, as I noted above, a score between −1.0 and +1.0. You can interpret the size of the effect under investigation using this score, with a correlation coefficient of < 0.1 a small effect, 0.3 a medium effect, and a score of 0.5 or higher a large effect.

KEY TERM

ONE-TAILED AND TWO-TAILED TESTS

Your test will explore a specific prediction (your hypothesis) that may be directional or non-directional in nature. A hypothesis such as 'a reduction in disposable income will result in lower spending on sports goods' is directional, that is we are explicit about the direction of the relationship. On the other hand, you may be testing the hypothesis that 'the introduction of a new manager will affect output in a sport manufacturing organisation'. This is non-directional, in that you cannot predict whether the change will be positive or negative. If this is the case, you need to select a two-tailed test. If you have a directional hypothesis then you need to select a one-tailed test, otherwise you increase your chance of making a type II error.

Choosing a Pearson or Spearman correlation

The Pearson correlation coefficient is used to analyse two variables collected at the interval or ratio level of measurement where the data are parametric in nature. Thus, a correlation between the height of a golfer and average drive length would use a Pearson's correlation. The Spearman's rank order correlation is the non-parametric equivalent of the Pearson's correlation, and is used with ordinal, or ranked, data. Thus you may be undertaking a project into golf performance, and be interested in the relationship between position in driving accuracy tables, and position in final money tables. As the data are ordinal and non-parametric, a Pearson's correlation is inappropriate, and a Spearman's test is required.

Regression analysis

Although a correlation may indicate a relationship between two variables, it does not provide any indicator of the magnitude of effect, for example what a likely outcome would be of an increase in the independent variable upon the dependent variable. Regression analysis between two variables effectively calculates a 'best fit line'. This line will subsequently predict the effect of one variable upon the other. Regression is undertaken through selecting 'analyse ➤ regression ➤ linear' on the SPSS menu. This will report first an 'ANOVA' which, essentially, will tell you the extent to which regression analysis predicts the effect of the independent variable on the dependent variable. If this is significant, then the regression model is a better predictor that simply using mean scores, and the subsequent coefficients (identified by B) allows you to identify the effect of a change in the independent variable upon the dependent variable. For more detail on this test, see Field (2013).

Testing differences

Tests of difference generally assess whether differences between two samples are likely to have occurred by chance, or whether they are the result of the effect of a particular variable. Thus, questions such

263

as whether males differ from females in terms of amount spent on sports-related merchandise, or whether undergoing a six-week period of relaxation techniques lowers pre-competitive anxiety among young golfers, would be answered through testing differences. The commonly used tests of difference are outlined below.

The independent-samples *t*-test

The independent-samples *t*-test examines whether the mean scores of two different groups can be considered as being significantly different. For example, you may be interested to compare the effects of mental rehearsal on golf putting performance. You randomly assign your participants to either the rehearsal or non-rehearsal group, and compare their scores to see if there is a significant difference. It can be used when:

- The data are interval or ratio in nature.
- The groups are randomly assigned (hence, you should use an ANOVA test, outlines below, rather than a *t*-test to compare differences between males and females, as gender is not randomly determined when you come to assign your groups).
- The two groups are independent of each other.
- The variance, or spread, in the two groups is equal.

THE INDEPENDENT-SAMPLES *t*-TEST USING SPSS

1 Select analyse from the menu.
2 Select compare means.
3 Select independent-samples *t*-test.
4 Select the independent variable and move it into the central box.
5 Choose the variable representing the groups you wish to compare and move it into the grouping variable box.
6 Click on define groups.
7 Type in the codes you have assigned for the two groups you want to compare (e.g. '1' for males and '2' for females).
8 Click continue.
9 Click OK. SPSS will now produce the results of the *t*-test.

The paired-samples *t*-test

Whereas an independent *t*-test measures differences between two groups, the paired *t*-test measures whether the mean of a single group is different when measured at different times, for example, whether the performance of a group on the putting task after mental rehearsal was significantly different from that before the rehearsal.

THE PAIRED-SAMPLES *t*-TEST USING SPSS

1 Select analyse from the menu.
2 Select compare means.
3 Select paired-samples *t*-test.
4 Select the paired variables (i.e. the before and after scores) and move them into the central box.
5 Click OK. SPSS will now produce the results of the *t*-test.

Analysis of variance

An analysis of variance (ANOVA) is similar in nature to the independent *t*-test; however, it allows you to ascertain differences between more than two groups. If you are looking to explore gender differences, then this is a more appropriate test to use than an independent *t*-test as it doesn't assume that participants have been randomly assigned to each group.

ANOVA USING SPSS

1 Select analyse from the menu.
2 Select compare means.
3 Select one-way ANOVA.
4 Select the variable and move it into the central box.
5 Select the independent variable and move it into the factor box.
6 Click OK. SPSS will now produce the results of the ANOVA.

The Mann–Whitney test

The Mann–Whitney is an alternative to the independent t-test, and is used when your data is ordinal and non-parametric. This test works on ranking the data rather than testing the actual score, and scoring each rank (so the lowest score would be ranked '1', the next lowest '2' and so on) ignoring the group to which each participant belonged. The principle of the test is that if the groups were equal, then the sum of the ranks should also be the same. If there are differences between the groups, the Mann–Whitney will identify them through the difference in rank scores.

THE MANN–WHITNEY TEST USING SPSS

1 Select analyse from the menu.
2 Select non-parametric tests.
3 Select 2 – independent-samples test.
4 Select the dependent variable and move it across into the appropriate box.
5 Choose the variable representing the groups you wish to compare.
6 Move it into the grouping variable box.
7 Click on define groups.
8 Type in the codes for the two groups to compare (e.g. '1' for males and '2' for females).
9 Click continue.
10 Tick the box for Mann–Whitney at the bottom of the dialogue box.
11 Click OK. SPSS will now produce the results of the Mann–Whitney test.

The Wilcoxon signed-rank test

This test is similar to the Mann–Whitney test. However, it examines differences where the two sets of scores are from the same participants (effectively it is a non-parametric alternative to a one-sample *t*-test).

The Kruskal–Wallis test

This is a non-parametric alternative to the ANOVA test, and can be used to identify differences between three or more independent groups.

Both of these tests can be accessed using analyse ➤ non-parametric tests, with the Wilcoxon signed rank test available under '2 related samples' and the Kruskal–Wallis test under 'K independent samples'.

Chi-squared test

The chi-squared test is a useful test for non-parametric nominal data. The chi-squared test compares the actual, or reported, frequencies of a given variable with the frequencies that would be expected if the data was to suggest no differences between groups. As an example, you may be interested in whether preferences towards sport vary between genders. The results may be as follows:

It would seem apparent from the table that there is a significant difference between the type of sports favoured by males and females. This can be confirmed by undertaking a chi-squared test.

THE CHI-SQUARED TEST USING SPSS

1 Select analyse from the menu.
2 Select descriptive statistics.
3 Select crosstabs.
4 Select one of the variables you wish to compare, and move it into the row box.
5 Select the other variable and move it across into the column box.
6 Click on statistics.
7 Tick the chi-squared box, and click continue.
8 Click 'cells'.
9 Check the 'expected' box, and click continue.
10 Click OK. SPSS will now produce the results of the chi-squared test.
11 If there is a significant result, then you need to examine the differences between your findings (observed) and what would be expected.

You need to ensure that you have a minimum of five cases in each cell, otherwise problems will arise in the accuracy of the test.

The above is a very simple guide to the different statistical tests that you may use. I have not included every test, and it may be that there are other tests that will be more appropriate. If your research involves statistical analysis, we strongly recommend that you read a specialist text, so that you gain a fuller understanding of the principles underlying each test.

TYPE I AND TYPE II ERRORS

When selecting a particular level of significance at which to reject the null hypothesis, be aware that there is a possibility of two types of error. These are:

- Type I error. This occurs when you reject the null hypothesis when it is, in reality, true. Thus, you would suggest a relationship where, in reality, none exists.
- Type II error. This occurs when you accept the null hypothesis when it is false. Thus, you would suggest no relationship, where a relationship does actually exist.

The likelihood of making a type I or II error depends on the level of significance that you choose. Thus, if you choose to operate at the 0.1 level of significance, then you are more likely to make a type I error. If you choose a level of significance of 0.01, then a type II error becomes more likely.

Choosing your test

I have included only some of the more commonly used tests. You should make sure you spend some time reading around the different types of test available to you, and when such tests are appropriate. You should also read up on what the tests actually say. It is no good obtaining a highly significant result from a test without knowing what that significant result actually means! It is important that you do choose the right test, otherwise your findings will lack any meaningfulness. The type of data that you collect will be important in your final choice of test:

- Nominal. Consider a chi-squared test if you are interested in differences in frequency counts using nominal data; for example, comparing whether month of birth affects the sport that someone participates in.
- Ordinal. If you are interested in the relationship between groups, then use Spearman's correlation. If you are looking for differences between independent groups, then a Mann–Whitney test may be appropriate. If the groups are paired, then a Wilcoxon signed rank test is appropriate; and if there are three or more groups, then consider a Kruskal–Wallis test.

268

- Interval or ratio. Are you looking to identify relationships between two variables? If so, consider the use of a Pearson's correlation. If there are three or more variables, then consider multiple regression. If you are concerned with differences between scores, then t-tests or ANOVA may be appropriate. If you want to identify differences within one group, then a paired-samples t-test should be used. If you are comparing two randomly assigned groups, then use an independent-samples t-test. If you are looking to compare two non-randomly assigned, or three or more groups, then use ANOVA.

Reporting the findings

You should always provide detail about the results beyond simply saying that the results were significant or non-significant. Consider first whether you need to report the findings within the text, or to tabulate the findings (preferable for anything other than simple results).

- For a correlation, you would generally report the correlation coefficient and the probability. If you have undertaken a one-tailed test, you should also state this, so you may report that 'there was a significant positive relationship between the number of times a sponsor's logo was seen by television viewers, and subsequent recall of that brand ($r = 0.47$, $p < 0.01$)'. It is also good practice to report the effect size (see Field 2013) for tests wherever possible.
- Paired and independent t-tests should be reported by stating the test statistic, the degrees of freedom, the probability value, and the effect size if possible.
- To report an ANOVA, report the F-ratio, the degrees of freedom, and the probability. For example, 'Analysis of variance demonstrated that there was a significant gender effect in the findings ($F (4, 245) = 3.93$, $p = 0.03$).
- For Wilcoxon signed-rank tests, Mann–Whitney and Kruskal–Wallis tests, report the test statistic, the degrees of freedom if appropriate (normally for Kruskal–Wallis), and the probability. Thus, you may report that 'a Kruskal–Wallis test demonstrated clear differences between pre-match meals and subsequent performance ($H(3) = 5.76$, $p = 0.04$)'.

- For chi-square, the test statistic should be reported, the degrees of freedom, and the probability value, e.g. 'those born in March were more likely to play cricket as their main sport ($X^2(1) = 29.89, p = 0.04$)'.

A final word on statistics

As a final note, I should stress that undertaking statistical analysis and producing significant results is not, in itself, the key part of your research. The important part is in being able to interpret your findings, that is being able to understand what they actually mean. Thus, if you have carried out a paired-samples t-test, then what does a significant result actually suggest? The interpretation is just as important as undertaking the correct test. Statistics are simply a tool to be used to assist you in your analysis. The second thing to remember is that non-significant results are just as interesting as significant results. It is fairly common for students to get a non-significant result and think that this is somehow 'wrong', or inferior to a significant result. This isn't the case, and will, in many cases, give you just as much of interest to examine when you discuss your findings.

Mistakes sometimes made in quantitative analysis

- Choosing an incorrect statistical test, often through applying parametric tests to non-parametric data.
- Designing the questionnaire so that the data is in the incorrect format for the appropriate statistical test, thus the format of the response may provide you with ordinal data when you require interval data.
- Misinterpreting a p-value, or deciding upon an inappropriate level of significance, and making a type I or type II error.
- Testing as many variables as possible to pick up any significant results without any theoretical rationale for selecting those variables.
- Deciding upon a level of significance after undertaking the analysis.

270

Summary

1 There are a number of ways in which you can analyse quantitative data. Descriptive statistics allow you to organise and summarise your data. Inferential statistics allow you to draw inferences regarding the association or difference between two or more variables. A number of computer packages exist to help you carry out descriptive or inferential statistics. SPSS for Windows is the most powerful.

2 Inferential tests will provide you with a 'p-value'. The p-value indicates the likelihood that any association or difference (depending upon the test) was down to chance or not. A p-value of 0.05 indicates that in 95 cases out of a 100 you could be confident that there was an actual difference or association, rather than a chance difference or association.

3 The importance of statistical analysis lies not in the analysis itself – although that has to be done correctly. Instead, it is the correct interpretation of the results that you obtain!

4 You should try to gain some experience using SPSS for Windows. Using some of the sample data files available with the package, try to undertake some descriptive and inferential analysis. Don't be too concerned with the subject matter of the data. Instead, it is more important that you begin to understand the principles of the package. Try to produce some tables and graphical output for some data you have created, or from an existing data set. Again, don't worry too much about what the data is saying, but simply try to gain confidence in using the programme.

ABOUT YOUR RESEARCH PROJECT

If you are undertaking quantitative analysis, can you identify the following:

1 What is the purpose of your analysis, that is, what exactly do you want to find out?

2 What statistical test will provide you with the result that you need?

3 Have you got the right data for this test (for example, in terms of ordinal or interval data for certain tests, parametric data where such data are required and so on)?

4 Have you assessed the likelihood of making a type I or a type II error?

Further reading

Acton, C. and Miller, R. (2009) *SPSS for Social Scientists* (2nd edn), Basingstoke: Palgrave Macmillan.

Field, A. (2013) *Discovering Statistics Using SPSS*, London: Sage.

Ntoumanis, M. (2009) *A Step-by-Step Guide to SPSS for Sport and Exercise Studies* (2nd edn), London: Routledge.

Vincent, W. (2005) *Statistics in Kinesiology*, Champaign, IL: Human Kinetics.

272

14 Analysing data II: qualitative data analysis

This chapter will:

- Introduce the basic principles of qualitative data analysis.
- Introduce the concepts of 'codes' and 'themes'.
- Describe the different types of coding that form the framework for qualitative analysis.
- Describe the ways by which you can graphically represent your qualitative analysis.
- Discuss some ways by which you can maximise the trustworthiness of your interpretations.

Introduction

Analysing qualitative data can prove to be much less straightforward – at least initially – than the seemingly more 'logical' and 'objective' analysis of quantitative data. This is partially due to the lack of a commonly accepted method of qualitative analysis, and also because, as you may have noted from your own reading, many researchers reporting qualitative research do not always make it clear how the analysis has taken place. Thus, there is often an air of mystery about qualitative analysis, especially when compared with the seemingly more straightforward and objective approaches to quantitative data analysis which follow tried and tested procedures. Essentially, the aim of both qualitative and quantitative data analysis is the same, that is to make sense of your data so that evidence can be obtained to answer your research question. Although quantitative and qualitative data are different in their nature, as Table 14.1 shows, the principles of analysis of each are, however, not entirely different.

Table 14.1 Similarities and differences between quantitative and qualitative analysis

Similarities	Differences
Analysis for both involves inference – that is they both reach a conclusion based on evidence.	Quantitative analysis is highly standardised and varies little between projects; qualitative analysis has many more possible approaches.
Both involve a systematic process.	Quantitative analysis takes place at the end of data collection; qualitative analysis takes place during data collection.
Both involve comparison, either internally or with related evidence from elsewhere.	Quantitative analysis tends to test hypotheses through the manipulation of numbers representing 'facts'.
Both strive to avoid errors, false conclusions and misleading inferences and description and seek valid explanations.	Qualitative analysis blends empirical evidence and abstract concepts in the form of words to explain or illustrate a theory or interpretation.
	Qualitative analysis is less abstract, and does not assume that real life can be measured by numbers.

Source: Adapted from Neuman (2000).

Stages of qualitative analysis

As I have noted, there is no single accepted method of analysing qualitative data. This section will provide a brief overview of one method of analysis. However, if you are analysing qualitative data it is worth having a look at texts such as Miles and Huberman (1994) or Silverman (2006) for more detail on the various methods of analysis available to you. The key, as always, is to ensure that your analysis is appropriate to achieve your research objectives.

Your data collection will invariably result in pages and pages of transcripts, field notes and so on. This needs to be focused, organised and interpreted. To do this, you will need to undertake the following steps:

1   Data familiarisation. Read your transcripts all of the way through at least 2–3 times. You may also want to listen to them again if appropriate. Essentially the idea is for you to firstly get to know your data 'inside out', and secondly, to begin the analytical process. As well as writing down your initial thoughts and ideas about your analysis, you also need to be aware at this stage about how such early analysis might impact upon the rest of the process, for example by leading you in a specific direction too early, or meaning that alternative theories or explanations might be overlooked. Such reflexivity is important in maximising the quality of your analysis.
2   Data reduction. At this stage, try to discard all irrelevant information, but do ensure that you have access to it later if required, as unexpected findings may need you to re-examine some data previously considered unnecessary. The amount of data you discard will depend upon how focused your data collection has been, if in doubt, do not discard.
3   Data organisation. You will have to organise your data firstly through coding, and subsequently through developing broader themes to make sense of the data itself. These issues are covered below.
4   Data display. To draw conclusions from the mass of data, Miles and Huberman (1994) suggest that a good display of data, in the form of tables, charts, networks and other graphical formats, is essential. Again, this is a continual process, rather than just one to be carried out at the end of the data collection. See Figures 14.1 and 14.2 to see how this can be done.

5   Conclusion drawing/verification. Your analysis should allow you to begin to develop conclusions regarding your study. These initial conclusions can then be verified, that is their validity examined through reference to your existing field notes, further data collection, or even critical discussion with your colleagues.

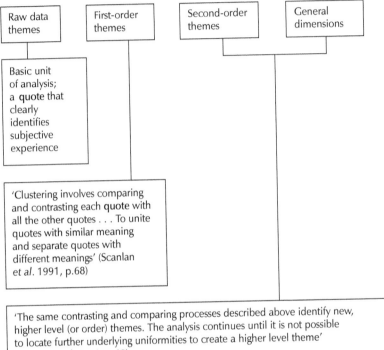

Figure 14.1 A framework for the thematic analysis of qualitative data

Developing codes and themes

Coding is the organisation of your raw data into 'conceptual categories'. As Miles and Huberman (1994, p.56) note: 'Codes are tags or labels for assigning units of meaning to the descriptive or inferential information compiled during a study. Codes are usually attached to "chunks" of varying size – words, phrases, sentences or whole paragraphs.' Each code is effectively a category or 'bin' into which a piece of data is placed, with the choice of bin reflecting the broader meaning of the data. Thus, for example, a piece of data that refers to an individual not wanting to take part in an activity because they feel they don't have the required skills might be coded as 'lack of confidence'. A statement from a participant about the rising costs at their gym might be coded as 'pricing concerns' and so on. Any further data with the same meaning would also be coded in the same way (i.e. put in the same 'bin'). Some codes will consist of a lot of data from a broad range of participants; other codes might have fewer data from only a few participants. Remember, though, that it's the qualitative meaning and importance of the data, rather than the quantitative significance of the data within a code, that is important.

Coding is the first stage to providing some form of logical structure to the data. Codes should be valid, that is they should accurately reflect what is being researched, they should be mutually exclusive, in that codes should be distinct, with no overlap, and they should be exhaustive, that is all relevant data should fit into a code of some description. Once you have coded your data, you can look for emerging themes. A theme is, essentially, a conceptual label for a group of linked codes, and is more abstract in nature. Thus, codes such as 'fear of failure', 'lack of confidence' and 'lack of interest' might all be grouped together under a theme of 'intra-personal barriers to participation'. In this case it would be a 'first order theme' as it has emerged from your codes. First order themes may then be grouped together in the same way if they are conceptually linked, for example first order themes of 'intra-personal barriers to participation' and 'structural barriers to participation' may be grouped together as a second order theme of 'general barriers to participation'. Themes may emerge from your conceptual framework if you have developed one prior to data collection, or inductively, through your own interpretation of the data. Whichever you choose, it is your job to convince the reader of the suitability of your themes. Themes should be insightful, and provide the reader with an idea of the underlying social processes, rather than simple one-word descriptions. Thus, if you are researching the experiences of athletes with a disability, and find data regarding the impacts of injury, then rather than naming your theme 'injury', ensure that is called 'reaction to injury'.

The following is a suggested process for developing your themes from your data:

1 The data is carefully read, all statements relating to the research question are identified, and each is assigned a code, or category. These codes are then noted, and each relevant statement is organised under its appropriate theme, either manually or on computer, along with any notes, or memos (see below) that the researcher wishes to add of their own. This is referred to as open coding.

2 Using the themes developed in stage 1, the researcher rereads the qualitative data, and searches for further statements that may fit into any of the codes, and subsequently become part of a theme. Alternatively, further themes may also be developed in this stage. This is also referred to as axial coding.

3 Once the first two stages have been completed, the researcher should become more analytical, and look for patterns and explanation in the themes. Questions should be asked such as:

   ● Can I relate certain themes (your 'first-order themes') together under more general themes (second-order themes')?
   ● Can I organise themes sequentially (for example, does code A happen before code B)?

- Can I identify any causal relationships (does theme A cause theme B)?

4 The fourth stage is that of selective coding. This involves reading through the raw data for cases that illustrate your analysis, or explain the themes developed. You should also look for data that are contradictory, as well as confirmatory, as it is important not to be selective. You must avoid what is referred to as confirmation bias, or the tendency to seek out and report data that support your own ideas about the key findings of the study.

While you are coding your data and developing your themes, you should also be prepared to write memos on an on-going basis. These are the ideas that occur to you while you are coding your data, for example concerning explanation, theorising, or other ideas about the data. They can be extremely helpful to you in trying to make sense of the data at a later date. You can write them directly on the transcripts, or keep a record of them elsewhere. Try to make your memos as detailed as you can, as this will help you with later analysis.

Using your codes and themes, your data may then be presented graphically as suggested by Biddle *et al.* (2001) where you demonstrate to the reader how the codes you generate have been clustered into themes. A simple example of how this may appear is provided by Roberts *et al.* (2001), who were interested in how comfortable golfers felt with their clubs. Their analysis is shown in Figure 14.2. Such a display is helpful for the reader to see the relationship between codes and themes and should always be presented within the study.

As you will notice, there is no indication of any numerical analysis, and at no stage are numbers assigned to any category. As Krane *et al.* (1997, p.214) suggest:

Placing a frequency count after a category of experiences is tantamount to saying how important it is; thus value is derived by number. In many cases, rare experiences are no less meaningful, useful, or important than common ones. In some cases, the rare experience may be the most enlightening one.

The layout and complexity of your thematic analysis will vary from project to project. Some data will result in a minimal number of codes, and look similar to that of Roberts *et al.* presented in this chapter. Other projects will result in many more first and second order themes. The important element is to let the data drive your analysis, and if the data suggests a level of complexity, then you should be guided by that.

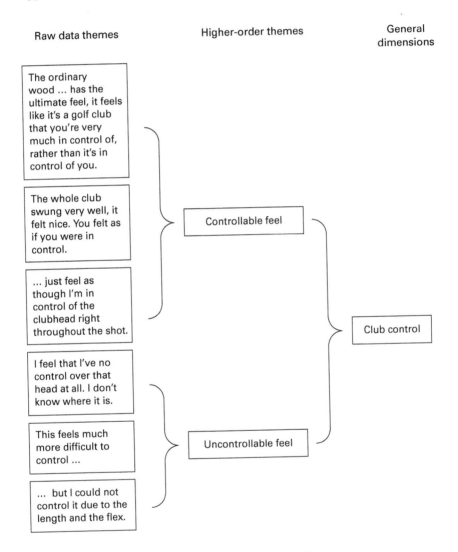

Figure 14.2 A qualitative analysis of golfers' perceptions

Presenting your analysis

When you write up your analysis, you will generally find it better to combine your results and discussion into one chapter or section. Assuming that you have both first- and second-order themes, then I would strongly recommend that you briefly summarise second-order themes one at a time, and then present each first-order theme that makes up that second-order theme in more detail. Begin by summarising your key findings for that first-order theme. Then present your evidence in the form of quotes from your participants, including any data that contradict such conclusions. Finally, provide a conclusion for each first-order theme. Using quotes can enrich your report, and bring your findings to life, often making the report much more readable. Although it essential to provide the reader with an idea of the voices of participants, you should resist the temptation to over-use them, however. As a rule of thumb, you should use direct quotes or observations:

- When they describe a phenomenon particularly well.
- To show cases or instances that are unusual.
- To show data that is unexpected.

You should also avoid including quotes without making clear reference to how such quotes refer to your analysis, so avoid having isolated quotes, and never finish a section with a quote.

Once you have discussed each of the themes, then it is important to revisit the data as a whole. You should try and bring everything together to discuss what everything means when taken together, and how this relates back to, and makes sense of your research question. Essentially this is where you answer the question 'what does it all mean?'. As with any analysis, don't let the reader have to make sense of it themselves. You are there to do this, and this is often a good way to conclude the discussion.

Computer analysis and qualitative data

A number of authors have suggested using computer software to analyse qualitative data, using packages such as NVivo. These packages typically help you manage and analyse qualitative data. They allow you to store and organise documents, attach ideas to text, and find patterns among your data. There are a number of issues related to the use of computer software for qualitative data analysis. First, although computer analysis may allow much quicker, and seemingly more objective, analysis, the process of manually 'tagging' specific quotations can often be considered desirable in that it gives you a 'feel' for the data, and allows increased familiarity with the transcriptions. Second, as Dey (1993, p.61) notes, 'the use of a computer can encourage a "mechanistic" approach to analysis. In this scenario, the roles of creativity, intuition and insight into analysis are eclipsed'. The research analysis may then become a routine and mechanical process (Lee and Fielding 1996). Third, much of the tagging that is carried out by such software requires words to be specified or coded beforehand by the researcher, which, given the wide range of possible answers, will be equally time consuming. Fourth, most of the available software only identifies the sentence within which a specific word or phrase occurs, and thus often fails to locate the context. Finally, the increased time incurred by manual tagging of transcripts is offset by the time required to develop competence in an appropriate computer software package. Some of the packages, although extremely powerful, do take some time to learn, even with specialised instruction.

You need to weigh up the pros and cons of taking the time to learn such a package before deciding on a particular approach. If you are likely to be undertaking a considerable amount of qualitative research over a reasonable period of time, then it may be worthwhile learning one of the packages. If you are engaged in a one-off piece of short-term research, then we would recommend manual analysis. If you do reject the use of computer software for analysis, you should not immediately assume that the quality of analysis is inferior to that done by computer. As Krane et al. (1997, p.215) note with regard to computer versus manual analysis:

> None of these procedures directly affects the value of the study; they are merely ways for the inquirers to work with their data ...

282

If individuals use NUD*IST or Hyperqual computer programs, or 3 × 5 cards and paste them to the wall, they are really doing the same thing conceptually.

Thus, provided the analysis is carried out correctly, as outlined above, the method of analysis is not related to the quality of the information obtained, and, in effect, the researcher is doing the same process, whether using a computer program or manual methods. It is equally likely that computer analysis may be done as well, or as badly, as manual analysis. To help you make your decision, have a look at something like Lewins and Silver (2007) which provides some useful background information.

Ensuring the trustworthiness of your data

Whereas the analysis of quantitative data is, on the outside at least, relatively objective and transparent, qualitative data analysis is open to considerably more interpretation and debate, especially with regard to the validity of the interpretation. There are a number of techniques that can be used to validate the interpretations, and Holloway and Wheeler (2009) summarise the means by which you can try to ensure the trustworthiness of your data. These include the following.

Member checking

One particular method of note is to ask those being investigated to judge the analysis and interpretation themselves, by providing them with a summary of the analysis, and asking them to critically comment upon the adequacy of the findings. While this is not a requirement of all qualitative analysis, it can be a useful exercise for the qualitative researcher to undertake. The issue arises, however, of what happens when subjects disagree with the analysis. In such instances, it is important to identify the source of disagreement, to assess whether such disagreement is indeed valid (it may be, for example, that participants have misunderstood some of the analysis, or they approach the analysis with a different agenda to the researcher). Thus, even agreement or disagreement with the analysis can be problematic. Despite this, however, member validation can be an important tool to the qualitative researcher. An alternative may be peer review, whereby a fellow researcher takes the place of the member, and seeks inconsistencies, bias, or possible errors in interpretation.

Searching for negative cases and alternative explanations

Interpretation should not focus on identifying only cases to support the researcher's ideas or explanations, but to also identify and explain cases that contradict.

Triangulation

Triangulation was introduced in Chapter 7, and is useful as a means to demonstrate trustworthiness in the analysis.

ENSURING TRUSTWORTHINESS OF DATA – PARENTS' PERCEPTIONS OF PHYSICAL ACTIVITY FOR CHILDREN WITH VISUAL IMPAIRMENTS

Perkins *et al.* (2013) were interested in how the perceptions of parents with visually impaired children impacted upon the participation of those children in physical activity. To do this, they interviewed 11 parents, and produced a number of first-order themes, such as 'living a healthy lifestyle' and 'building confidence', as well as being able to group such themes into second order themes, such as 'holistic benefits of physical activity'. To enhance the quality of their analysis, they undertook a number of activities, including:

- Member checking – this involved sending the transcripts back to the participants to ensure that the interviews were an accurate account of the participant's perceptions.
- In addition data were analysed by multiple researchers, first independently of one another; and subsequently together until a consensus on the themes was reached.
- They also conducted a search for negative cases by looking for responses that were counter to or did not align well with their themes.
- Finally they consulted an external reviewer who reviewed the themes to ensure that they reflected the purpose of the study and corresponded with the research questions.

The audit trail

To ensure reliability (in the qualitative sense, see Chapter 6) all research should have an audit trail by which others are able to judge the process through which the research has been conducted, and the key decisions that have informed the research process. This should include rich (or 'thick') descriptions of the setting, and participants, the context within which data were collected, and a clear description of the rationale for any decisions made regarding the data collection or analysis.

Reflexivity

Reflexivity means that researchers critically reflect on their own role within the whole of the data collection process, and demonstrate an awareness of this, and how it may have influenced findings, to the reader.

In addition, you should also ensure that your written account of the research:

- Is contextually complete – Your account makes full reference to the context within which the group exists through rich description of the setting, identification of any idiosyncratic features and so on.
- Tells a 'good story' to the reader.
- Provides 'verisimilitude' – Does it provide the reader with a sense of almost 'being there', and give them a feeling of understanding of the culture?

A good qualitative analysis places the emphasis clearly upon the data, and it is vital that it is not hidden away, but takes primacy within your analysis. This should be apparent in your presentation of the data, and the error of not reporting enough data is more common than that of reporting too much.

Summary

1   Although qualitative and quantitative data are different in nature, the analysis of both involves inference, systematic analysis and comparison. Both try to seek valid conclusions and avoid errors.
2   There are a number of ways of approaching qualitative analysis.
3   Analysing qualitative data should be an on-going process throughout, as well as after the collection of data.
4   There are three key stages to qualitative data analysis: data reduction, data display and conclusion drawing/verification.
5   Data reduction takes place through the process of coding. Coding involves assigning units of meaning to data chunks, and can be open, axial or selective. These codes can then be displayed or organised to allow the drawing of conclusions.
6   Your analysis can be done either manually or by computer. There are advantages and disadvantages to each, but the final analysis should be the same whichever method you adopt.
7   There are a number of means by which you can maximise the trustworthiness of your data, these being member validation, searching for negative cases and alternative explanations, triangulation, having an audit trail, and reflexivity.

Activity

1   Carry out and transcribe a short interview with someone you know who is keen on sport. Question them on their experiences of playing and/or watching sport. Now try to code the interview, first using open, and then axial coding.
2   Can you draw any conclusions from your coding?
3   Now undertake selective coding to explain, support or refute your conclusions.
4   Ask a colleague to undertake the same process in terms of open and axial coding. How reliable are the results?
5   Try to produce a graphical display of your findings.

286

If your research project involves the analysis of qualitative data, you need to consider the following points:

- How will you maximise the trustworthiness of your data? Have you considered strategies such as member validation?
- In your write-up of the research, have you made the processes by which your data was analysed clear to the reader? Have you a clear audit trail? Have you demonstrated reflexivity?

Further reading

Denzin, N. and Lincoln, Y. (eds) (1994) *Handbook of Qualitative Research*, London: Sage.

Denzin, N. and Lincoln, Y. (eds) (1998) *Collecting and Interpreting Qualitative Materials*, London: Sage.

Lewins, A. and Silver, C. (2007) *Using Software in Qualitative Research: A Step-by-Step Guide*, London: Sage.

Miles, M. and Huberman, A. (1994) *Qualitative Data Analysis,* Thousand Oaks, CA: Sage.

Silverman, D. (2006) *Interpreting Qualitative Data*, London: Sage.

15 Writing the research report

This chapter will:

- Introduce the process of writing up your research.
- Outline the structure of a typical research report.
- Identify some of the areas where you should be assessing the quality of your written report.
- Describe some of the issues related to oral and poster presentations of your research.
- Suggest some alternative means by which you can disseminate the findings of your research.

Introduction

An important part of your research is being able to communicate what you have done through presenting it, whether in the form of a written report, dissertation, journal article, presentation or other format. It does not matter how good your data collection and analysis has been if the report is poorly written – you must ensure that you do not let yourself down in the final write-up. This chapter will guide you through the process of writing up, and highlight some of the problems that you may face, so that you can present a final report that will do the many hours spent undertaking the research justice.

Writing the research report

Writing the research report is a difficult and time-consuming task, and will generally take much more time than you think. The six main pieces of advice to bear in mind in terms of your overall strategy for approaching the process are:

1   Begin writing up the report as soon as you can. Do not leave it until you have finished your data collection before you start writing up. Many sections, for example the literature review and the methodology can be drafted during or even before data collection.
2   Write down ideas as soon as you get them, rather than leaving them to the writing-up stage. As I noted at the end of Chapter 1, you should be keeping a research diary where you can safely note any ideas. Not all of your ideas will be useful, but it is certain that some of them will be! Don't imagine that you will be able to remember these ideas at a later date.
3   Be aware of the nature of the report and the intended audience. If it is for an assessed piece of coursework, then ensure you have read and understood the criteria laid down by your institution in terms of content, presentation, length and so on. Look at the relative weightings of each section to see which elements assume greater importance. If you are writing for a journal, ensure that your research fits within the

scope of that journal's objectives as well as its editorial requirements. If you are producing a report or piece of consultancy, ensure that you are clear about the requirements of your audience.

4   You will need to rewrite your report a number of times. You should allow for this when planning your research timetable, and not become discouraged when the first draft is not perfect.

5   Have a clear schedule of when certain sections are to be completed, and ensure you monitor your progress against this schedule.

6   Make sure before you begin writing up that you have an adequate strategy for backing up your work, whether on memory sticks or using online storage, and that you make backups of your work at every available opportunity. Whatever you do, don't assume that whatever you save on a hard drive will be safe! You should keep your backups in a separate location. It is no good keeping them with your laptop on whose hard drive your work is saved – if the laptop does go missing, then you have lost all of your work.

The actual process of writing the report is a difficult task, and generally much more time consuming than most inexperienced researchers imagine. There are a number of stages that you will need to undertake:

1   Firstly clarify the nature of the report, and its intended audience. If any examples of past reports are available, read as many as you can. Try to identify what was good/bad about them, and ensure that you bear these evaluations in mind when compiling your own report. If there are specific marking criteria, then make sure you clearly understand them before you start writing.

2   As well as the content of past reports, familiarise yourself with the layout and technical requirements, for example maximum word length, required formatting, such as double spacing or specific referencing style, so that you have an idea of the final product before you start.

3   Prepare an outline plan. At the bare minimum, this should be a list of chapter headings. Ideally you should be able to have more detail – include likely subheadings as well. The more detailed your initial outline, the easier you will find the process of writing up the first draft of the report.

4   Write a first draft of the report. You should not anticipate the first draft being your final submission!

5   Evaluate the content of the first draft, either through reading it yourself or – preferably – getting somebody else to read it with a critical eye. Ask

this 'critical friend' to comment upon the content (although remember they will almost certainly – at this stage – be less knowledgeable than you about the subject matter) as well as the flow of the work, clarity of argument, layout and presentation, and the overall 'feel'.

6   Rewrite and re-evaluate the report as appropriate. You may need to do this more than once!

7   Final editing and proof reading. Once you have got this far, the temptation is to skip over the final proof reading. Do carefully read over to check spelling and grammar, and get someone else to do the same (once you have read your own work several times, it becomes very difficult to take in what you have read). Don't rely on the spell-checker that comes with your word processing package. It is a useful tool, but will not pick out every mistake, for example when you type 'there' instead of 'their'.

8   Submission of the report. Now you can relax! Unless you are to be orally examined, don't read a copy of the report for some time … you will only pick up errors that you didn't see, sections that you feel could have been written better and so on. Instead, you should enjoy the achievement of completing the research!

When writing the report, do not feel that you have to complete one chapter or section before starting another. It can be a good idea to be working on several sections simultaneously, so that if you do – as is likely – get 'writer's block', then you can carry on writing. Often, it then becomes easier to go back to the problematic section. Nor should you attempt to write the report in the same order as it is to be presented. Early sections, such as the abstract and the introduction, for example, are better left until towards the end of the writing-up process. There is no set way to go about the process of writing a report, and it is often a case of personal preference. Do try, however, to ensure that you have all the sections (literature review, methodology and so on) on a single file, as this will encourage you to see the written report as one coherent flowing document, rather than as a series of sections.

Structuring the written report

It is possible to structure a report in different ways, depending upon the nature of the research. You may find that your approach lends itself to a different layout from the one suggested here, for example if you have undertaken an qualitative piece of research, in which case you may wish to combine your results and discussion into a more integrated section. If you consider that a different approach is necessary, then discuss this with your tutor or research supervisor. A commonly used structure for an undergraduate dissertation is as follows:

1 Abstract
2 Acknowledgements
3 Table of contents
4 List of tables and figures
5 Introduction
6 Literature review
7 Research methodology
8 Results
9 Discussion
10 Conclusions and recommendations
11 References and/or bibliography
12 Appendices.

1 Abstract
This is, essentially, a summary of the research. It describes the topic under examination and outlines the research question or hypothesis, objectives, and methods of the study. It should also give a brief résumé of the main conclusions and recommendations. The abstract is a brief section, and should be within the word limits set down by your institution, journal, etc., often between 150 and 250 words (slightly longer for a postgraduate thesis). It is often the basis upon which others will assess the usefulness of the research, so you should ensure that you include all relevant details.

What should my abstract include?

- The aim of the research.
- The background to the research, and the focus of past literature.
- What is distinctive about your study, how it adds to or extends existing knowledge.
- A brief outline of the methodology you adopted.
- Your key findings/conclusions.
- How this has added to knowledge or understanding.

2 Acknowledgements

Your report should thank various people who have helped in the research. You might include specific individuals who have given information, offered insightful clues, or have been especially supportive. If funding has been provided, then acknowledgement should be made here. Gratitude may also be expressed to groups of people, such as those who formed the sample group. It is best to avoid tendencies towards the extremes of either flippancy or sycophancy. Sometimes, for example in a journal article, acknowledgements may be placed after the main body of the report.

3 Table of contents

The contents page gives the reader the first view of how the report is structured and how you have attempted to develop the topic. It should list sequentially the chapters and the major subdivisions of chapters, each identified by a heading and located by a page number. Contents are not always required, for example for journal articles.

4 List of tables and figures

Throughout the written report you may want to present material in tabulated (tables) or diagrammatic (figures) form. For example, if you have undertaken any quantitative analysis you will need to report the analysis in the form of tables. The location of this material needs to be listed, with separate lists for figures and tables.

5 Introduction

The introduction is there to make the reader think that this is a study that needs doing and is worth reading. It should describe the subject under investigation, the purpose of the research and why you are doing the research, essentially what you are doing, why you are doing it and how you are doing it. In the introduction you should provide some academic justification for the choice of topic if possible, as well as any particular personal justification. You should include a summary of how you are going to treat the chosen topic and, importantly, set out and explain (especially if your terminology requires clarification) your research question or hypothesis and your subsidiary questions or objectives, including defining any key terms or concepts. Finally, it may be useful to show your intentions by briefly running through your intended chapters or sections. What you must not neglect, or hide away, is what Creswell (1994) refers to as your purpose statement. The purpose statement is the statement that establishes the direction of the research, and highlights the objectives that are hopefully to be met. You can often start this with the phrase 'the purpose of this study is to …'. For a quantitative purpose statement, Creswell suggests including the following:

- The theory or model that is to be used in the study.
- The specific research design (cross-sectional, experimental, etc.).
- The variables to be tested, and their relationship with each other (begin with the independent variable, followed by the dependent variable).
- The unit of analysis, or the sample that you are investigating.

For a qualitative study, Creswell suggests the following:

- Use words such as develop, understand, and so on, that convey the emergent sense of the research, rather than words such as test, or measure.
- Clearly state and define the central concept or idea being researched.
- Describe the research design and method of data collection to be used, for example an ethnographic design, involving participant observation, etc.
- Identify the unit of analysis, such as the setting, organisation, group and so on.

6   Literature review

After an introductory chapter, most reports will include one or more chapters where you draw upon and consider theories, arguments and findings from the literature and which obviously relate in some way to your question or hypothesis (see Chapter 5). As suggested earlier, the literature review should not just be a list of all of the literature you have discovered, rather it should be a critical appraisal of existing work, and you should be explicit as to how your study is related to, or has emerged from this literature. A number of research objectives should emerge from your literature review. It is essential to state these clearly, and to show how they have developed. A common weakness in literature reviews is to list or summarise existing literature, then conclude with a number of research objectives that are unrelated to the literature. You should ensure that there is a strong link between your written literature review and your research objectives.

7   Research methodology

The literature review should 'set the scene' in terms of how your research relates to, and emerges from existing knowledge and understanding. The methodology should outline how your objectives are to be achieved. Although the methodology may be one of the shorter sections, it is crucial to the entire project. You must address the area of research methods, including a justification of the methodology chosen and an explanation of how the data was gathered. Generally the methodology section or chapter will consist of a number of sections:

294

- An outline of your underlying methodological assumptions. You may wish to justify your epistemological stance, for example, or your use of qualitative rather than quantitative data. You don't, however, need to provide lots of basic description about the nature of positivist approaches, or the characteristics of qualitative data in general.
- Your research design. Explain your choice of research design, making it clear what data is to be collected, and at what times.
- Methods. You should describe your choice of method, such as an online questionnaire, and outline some of the design issues. What questions were included and why? If you have adopted an existing questionnaire or interview schedule, then explain why you have done this, perhaps referring to issues of reliability and validity. You may also – depending upon the nature of the report – include details about the piloting or pre-testing procedure.
- Sample. You should include details of your sample or participants, how you achieved the sample, and any limitations of your sampling method.
- Procedures. Describe how the research was carried out, for example whether questionnaires were posted or handed to participants, what instructions were given and so on.
- Methods of analysis. You should briefly outline your methods of analysis, for example a description of the statistical tests to be used and a justification of their appropriateness.
- An overview of the ethical issues that emerged, and how these issues were addressed.
- You may also consider including an evaluation of the methodology, highlighting the strengths and weaknesses, and making any limitations clear to the reader.

Qualitative methodologies should always include a section about reflexivity, that is the role of the researcher, their characteristics, experience and values, and how this will have impacted upon all aspects of the data collection and analysis.

The methodology section or chapter needs to include a lot of detail in a relatively short space (often about 1,500–2,000 words in a 10,000-word undergraduate project). One rule of thumb that you can use to check whether you have included enough detail is whether another researcher, through reading only your methodology and equipped with copies of your data collection instruments, could undertake the same research and gain similar results. You should also justify your key decisions throughout. Rather than just present generic justifications (such as 'questionnaires were adopted because of their ability to reach a geographically dispersed sample'), you should explain why you have made the methodological choices specifically for your study.

8   Results

Do not simply report every finding here – report only those results that are relevant to your study. In terms of the presentation of results, think about how to put your findings over as clearly as possible. You may want to look at past research reports to see how they have presented their results. The purpose of the data analysis is to develop a series of logical and convincing answers to the research question(s) that have emerged from the literature review. You should not therefore present data that does not relate to your research, even if you think it would be 'interesting'. Be careful in your graphical treatment of data – it is very tempting to include as many charts and graphs as possible, and to try to make them extremely impressive in terms of colour, layout and so on. In practice, it is often the case that the chart with minimal detail is often the clearest to understand. You should only consider the use of colour if it clarifies a particular chart, a situation which is actually rare (and in many instances, such as when you submit to an academic journal, you will be restricted to black and white line drawings anyway!).

9   Discussion

The purpose of this chapter or section is to discuss the implications of your results in light of your research objectives. Remember when you are writing this section that it is all about what the results mean, rather than what they say. Berg and Latin (2008) identify four components of a typical discussion:

- A restatement of the results. Keep this as brief as possible.
- Relating the results to theory, either deductively, in comparing your findings to your underlying theoretical framework, or more inductively, developing your own theoretical framework.
- Assessing the limitations of the study (I would go further and suggest that the strengths of the study could be discussed as well).
- Discussion of the implications of the findings.

A common error at this stage is simply to discuss your own findings – what they mean and so on without any reference to existing knowledge. Do remember, however, that you are building on such existing knowledge, so refer back to what has been discussed in your literature review. Do your results find support in the literature? Were they predicted by the literature? If they did and were, then how does your research add to the literature? If your findings differed from your expectations, then are there any possible reasons why? Does the particular theory or model you've used still hold true in light of your research? If not, to what extent is this a limitation of the theory or model, or a possible limitation of your research? If the theory or model seems flawed, then how can it be refined to explain your findings? When discussing such issues, it is important to ensure that the discussion is grounded on your own observations, analysis and reading of the literature. By doing this, your arguments are more likely to be well constructed and convincing.

10 Conclusions and recommendations

Your discussion of findings/literature should lead to a final conclusion chapter or section. Your conclusions are very important and often receive inadequate attention. Importantly, they should stem from the findings/discussion, and lead to consistent, sensible recommendations if applicable. All the matters you wish to discuss and develop in the concluding section should be related to and follow logically from what's gone before. The conclusion should include a summary of your main arguments, drawing together the various themes and issues so that they can be brought to bear on the defined objectives or subsidiary questions of the study. The original research question or hypothesis should be revisited at this stage, and the dialogue would explain the extent to which this has been addressed within the context of the study. Strengths and limitations of your project and what, in hindsight, you might have done differently should be included.

When you have completed the first draft of your introductory chapter and your conclusions, try to read them together. Ideally, reading the introduction followed by the conclusions should make sense without reading anything in between – remember, the introduction should set the scene to the research question, and the conclusion will provide the answers! Depending upon the nature of your project, recommendations often follow a conclusion, but not in all cases. Recommendations based on the research itself are more likely to be included where your project is of a practical nature (e.g. in terms of the potential application of your findings to industry or education). Recommendations for further research are generally an excellent way to finish off the main body of the research and I would strongly advise you to include one or two suggestions for how future researchers could extend the work that you have done.

11 References and/or bibliography

Some confusion exists over the difference between 'references' and 'bibliography' and whether it is a requirement to include both lists. In reality, the terms are often used interchangeably – the minimum requirement is normally for a list of references, which contains all items cited in the text in alphabetical order of author. If you want to use both a list of references (references cited in your own text) and a bibliography (items not necessarily cited, but deemed relevant to the research), then this may be in order. Including the latter can be advantageous as a bibliography can demonstrate the width of literature that you have accessed, which may not always be clear from doing a reference list alone. You should check the requirements of your own institution if there is any doubt. Whatever you do, it is critical that you reference any work that you are citing accurately, giving a detailed description of the source from which you obtained the information. You must acknowledge sources and clearly differentiate between ideas or words that are your own and those that originate from others.

12 Appendices

You should locate in the appendices all that information which gives any additional support to the arguments you are constructing. It is important, however, that you put all the crucial information you wish to be read in the main text, rather than hiding it away in an appendix. All appendices that you do include should be referred to in the text. You may also want to include copies of correspondence, details of organisations, people you have contacted, details of interviewees, etc. Your research instruments, such as copies of questionnaires or interview schedules, should also be included in an appendix.

THE PURPOSES OF THE MAIN SECTIONS OF YOUR WRITTEN REPORT

- Abstract – what is the study about, how did you do it and what you found.
- Introduction – what you are doing, why you are doing it and how you are doing it.
- Literature review – what is known about the subject of your research, what isn't known, and how your research relates to the existing literature.
- Methodology – how you collected the data to answer that question and why you used that method.
- Results – what the data say.
- Discussion – what the data mean, and how the data relate back to the literature you discuss earlier in the report.
- Conclusion – what the answer to your research question was.

Language and writing style

The issue of language and style can often be overlooked in a research report. What you should be aiming for is to present a well-written, readable report that will actually interest your readers. There are four very general styles that can be identified:

1   The 'dry' and objective style. This is characterised by reporting everything in a totally objective manner, with no sense of humour or enthusiasm for the research. This style is difficult to read, especially in an extended report, and makes it quite difficult for the reader to actually complete the report! Try to avoid this style if at all possible.
2   The informal style. Here, the researcher feels that they have to chat to the reader. The language used is informal, as if the writer were explaining the research to his or her friends over lunch. Again try to avoid this style!
3   The 'long-winded' style. Also referred to as verbosity, this sometimes happens when writers try to imitate some of the more complex pieces of literature that they have come across in their reading, or, alternatively, to impress the reader with their use of complex academic language. This type of report uses technical jargon when perfectly acceptable words in plain English exist, in an effort to impress. Such reports can be difficult to read, and it may be harder for the reader to accurately assess what the researcher is actually saying! Holt (1989, p.357) identifies an example of this style, when he refers to a paper that suggests that 'Massification as the negation of publics designates that moral inter-subjectivity as a process of need expression and sublimation is replaced by corporatized, desublimating modes.' Remember – write to express, rather than to impress!
4   The 'elegant' style. This is the style towards which you should strive. It lies somewhere between the dry and informal, and it allows the information to be presented in a manner which is readable and interesting. Technical terms can be used where appropriate, but sparingly. This style often conveys the researcher's own sense of enthusiasm, and makes for an interesting, yet 'academic' read.

You also need to be confident in writing up. Remember that by this stage, you should have some degree of expertise both in the subject matter and research methodology. This expertise should come out in your writing. Avoid being over confident, and making grand or unsupported claims, but think about how your writing style can convince the reader that you have the credibility as a researcher.

Assessing your own research report

Before your report is read or assessed by others, such as your examiners, it is important that you critically evaluate its content beforehand. This can sometimes be a time-consuming task, and you should allow yourself as much time as you can for this stage, especially if it is likely that you will find significant errors, or if you think that a significant rewrite is required. There are a number of specific questions that you should ask yourself with regard to the content of your report. These are as follows.

Setting the scene

- Does your abstract give a clear idea of what is in the report? Has it clearly described the background to the study, what is distinctive about what you are doing, the methodology adopted, the main conclusions that have emerged, and how your study adds to knowledge?
- Is your table of contents well structured and does it give an accurate picture of what's included? Have you included a list of tables and a list of figures if appropriate?
- In your introduction have you introduced your research adequately? Is it totally clear to the reader what the aim of the research is? Have you got a clearly constructed and suitable research question or hypothesis which leads to a set of clear and related subsidiary questions or objectives?
- Are you happy that you have 'set the scene' for the reader? What is the rationale behind your research report? Have you clearly identified this? Why should the reader read your piece of work? Is it saying something worthwhile?

Your use of the literature

- Have you got a logically structured review of literature, starting off with a broad outline of the key concepts, focusing towards more specific literature as the review progresses?

- Is your issue or focus underpinned by theory? Is it clear which theory or model you have adopted?
- How up to date are your references? Have you included the most up-to-date work in your area?
- Have you managed to identify and get hold of the work of key writers in your particular area? Have you ensured that you have paid due attention to 'classic' sources?
- Have you used a variety of sources or are you over-reliant upon certain authors? Have you included or acknowledged competing theories or viewpoints, or simply selected literature that supports your hypothesis?
- Is it clear to the reader how your research relates to what has been done before, or builds upon existing knowledge?
- In your literature review do you merely identify and describe, with no real critical edge? Have you been analytical enough?
- Have you explored all possible sources?

Your methodology

- Have you clearly explained your broad epistemological assumptions? Does the methodology reflect these assumptions throughout?
- Do you clearly identify and explain your choice of research design?
- Have you explained the rationale behind your chosen means of collecting information? If it is an existing instrument, whose is it? Why did you choose it? Is it clear to the reader why your methods were the most appropriate ones for your research question?
- Have you made it clear who the subjects are? And to what population these subjects belong? Is it clear how they were selected?
- Did you undertake any piloting of your data collection instruments? What was the outcome of any piloting? If so, have you reported these in your write-up?
- Have you been explicit in outlining how data were analysed?
- Have you evaluated the methodology? Can you identify what was strong and what was weaker?
- Are you making assumptions? You know what you did in terms of research methods, but would the reader? Have you expressed yourself clearly and given adequate details? Would someone else be able to replicate your study on the basis of the information you've given?
- Have you justified your key decisions?

Discussion and conclusions

- Are your findings clearly presented? Have you included tables for your descriptive and inferential analysis of quantitative data?
- If you have included graphs, charts and so on, are these appropriate? Do they add anything?
- Is the content of each chart clear? Is it clear how each chart relates to your research objectives?
- How have you analysed your findings? If you have undertaken quantitative analysis, which statistical tests have you used? Are you sure these are the correct tests? Have you interpreted the results correctly? For qualitative analysis, have you demonstrated that you have analysed your data in a systematic manner?
- In your discussion, do you adequately revisit the literature and relate your findings to the literature, or do you simply discuss what you found?
- Are your arguments coherent, logical and sound? Are they consistent with the evidence that you have collected?
- Have your conclusions clearly emerged from the evidence collected and discussed? Have you acknowledged unexpected evidence, or evidence that contradicts your chosen theory or model?
- Do you return to your research question or hypothesis?
- Do you evaluate the research? Have you identified the strengths and the limitations of the project?
- Are any recommendations you make based upon your findings? Are they feasible and practical? Have you identified recommendations for further research?

General presentation of the report

- Is your content well planned and logically structured?
- Is the work well presented? Have you used an appropriate font, and followed the guidelines of your institution in terms of margins, double spacing and so on?
- Have you made appropriate use of supportive materials to enhance presentation (i.e. graphs, tables, illustrations)?
- Have you conducted a thorough read through, to eliminate careless spelling and typographical errors, poor grammar and poor sentence construction?

- Are you writing in the most appropriate tense? Is your writing too informal?
- How well do you communicate your ideas? Does what you write make sense?
- Do you link your various chapters and make use of signposting to help the reader?
- Have you set out your references and/or bibliography with the required detail and in the recommended format?
- Have you acknowledged all sources used, and made it clear when it's your views that are being expressed, or the views of others?
- Have you made appropriate use of appendices? Are there any unnecessary appendices?
- Have you ensured that your report is as stimulating and as interesting as possible? Have you conveyed your enthusiasm to the reader throughout the project?

Defending your research

It may be the case that you are called upon to defend your research orally, generally through what is referred to as a viva voce (or just viva). This is still rare at undergraduate level, although it is a requirement of higher degrees such as a doctorate. Alternatively, you may be asked to give a short presentation about your research (this is often a useful way to answer questions where there are doubts about the authenticity of some aspect of the research).

The viva voce

The difficulty with preparing for an examination of this nature is that it is simply not possible to predict with total accuracy the questions that will be asked! The best advice is that you simply have to know your research inside out. You should be able to anticipate some of the questions, for example on the main findings of the research and so on, and prepare for them. If you are asked a question that you can't answer straight away, then stop and carefully consider your answer rather than rush into a response. Write down the question if necessary, and ask the examiner for clarification of what he or she means if you are not sure. If you really cannot answer the question, then don't panic! The examiners are not expecting a perfect response to every question anyway. You should put such questions to the back of your mind and concentrate upon the rest of the viva – remember, one question that you cannot answer will not lead to a failed exam!

COMMON VIVA QUESTIONS

The following are some of the questions that do appear regularly at viva examinations. It is by no means an exhaustive list, and you should always expect the unexpected, or unusual questions as well!

- How did you come to research this topic?
- How has the research contributed to knowledge in this area?
- What were the important research decisions that you made?
- On what basis did you make these decisions?
- How did you choose which theory to focus upon?
- How did you come to decide upon a particular methodological approach?
- What are the most interesting findings from the research? And the most unexpected?
- What would you have done differently if you had repeated the research?
- What have you learnt personally from doing the research?

Presenting your research

An alternative to the viva is to present your research in front of a small audience. Not everyone in the audience may have read your work, and you may well be addressing differing levels of expertise. Presentations of this nature are often short, and need to be well rehearsed. There are a number of common errors in presentations that you should be aware of when preparing:

304

- Putting too much detail on your overheads or slides. Stick to the key points. Often people will put a lot of detail on each slide, and simply read the slides out loud. Sticking to the essentials will help prevent this, and help you maintain eye contact with your audience.
- Using material that is difficult to read. Ensure that you have a sufficiently large and easily readable font. Fonts such as Arial are better for presentations than fonts such as Times New Roman. If in doubt about the font size, then err on the side of caution and use a minimum font size of 24 points, and avoid complex models or diagrams. Use handouts for such material if they are to be included.
- Having too many slides. If you are presenting for 10 minutes, then you simply will not get through 10 or 15 slides! Ensure you have a run through beforehand to check your timing, especially if you are presenting at an institution that will simply cut you off without warning at the end of your allocated time slot! Even if you are not cut off, over-running can show a lack of respect to any following speakers, so it is imperative to keep to time.

You may wish to adopt the following structure if you are called upon to present your research:

Slide 1 – Introduction, main aims and objectives of the research.
Slide 2 – A brief outline of your theoretical approach.
Slide 3 – The key features about your methodology.
Slide 4 – Your important/significant results.
Slide 5 – Two or three bullet points for discussion.

You will find that using five slides, with only one or two points on each slide will be more than adequate, provided you are able to talk about your own research freely.

Presenting a research poster

A poster summarises your research project on a single large sheet of paper (typically A0). It also has other functions, perhaps most importantly to attract people to read about your research in the first place, and also to stimulate subsequent discussion between you, as the presenter, and the audience who may, in many cases, have limited knowledge of the subject matter. Thus, your poster has to demonstrate a balance between content and attractiveness.

Designing your poster

First, identify the main message that you want the poster to put over. Then identify the essential elements that will need to be included for this message, for example background, methodology, key findings and so on. Some institutions have set requirements of the layout and what should be included, so if this is the case you should ensure you follow these. Otherwise, you will need to put together an initial draft design of your own. The guidelines you need to follow are:

- Keep the poster simple. Put across your message in as few words as possible, while providing all relevant detail. Your audience will not want to read long blocks of text, so think about how to communicate in as concise a way as possible.
- Keep your results as clear as possible. Present data in graphical format, rather than text or in tables. Ensure that the labelling of graphs is large enough, and ensure that the results are clear when read in isolation from the rest of the poster.
- Avoid the temptation to use too many colours. Try to use 3–4 at most, and avoid overly bright colours. Keep backgrounds light, and text dark. Make sure there is enough contrast between content and background.
- Fonts such as Ariel and Verdana are good for posters. Avoid obscure or unusual fonts. You will be trying to attract an audience from some distance, so make sure your font is large enough. A title will have a font size of approximately 100 points, 30–36 for headings and 20–24 for text.
- Use bullet points/tables to aid clarity.
- Leave a minimum 3 cm white border around the poster to frame your work.
- Use blank space to make the poster more attractive.
- Consider the use of a QR code on the poster that people viewing your poster can use to access certain information, such as reference lists, a biography of the researcher and so on.

As well as thinking about what will make the poster attractive, also consider what will put people off coming to view your poster. Things such as too much dense text, unclear results, and a message that is difficult to identify from a brief glance will all impact negatively upon interest in your research.

Other ways of reporting your research

Given all of the time and effort that you will have put into the research, its important to think about how your findings could be communicated beyond the limited audience involved in assessing your written report or presentation. If you feel that you've made even a modest contribution to knowledge, understanding or practice then it's important to disseminate it. There are a number of ways you could consider doing this:

1   If you feel like the work has real merit, and makes a significant contribution, then you could always discuss with your supervisor the possibility of writing it up and submitting it to a peer-reviewed journal. There is a growing volume of research being published in such journals that has emerged from student research, so it's worth considering this if the work is of sufficient standard.

2   If the work doesn't quite have the merit for a fully peer-reviewed journal, then many universities will run their own in-house journals for publishing good student research. These journals will still go through a peer-review process, but it is likely to be less demanding. Ask your supervisor if your institution does have such a journal, it is often an excellent opportunity.

3   You can always present your work at a conference such as the British Conference for Undergraduate Research (BCUR). This conference allows students from all disciplines to present papers, posters and workshops to other undergraduate researchers, and there is generally a good presentation from students studying sport-related topics.

4   Use social media. Report the key findings (remember any ethical issues related to aspects such as confidentiality and anonymity) through your Twitter account, or blog for example. This can often be an excellent way to attract interest in your research. You can also download a video summary of your research and download to a

site such as YouTube. If you use social media to communicate your findings, remember your audience will differ from that who would normally assess your research. Don't present things in an overly academic way, but don't over simplify or dumb it down.

5   If you carried out the research for an organisation or sporting body of some sort, think about how they are going to disseminate the findings. You should also find out if they are going to implement any changes as a result of your research, this way you can assess any impact of what you have done.

Summary

1   Writing the report is the culmination of a lot of time and energy spent doing the research, so make sure that you do yourself justice!

2   Writing the report will almost certainly take longer than you think.

3   You will generally have to go through the process of writing and rewriting a number of times until you are happy with the result.

4   There is normally no single acceptable structure for your research report. A typical undergraduate dissertation may follow the order of abstract, acknowledgements, table of contents, list of tables and figures, introduction, literature review, methodology, results, discussion, conclusion and recommendations, references and/or bibliography and appendices.

5   Take care with your writing style. Avoid the extremes of informality, dryness or jargon.

6   While you are writing the report, you have to be self-critical, and read your work with an eye to continually improving its content.

7   Consider other ways of presenting your research, and consider how to present your research in a way that is both informative and interesting.

You should obtain, if appropriate, a copy of the marking criteria used by your institution. Carefully, and critically, assess your own performance against the criteria. Identify the areas where you are happy that you fulfil the criteria, and also those areas that you are not sure about. Identify what you see to be the strengths and the weaknesses of the research. Now is the time to look at the weaknesses – are they remediable? If the weaknesses are things such as a lack of literature, poor structure and so on, you should address these and redo the activity. Get a colleague to read your research report. What do they think? Often they will be able to spot things that you will have missed – once you have read a section more than a few times, it becomes extremely difficult to take in everything you are reading.

Further reading

Weyers, J. and MacMillan, K. (2009) *How to Write Dissertations and Research Projects*, Upper Saddle River, NJ: Prentice Hall.

16 Practical issues

This chapter will:

- Outline the different types of research that you may undertake as a student.
- Describe some of the initial considerations that you should make about your research project.
- Outline some of the issues that you may need to consider when trying to gain collaboration for your research.
- Discuss the role of your tutor or supervisor in your research project.

Introduction

This chapter is designed for those undertaking research as part of a taught degree, for example a final-year dissertation at undergraduate level. If this is the case, then this is probably the first significant piece of research that you will have to do. This chapter will highlight some of the specific issues that you may want to consider before starting your research, and also make continual reference to throughout the research process.

The types of student research

Student research takes on a number of forms, each with its own requirements, depending both upon the nature of the course and the institution within which the research is being conducted. This section can only give a broad overview of the issues, and you should ensure that you read your own institution's regulations carefully before you start the research.

Student research can be broadly separated into two forms. First, the research may be the culmination of a period of taught study, generally at undergraduate or masters level. The research produced for the purpose of these degrees is referred to as a dissertation. The dissertation gives students the opportunity to conduct an in-depth study of a particular topic, synthesising various course elements, yet pursuing one area of interest in depth. The dissertation allows students scope for expression of skills, knowledge and abilities, and offers the chance to develop – in an original and creative way – areas of particular interest. The dissertation also performs the important integrative function of bringing together different elements from the course, testing the ability and discipline of the student in producing a detailed piece of work through a sustained period of independent study.

Other types of award are based entirely upon the production of a research report – in this instance a thesis – and an accompanying defence of the research with two or more examiners who are expert within the field (the viva voce). These awards are normally at masters level (MRes/MPhil) or doctoral level (PhD or DPhil). The objectives of these programmes are naturally considerably more advanced, with the criteria generally requiring the student to have satisfactorily completed a research training programme and to have investigated and evaluated or critically studied an appropriate topic over normally a minimum of one year (MRes), two years (MPhil) or three years (PhD/DPhil).

The research project – at whatever level – is an important part of any programme of study, as it allows you to both develop and demonstrate a number of key transferable skills. The transferable skills that you could expect to develop and demonstrate as part of a research project are as follows:

- To demonstrate familiarity with the core knowledge base of a particular field of sport-related study.
- To be able to evaluate that core knowledge base, its strengths, weaknesses and omissions.
- To be able to create a suitable methodology to achieve a series of research objectives.
- To be able to describe, analyse and interpret data from such a methodology using appropriate techniques.
- To be able to draw appropriate conclusions from evidence.
- To produce a complex piece of work which demonstrates a grasp of vocabulary of the subject and deploys a range of skills of written expression appropriate to the subject.
- To be able to decide on action plans and implement them effectively.
- To manage time effectively in order to achieve intended goals.
- To use appropriate IT resources independently.
- To deliver a paper or presentation which succeeds in communicating a series of points effectively.
- To produce creative and realistic solutions to complex problems.

Thus, by undertaking a piece of research, you are likely to show a potential employer that you possess a wide range of desirable skills that you may not develop to the same extent elsewhere during your academic career. Potential employers are likely to look at any research project you have undertaken – especially a dissertation or thesis – much more closely than taught modules, and you should bear this in mind when you commence your research programme.

Initial considerations

Whatever programme of study you are on, you will almost certainly have to present a proposal for your research project at an early stage, either in the form of a written or verbal presentation, which may in itself be assessed or non-assessed. Even for a non-assessed piece of work it is important to be as detailed and as thorough as possible as it is at this stage that you should highlight any potential problems. You should remember that your research will be restricted in terms of time and resources, and poor planning can lead to difficulties later. At this stage, you may want to consider the criteria in Table 16.1, and assess your intended project against such criteria.

Table 16.1 Criteria for consideration at the planning stages

Research topic

- Is it focused enough? Avoid making it too broad
- Is it realistic? Will you get the co-operation you need?
- Is it related to your programme of study?

Background

- Is there a well-defined theoretical background?
- What particular theories or models are you going to use?
- Have you defined your concepts?
- How will you measure these concepts?
- Have you mentioned at least one or two key authors?

Research design

- What design will you use?
- What type of data will you collect?
- What methods do you anticipate using?
- Can you justify your methodology?

Sampling

- Who will be your sample?
- What is your desired sample size?
- How will you choose them?
- Have you got confirmed access to your sample?

General

- Have you got the collaboration/access you need?
- Do you have the appropriate skills to carry out such research?

What characterises a good piece of student research?

Identifying what makes a piece of research 'good' or 'bad' is an important skill to develop. First, it is important for you to be able to assess the work of others. Second, you will also have to assess your own research. Finally, it is important to know how others will be assessing your work. It is important to know upon what criteria you are to be assessed before you start your research. Although there are some general areas upon which your research will be judged, which I will outline later, there may also be specific requirements of your institution, organisation, etc., and you should familiarise yourself with these at the earliest possible stage. Generally speaking, there will be four areas upon which you will be assessed:

1 Your understanding of existing knowledge, the use of existing ideas, and the development of your own research question from relevant literature, based upon logical argument and rational thought.
2 The use of an appropriate methodology to collect valid and reliable data with which to answer that question.
3 The development of sound conclusions based upon your data.
4 The associated transferable skills.

Read any marking criteria as soon as you can. What are the areas being assessed? What are the relative weightings of each, and which elements are given the highest importance? From the marking criteria you should be able to identify what examiners are seeking in terms of an 'excellent' piece of work. Try and identify what makes the difference between a good and an excellent piece of work. By knowing this before you start, you can focus on achieving excellence throughout the research process.

Originality and generalisability

There may also be the requirement with certain research projects (for example at masters or doctoral level) to make a 'contribution to human knowledge', through the development of new theories, methods, etc. At

314

undergraduate level, there is not the need to make such a contribution, and the extent of 'originality' required is minimal (although you should aim to make your project 'original' in some way, for example in one of the ways suggested in Chapter 4). It is also a good idea in most cases to ensure that your project has some relevance beyond the context within which it was carried out, for example in terms of your findings being representative beyond your sample or setting.

The research timescale

You also need to consider the timescale for your research. From my experience, students often underestimate the time required to undertake a piece of research, and it is important to be realistic rather than optimistic. Take for example the following activities:

- Locating relevant literature using an online database. This can be an on-going, and seemingly endless task. You may need to spend an entire day locating literature on one specific area of the project. You may then have to order this (for example from the British Library) which could mean up to a fortnight before you even get a look at the key literature.
- Reading a single journal article. To read such an article could take you anything from an hour upwards, especially at the beginning of the research, when you are still developing your own understanding of the subject, where you may find yourself struggling with an article for three hours or more.
- Designing an initial questionnaire/interview schedule. A good questionnaire or interview will take a substantial period of time to develop, even once you have developed an understanding of the concepts that you are researching.
- Piloting an initial questionnaire. This may take several weeks – remember that it is up to your respondents to get the questionnaire back to you, which they may need to be reminded of several times!
- Undertaking a postal survey. Even using a pre-designed questionnaire, you will need to post the questionnaires to your sample (taking several days). They will then need to complete the questionnaires (up to two weeks for those who remember) and return them to you (several more days). You will then have to repeat the process

for those who didn't return the questionnaires in the first round (another two to three weeks). Even an online survey will involve a period of time where you allow respondents to complete the questionnaire, which will be a minimum of two weeks.

- Writing up an interview. Even if you are a good typist, you should allow yourself about four to five hours to transcribe a one-hour interview, often more, especially if the recording is not clear, or if there is background noise.
- Entering the results from one hundred questionnaires onto a statistical analysis package. Obviously this is dependent upon the length and complexity of the questionnaire, but you may need to allow yourself several days to do this.

These are just some of the activities you may find yourself undertaking as part of a research project. You need to timetable as many of the activities that you think you will be undertaking as soon as possible, and ensure that your objectives are feasible within the time available to you.

Gaining collaboration and access

Developing a focused, feasible research proposal is, unfortunately, only part of the story. As part of your research, it is very likely that you will have to negotiate access to a sports-related body, whether it is a sports team, a school, sports organisation, local authority and so on. Securing good relations at an early stage can be extremely beneficial to you, and can make the whole research process seem a lot easier, so it is worth considering three questions:

1 What organisation/school/team, etc. do I need to gain access to?
2 How likely are they to provide access?
3 What is the best way to gain access?

The issue of access is important, and one that you should think about sooner, rather than later (it is no good completing your literature review, designing your questionnaire and so on, only to find out that you have no way of accessing your intended sample!). The two pieces of advice I can give are:

316

1   Be realistic. You may think that professional sports teams would be only too willing to distribute your questionnaires among their players and/or supporters. In reality, professional teams, governing bodies, etc. are often inundated with requests from students (often with requests such as 'please could you suggest an area for my dissertation'!) and your chances of a positive response are minimal in most cases. If you do require assistance, then consider regional or local – rather than national – bodies. They are much more likely to be interested in your research, and may be more willing to provide assistance.

2   Try to gain the co-operation of whichever body you choose at the earliest appropriate stage. This does not mean that you should approach them as soon as you have a rough idea of your research question. They are much more likely to be impressed if you can provide the following information:

- What is the rationale behind the research? Why is it important?
- What is the expertise of the researcher to undertake such a research project?
- What are the benefits for the particular body if they provide you access?
- What is the anticipated methodology? What data would you need to collect, and from whom?
- What is the timescale of the research?
- Will the organisation have the opportunity to view the research report before it is submitted?
- Will a copy be available to them after the research is completed?
- How will confidentiality be ensured if the research involves sensitive information?

The first step is generally to telephone or email the organisation to identify the appropriate person to contact. If you are using a personal acquaintance (for example you may know someone who works for a particular organisation), then you should also find out whether they are the best person to deal with, or if there is someone else in the organisation that you should be in contact with. (There is no harm at this stage in approaching several different organisations to maximise your chances of access. Do ensure that if you receive an offer of help that you have to decline, then you should respond in writing explaining your reasons and thanking them for the offer.)

Your next stage, even if verbal agreement has been given, is to write to the appropriate individual within the organisation. Include the information about the project mentioned above. Put as much detail as you can into this letter. Following this, you should wait until you receive a response in writing before assuming that co-operation is assured! Finally, you should confirm your acceptance in writing, and make arrangements for the next stage, which will often be a face-to-face meeting with the organisation.

The role of your tutor

So far, it may seem the case that you are on your own, that coming up with a suitable proposal is your task, and that you are left to sink or swim. Thankfully this is not normally the case! Normally you will be allocated a tutor (also referred to as a supervisor) who will provide guidance throughout the research. The student–tutor relationship can be crucial to the success of the project in many cases. It is important to strike the right balance – a final-year dissertation, for example, is designed to test the student's ability to carry out a piece of in-depth research independently, yet you are not expected to undertake the task without any help or assistance at all. Different institutions have differing guidelines.

Frequently asked questions on dissertation tutors and their role

Q. What will my tutor do?

A. Your tutor will help you complete the research by providing guidance on key areas of the research. Your tutor will tell you if you are on the right track, or if anything is wrong. It is not the tutor's role, however, to give you a topic to research, to suggest the detailed methodology, to interpret the results for you, or to keep in contact with you.

Q. How often should I see my tutor?

A. It is up to you and your tutor. Past experience has shown that no or minimal contact correlates with failed work. You should be aiming to see your tutor at least once every two weeks, sometimes more regularly,

318

especially during key stages of the research. If there is a problem then you must make alternative arrangements with your tutor. You should always have an agenda for your meeting – do not turn up without a clear idea of what you want to discuss.

Q. What sort of things will I discuss with my tutor?

A. The function of meetings will differ, depending upon the stage that you are at. Once you have decided upon your research question, it is often a good idea to produce written work on a regular basis, which can form the focus of the meeting. Do not expect the meeting to consist of your tutor giving you advice, or telling you what to do. It is up to you to discuss and debate your project with them, and to lead the meetings. You must have an objective for each meeting with your tutor. You should discuss progress and attempt to resolve any issues that might detract from your ability to work towards maximum performance. Examples of these issues are:

- Recommendation of suitable references.
- Amendment of project objectives.
- Advice on carrying out research.
- Advice on suitability of research instruments, e.g. questionnaire/ interview schedule.
- Advice on planning/scheduling your work, setting deadlines.
- Debate about theoretical issues.
- Making personal contacts.

Q. Can I bring in work for my tutor to check on the day of my appointment, or should I hand it in prior to the meeting?

A. Usually you will have a relatively short time allocated to you, thus you should not expect your tutor to give you feedback on the spot. Often it is a good idea to give work to your tutor in plenty of time. To do this, you will need to be well prepared!

Q. Is the tutor responsible for getting me to complete the research?

A. No. While the tutor acts as adviser and facilitator, the onus is clearly on you: to be responsible for your own progress; to keep in contact with your tutor; and to come to an agreement on frequency of attendance. Ideally, you should see your tutor at regular intervals. While it is difficult to come up with an optimum amount of contact, as suggested before, past experience has shown that no or minimal contact correlates with failed project work. Equally, the tutor does not expect you to be camped on her or his doorstep, nor to do the work for you!

Q. The skills being tested as part of the project include communication skills. Will my tutor check my spelling and grammar in my draft?

A. No. They will not have time to check for grammatical errors. It is up to you to have this done, through the use of spelling/grammar checkers in your word processing package, and through using someone who is skilled in the use of English. You should not rely on spellcheckers, as they will not always pick out incorrect usage of words, e.g. there/their.

Q. Will my tutor mark individual chapters for me before I hand in the final submission?

A. No. While tutors may be prepared to look at drafts, or rough sections of your work, do not expect any pre-marking. You should also be aware that even if you have completed a number of individual chapters each of a good standard, that is no guarantee of a good grade. It is how the chapters link together as a holistic piece of work that is important. Thus, you may have a detailed and well-written methodology chapter, but if your chosen methodology is not appropriate to the research objectives developed from your review of literature, then the worth of the chapter is significantly reduced. Remember that all work that you hand to your tutor should be word-processed.

Q. Will my tutor tell me what to do if I have a problem with my project?

A. Your tutor will help you solve the problem, but do not expect them to solve the problem for you. Problem solving is part of your work. Your tutor may suggest materials to read, refer you to someone else who may be able to give advice, or give you some ideas on how to solve the problem. You should, whatever happens, make the most of your tutor – remember, they are there to help you! Conflict can, and does, happen, however, between tutor and student, often as a result of differing expectations. Phillips and Pugh (1994) provide a useful list that is informative for both students and tutors. They suggest that tutors expect students to:

- Be more independent than the student expects.
- Produce regular written work.
- Seek help from others, not just the tutor.

- Organise and attend meetings regularly at their own initiative.
- Follow advice given in those meetings.
- Report progress honestly.
- Be enthusiastic!

For their part, students expect their tutors to:

- Actively supervise them.
- Have a good knowledge of the subject area.
- Be friendly, open and supportive.
- Read and understand written work provided by the student.
- Be constructive in their criticisms.
- Recommend appropriate reading.

Thus, the student–tutor relationship is clearly a two-way process, and you should approach it as such. However, you need to remember that overall responsibility for the completion of the research project lies with the student!

Common faults in student research

It is a good idea at this stage to alert you to some of the most common faults that are found in research projects, so that you may be aware of them before you commence, rather than reading about them when your research is almost complete! Although by no means an exhaustive list, these are the sorts of issues that you should consider, and hopefully avoid!

- Poor time management. Often the time required to complete a piece of research is underestimated. Although the written research report may often be relatively short, the time required for the entire research process is disproportionate. It is simply not possible to leave a research project until the last minute and complete it successfully.
- The research question is too broad. If the topic is too broad, then it is difficult to cover it in sufficient depth. You must be focused, and be realistic in terms of what you can achieve. Often students are

concerned that a focused question is unlikely to be able to provide them with the 10,000 or so words required by their institution. In reality, this is rarely a problem!

- The research is too descriptive. Often there is insufficient theoretical content to allow you to analyse and explain your findings. What theories are you using to inform your research? If you are unsure, then it is likely that your research will be descriptive rather than analytical.
- Not acknowledging the research process. There should be clear links between each section, and the research should follow a logical process, as highlighted in Chapter 2. The final written report should not read as a collection of unrelated chapters, but as an integrated piece of work.
- Coming to conclusions that are not based upon the evidence. Remember that research adds to knowledge through considering evidence gathered with the purpose of answering your research question.
- Limited sources. Good research shows evidence of wider reading. Do not simply use sport-related books as your main source of information. You should also be using texts from your theoretical discipline (e.g. sociology or marketing), and also a wide range of journal articles.
- Lack of objectivity. The research can be based too much on personal opinion, anecdotal evidence and a lack of detachment. Often, the conclusions may not be based upon the evidence that is presented, rather they are selected to highlight a particular opinion of the author.
- Poor presentation. This is often a problem with rushed reports! The research report has to be acceptable in terms of spelling, grammar, punctuation, layout and overall appearance. If the report is being undertaken for a particular body or institution, ensure that you have adhered to its particular requirements (e.g. word limits, referencing format and so on).

Summary

1 You can undertake research as a student for a number of purposes. A research project may be carried out to complete your study at undergraduate level and for most masters degrees. Alternatively, the research may form the basis of the entire degree, such as for some masters and most doctoral degrees.

322

2   As a student, there are a number of key issues that you must consider about your research. Is it feasible given your timescale? Do you have the necessary resources to complete the research?

3   One key issue is that of gaining collaboration. This is an important task, and must be carried out carefully and thoughtfully. You need to be realistic in terms of your chosen partners.

4   Use your tutor or supervisor appropriately. They are not there to do the research for you – but they can ensure that you are on the right track and give useful advice.

ABOUT YOUR RESEARCH PROJECT

Once you have been allocated your tutor or supervisor, you should ensure that you clarify each other's expectations at an early stage. What do you want from your tutor? What does your tutor expect from you? Doing this at an early stage can help prevent misunderstandings later on! If possible, write down each other's expectations for reference throughout the project.

Further reading

Phillips, E. and Pugh, D. (1994) *How to Get a PhD*, Buckinghamshire: Open University Press.

Although aimed at PhD students, there is a lot of valuable information of use to the undergraduate researcher, especially at the beginning of a research project.

Bibliography

Acton, C. and Miller, R. (2009) *SPSS for Social Scientists* (2nd edn), Basingstoke: Palgrave Macmillan.

Albert, E. (1999) 'Dealing with danger', *International Review for the Sociology of Sport* 34 (2), 157–71.

Allender, S., Cavill, N., Parker, M. and Foster, C. (2009) 'Tell us something we don't already know or do! The Response of Planning and Transport Professionals to Public Health Guidance on the Built Environment and Physical Activity', *Journal of Public Health Policy* 30, 112–16.

Anderson, L. (2006) 'Analytical autoethnography', *Journal of Contemporary Ethnography* 35 (4), 373–95.

Andrews, D., Nonnecke, B. and Preece, J. (2003) 'Electronic survey methodology: A case study in reaching hard to involve Internet users', *International Journal of Human–Computer Interaction* 16 (2), 185–210.

Atkinson, P. and Hammersley, M. (1994) 'Ethnography and participant observation', in Denzin, N. and Lincoln, Y. (eds) *Handbook of Qualitative Research*, London: Sage, pp.248–61.

Baker, T. (1994) *Doing Social Research*, New York: McGraw-Hill.

Bandura, A. (1977) *Social Learning Theory*, Englewood Cliffs, NJ: Prentice Hall.

Barker, J., McCarthy, P., Jones, M. and Moran, A. (2011) *Single Case Research Methods in Sport and Exercise Psychology*, London: Routledge.

Berg, K. and Latin, R. (2008) *Essentials of Research Methods in Health, Physical Education, Exercise Science and Recreation* (3rd edn), Baltimore, MD: Lippincott, Williams and Wilkins.

Biddle, S., Markland, D., Gilbourne, D., Chatzisarantis, N. and Sparkes, A. (2001) 'Research methods in sport and exercise psychology: Quantitative and qualitative Issues', *Journal of Sport Sciences* 19 (10), 777–809.

Birrell, S. and Loy, J. (1979) 'Media sport: Hot and cool', *International Review of Sport Sociology* 14 (5), 5–19.

Brackenridge, C. (1999) 'Managing myself', *International Review for the Sociology of Sport* 34 (4), 399–410.

Bray, S., Martin, K. and Widemeyer, W. (2000) 'The relationship between evaluative concerns and sport competition state anxiety among youth skiers', *Journal of Sport Sciences* 18 (5), 353–61.

Brewer, J. (2000) *Ethnography*, Buckingham: Open University Press.

Brinkmann, S. and Kvale, S. (2014) *Interviews: Learning the Craft of Qualitative Research Interviewing*, London: Sage.

Brown, N. and Billings, A. (2013) 'Sports fans as crisis communicators on social media websites', *Public Relations Review* 39 (1), 74–81.

Brownell, S. (2006) 'Sport ethnography; A personal account', in Hobbs, D. and Wright, R. (eds) *The Sage Handbook of Field Research*, London: Sage, pp.243–54.

Brustad, R. (2002) 'A critical analysis of knowledge construction in sport psychology', in Horn, T. (ed) *Advances in Sport Psychology* (2nd edn), Champaign, IL: Human Kinetics, pp.21–38.

Brymer, E. and Schweitzer, R. (2013) 'The search for freedom in extreme sports: A phenomenological exploration', *Psychology of Sport and Exercise* 14 (6), 865–873.

Buckley, C. (2007) 'Doing Your Undergraduate Dissertation Using Qualitative Research: Tutor Reflections', *Journal of Qualitative Research in Sports Studies* 1 (1), 89–93.

Butterworth, A. and Turner, D. (2014) 'Becoming a performance analyst: autoethnographic reflections on agency, and facilitated transformational growth', *Reflective Practice: International and Multidisciplinary Perspectives*, advanced online publication, doi: 10.1080/14623943.2014.900014.

Carey, D., Smith, G., Smith, D., Shepherd, J., Skriver, J., Ord, L. and Rutland, A. (2001) 'Footedness in world soccer: An analysis of France '98', *Journal of Sport Sciences* 19 (11), 855–64.

Carless, D. and Douglas, K. (2007) 'Narrative, identity and mental health: How men with serious mental illness re-story their lives through sport and exercise', *Psychology of Sport and Exercise* 9 (5), 576–94.

Case, R., Dey, T., Lu, J., Phang, J and Schwanz, A. (2013) 'Participant spending at sporting events: An examination of survey methodologies', *Journal of Convention and Event Tourism* 14 (1), 21–41.

Chelladurai, P. (1990) 'Leadership in sports: A review', *International Journal of Sport Psychology* 21 (4), 328–54.

Chelladurai, P. and Saleh, S. (1980) 'Dimensions of leader behaviour in sports: Development of a leadership scale', *Journal of Sport Psychology* 2, 34–45.

Chen, N., Ji, S. and Funk, D. (2014a) 'An extended study on destination image decay of sport tourists over time', *Journal of Destination Marketing and Management* 2 (4), 241–252.

Chen, Y., While, A. and Hicks, A. (2014b) 'Physical activity among older people living alone in Shanghai, China' *Health Education Journal* advanced online publication, doi: 10.1177/0017896914523943.

Cialdini, R., Borden, R., Thorne, A., Walker, M., Freeman, S. and Sloan, L. (1976) 'Basking in reflected glory: Three (football) field studies', *Journal of Personality and Social Psychology* 34 (3), 366–75.

Clarke, G. and Humberstone, B. (1997) *Researching Women and Sport*, London: Macmillan.

Clarke, M., Riley, M., Wilkie, E. and Wood, R. (1998) *Researching and Writing Dissertations in Hospitality and Tourism*, London: Thomson Business Press.

Coakley, J. (2009) *Sport in Society: Issues and Controversies* (10th edn), Boston, MA: McGraw-Hill.

Coakley, J. and Dunning, E. (eds) (2000) *Handbook of Sports Studies*, London: Sage.

Cooper, D. and Schindler, P. (1998) *Business Research Methods* (6th edn), Boston, MA: McGraw-Hill.

Creswell, J. (1994) *Research Design: Qualitative and Quantitative Approaches*, Thousand Oaks, CA: Sage.

Cronin, O., Jordan, J., Quigley, F. and Molloy, M. (2013) 'Prepared for sudden cardiac arrest? A cross-sectional study of automated external defibrillators in amateur sport', *British Journal of Sports Medicine* 47 (18), 1171–4.

Culver, D., Gilbert, W. and Trudel, P. (2003) 'A decade of qualitative research in sport psychology journals: 1990–1999', *The Sport Psychologist* 17 (1), 1–15.

Dean, R. and Whyte, W. (1978) 'How do you know if the informant is telling the truth?', in Bynner, J. and Stribley, K. (eds) *Social Research: Principles and Procedures*, Harlow: Longman, pp.179–88.

Dennis, P. and Carron, A. (1999) 'Strategic decisions of ice hockey coaches as a function of game location', *Journal of Sport Sciences* 17 (4), 263–8.

Denzin, N. (1989) *Interpretive Biography*, London: Sage.

Denzin, N. and Lincoln, Y. (eds) (1994) *Handbook of Qualitative Research*, London: Sage.

Denzin, N. and Lincoln, Y. (eds) (1998) *Collecting and Interpreting Qualitative Materials*, London: Sage.

De Vaus, D. (2001) *Research Design in Social Research*, London: Sage.

Dey, I. (1993) *Qualitative Data Analysis*, London: Routledge.

Dijksterhuis, A. and van Knippenberg, A. (1998) 'The relation between perception and behavior, or how to win a game of Trivial Pursuit', *Journal of Personality and Social Psychology* 74 (4), 865–877.

Dingwall, R. (1997) 'Accounts, interviews and observations', in Miller, G. and Dingwall, R. (eds) *Context and Method in Qualitative Research*, London: Sage, pp.51–65.

Dismore, H. and Bailey, R. (2005) '"If only": Outdoor and adventurous activities and generalised academic development', *Journal of Adventure Education and Outdoor Learning*, 5 (1), 9–19.

Dixon, A., Henry, T. and Martinez, J. (2013) 'Assessing the economic impact of sport tourists' expenditures related to a university's baseball season attendance', *Journal of Issues in Intercollegiate Athletics*, 6, 96–113.

Donnelly, P. and Young, K. (1988) 'The construction and confirmation of identity in sport subcultures', *Sociology of Sport* 5 (3), 223–40.

Eagly, A. and Johnson, B. (1990) 'Gender and leadership style: A meta-analysis', *Psychological Bulletin* 108 (2), 233–56.

Edwards, A. and Skinner, M. (2009) *Qualitative Research in Sport Management*, Oxford: Butterworth-Heinemann.

Ehsani, M., Amiri, M. and Hossini, R. (2012) 'The relationship between leadership styles of coaches with coaching efficacy among elite Iranian judokas', *International Journal of Sport Studies* 2 (8), 399–405.

Eichler, M. (1988) *Nonsexist Research Methods*, London: Routledge.

Elias, N. (1986) 'Introduction' in Elias, N. and Dunning, E. *Quest for Excitement*, Oxford: Basil Blackwell, pp.19–62.

Eysenbach, G. and Till, J. (2001) 'Ethical issues in qualitative research on Internet communities', *British Medical Journal*, 323 (7321), 103–5.

Field, A. (2013) *Discovering Statistics Using SPSS*, London: Sage.

Finn, M., Elliott-White, M. and Walton, M. (2000) *Tourism and Leisure Research Methods: Data Collection, Analysis and Interpretation*, Harlow: Longman.

Fishwick, L. and Leach, K. (1998) 'Game, set and match: Gender bias in television coverage of Wimbledon 1994', in Scraton, S. and Watson, R. (eds) *Sport, Leisure Identities and Gendered Spaces*, Eastbourne: Leisure Studies Association, pp.31–44.

Fontana, A. and Frey, J. (1998) 'Interviewing: The art of science', in Denzin, N. and Lincoln, Y. (eds) *Collecting and Interpreting Qualitative Materials*, Thousand Oaks, CA: Sage, pp.47–78.

Frankfort-Nachimas, C. and Nachimas, D. (1996) *Research Methods in the Social Sciences* (5th edn), London: Arnold.

Gall, M., Borg, W. and Gall, J. (1996) *Educational Research: An Introduction* (6th edn), White Plains, NY: Longman.

Gallmeier, C. (1988) 'Methodological issues in qualitative sport research: participant observation among hockey players', *Sociological Spectrum* 8 (3), 213–35.

Gilchrist, P. and Ravenscroft, N. (2011) 'Paddling, property and piracy: the politics of canoeing in England and Wales', *Sport in Society* 14 (2), 175–92.

Gilhespy, I. (2006) 'The status of visual data in research methods textbooks for sport and leisure programmes', *Journal of Hospitality, Leisure, Sport and Tourism Education* 5 (2), 71–6.

Gill, F. and Johnson, P. (1997) *Research Methods for Managers* (2nd edn), London: Paul Chapman.

Giulianotti, R. (1995) 'Participant observation and research into football hooliganism: Reflections on the problems of entrée and everyday risks', *Sociology of Sport* 12 (1), 1–20.

Greene, J., Caracelli, V. and Graham, W. (1989) 'Toward a conceptual framework for mixed-method evaluation designs', *Educational Evaluation and Policy Analysis* 11 (3), 255–274.

Greenwald, A., Gonzalez, R., Harris, R. and Guthrie, D. (1996) 'Effect sizes and p Values: What should be reported and what should be replicated', *Psychophysiology* 33 (2), 175–83.

Grills, S. (1998) 'An invitation to the field: Fieldwork and the pragmatists' lesson', in Grills, S. (ed.) *Doing Ethnographic Research: Fieldwork Settings*, Thousand Oaks, CA: Sage, pp.3–18.

Gruneau, R. (1989) 'Making spectacle: A case study in television sports production', in Wenner, L. (ed.) *Media, Sports and Society*, Newbury Park, CA: Sage, pp.134–54.

327

Hallmann, K., Feiler, S., Muller, S. and Breuer, C. (2012) 'The interrelationship between sport activities and the perceived winter sport experience' *Journal of Sport and Tourism* 17 (2), 145–163.

Hammersley, M. and Atkinson, P. (2007) *Ethnography: Principles in Practice*, London: Routledge.

Hannabus, S. (1996) 'Research interviews', *New Library World* 97 (1129), 22–30.

Hart, C. (2009) *Doing a Literature Review: Releasing the Social Science Research Imagination*, London: Sage.

Heitzler, C., Martin, S., Duke, J. and Huhman, M. (2006) 'Correlates of physical activity in a national sample of children aged 9–13 years', *Preventive Medicine* 42 (4), 254–60.

Henderson, K., Ainsworth, B., Stolarzcyk, L., Hootman, J. and Levin, S. (1999) 'Notes on linking qualitative and quantitative data: The cross cultural physical activity participation study', *Leisure Sciences* 21 (3), 247–55.

Hing, N., Vitartas, P., Lamont, M. and Fink, E. (2014) 'Adolescent exposure to gambling promotions during televised sport: An exploratory study of links with gambling intentions', *International Gambling Studies*, advanced online publication, doi: 10.1080/14459795.2014.902489.

Hoffman, S. (1992) (ed.) *Sport and Religion*, Champaign, IL: Human Kinetics.

Holloway, I. and Wheeler, S. (2009) *Qualitative Research in Nursing and Healthcare*, Oxford: Blackwell.

Holmes, R. (1998) *Fieldwork with Children*, Thousand Oaks, CA: Sage.

Holt, N. and Sparkes, A. (2001) 'An Ethnographic Study of cohesiveness in a college team over a season', *The Sport Psychologist* 15 (3), 237–59.

Holt, N., Scherer, J. and Kock, J. (2013) 'An ethnographic study of issues surrounding the provision of sport opportunities to young men from a western Canadian inner-city', *Psychology of Sport and Exercise* 14 (4), 538–48.

Holt, R. (1989) *Sport and the British*. Oxford: Blackwell.

Hoobler, J., Lemmon, G. and Wayne, S. (2014) 'Women's managerial aspirations: An organizational development perspective', *Journal of Management* 40 (3), 703–730.

Hooley, T., Marriott, J. and Wellens, J. (2012) *What is Online Research?* London: Bloomsbury.

Houlihan, B. (2007) *Sport and Society: A Student Introduction* (2nd edn), London: Sage.

Hussey, J. and Hussey, R. (1997) *Business Research*, Basingstoke: Macmillan.

Hutchins, B. and Rowe, D. (2012) *Sport Beyond Television*, Abingdon: Routledge.

Ingham, A. and Donnelly, P. (1992) 'Whose knowledge counts?', in Yiannakis, A. and Greendorfer, S. (eds) *Applied Sociology of Sport*, Champaign, IL: Human Kinetics, pp.247–55.

Ireland, R. and Webb, J. (2007) 'A cross-disciplinary exploration of entrepreneurship research', *Journal of Management* 33 (6), 891–927.

Jakobsen, J., Solberg, H., Halvorsen, T. and Jakobsen, T. (2013) 'Fool's gold: Major sport events and foreign direct investment', *International Journal of Sport Policy and Politics*, 5 (3), 363–380.

Jankowicz, A. (1995) *Business Research Projects* (2nd edn), London: Chapman-Hall.

Jankowicz, A. (2000) *Business Research Projects* (3rd edn), London: Thomson.

Jarvie, G. (2012) *Sport, Culture and Society*, London: Routledge.

Jayaratne, T. (1993) 'Quantitative methodology and feminist research', in Hammersley, M. (ed.) *Social Research: Philosophy, Politics and Practice*, London: Sage, pp.109–23.

Jones, C. (2014) 'Sports ethics: drunken role models: Rescuing our sporting exemplars', in Neil, R., Hanton, S., Fleming, S. and Wilson, K. (eds) *The Research Process in Sport, Exercise and Health: Case Studies of Active Researchers*, London: Routledge, pp.5–20.

Jones, I. (1997) 'Mixing qualitative and quantitative methods in sports fan research', *The Qualitative Report* 3 (4), available at http://www.nova.edu/ssss/QR/QR3-4/jones.html (accessed 09/05/14).

Jones, I., Brown, L. and Holloway, I. (2013) *Qualitative Research in Sport and Physical Activity*, London: Sage.

Jones, R., Murrell, A. and Jackson, J. (1999) 'Pretty versus powerful in the sports pages', *Journal of Sport and Social Issues* 23 (2), 183–92.

Jowett, S. and Frost, T. (2007) 'Race/ethnicity in the all-male coach–athlete relationship: Black footballers' narratives', *International Journal of Sport and Exercise Psychology* 5 (3), 255–69.

Keegan, R., Harwood, C., Spray, C. and Lavallee, D. (2014) 'A qualitative investigation of the motivational climate in elite sport', *Psychology of Sport and Exercise* 15 (1), 97–107.

Kellehear, A. (1993) *The Unobtrusive Researcher*, St Leonards, NSW: Allen & Unwin.

Keogh, J., Power, N., Wooller, L., Lucas, P. and Whatman, C. (2014) 'Physical and psychosocial function in residential aged care elders: Effect of Nintendo Wii sports games', *Journal of Aging and Physical Activity* 22 (2), 235–44.

Kerrigan, F., Larsen, G., Hanratty, S. and Korta, K. (2014) 'Gimme shelter': Experiencing pleasurable escape through the musicalisation of running' *Marketing Theory*, advanced online publication, doi: 10.1177/1470593114521451.

Kim, J. and Taggart, A. (2004) 'Teachers' perception of the culture of physical education: Investigating the silences at Hana primary school', *Issues in Educational Research*, available at http://www.iier.org.au/iier 14/kim.html (accessed 09/09/09).

King, N. and Horrocks, C. (2010) *Interviews in Qualitative Research*, London: Sage.

Knowles, A., Niven, A. and Fawkner, S. (2014) 'Once upon a time I used to be active: Adopting a narrative approach to understanding physical activity behavior in adolescent girls', *Qualitative Research in Sport, Exercise and Health* 6 (1), 62–76.

Kozinets, R. (2010) *Netnography: Doing Ethnographic Research Online*, Los Angeles, CA: Sage.

Krane, V., Anderson, M. and Stean, W. (1997) 'Issues of qualitative research methods and presentation', *Journal of Sport and Exercise Psychology* 19 (2), 213–18.

Kvale, S. (1996) *Interviews: An Introduction to Qualitative Research Interviewing*, Thousand Oaks, CA: Sage.

Kvale, S. (2007) *Doing Interviews*, London: Sage.

Lee, R. and Fielding, N. (1996) 'Qualitative data analysis: Representations of technology: A comment on Coffey, Holbrook and Atkinson', *Sociological Research Online* 1 (4), available at http://www.socresonline.org.uk/1/4/1f.html (accessed 09/09/09).

Leedy, P. (1985) *Practical Research: Planning and Design*, New York: Macmillan.

Leonard, W. (1998) *A Sociological Perspective of Sport* (5th edn), Boston, MA: Allyn and Bacon.

Lewins, A. and Silver, C. (2007) *Using Software in Qualitative Research: A Step-by-Step Guide*, London: Sage.

Lincoln, Y. and Guba, E. (1985) *Naturalistic Inquiry*, Newbury Park, CA: Sage.

Lloyd, B., Matthews, S., Livingston, M., Jayasekara, H. and Smith, K. (2013) 'Alcohol intoxication in the context of major public holidays, sporting and social events: a time-series analysis in Melbourne, Australia, 2000–2009', *Addiction* 108 (4), 701–9.

Lonsdale, C., Hodge, K. and Rose, E. (2006) 'Pixel vs paper: Comparing online and traditional survey methods in sport psychology', *Journal of Sport and Exercise Psychology* 28 (1), 10–108.

Lucas, S. (2000) 'Nike's commercial solution', *International Review for the Sociology of Sport* 35 (2), 149–64.

MacClancy, J. (1996) 'Nationalism at play', in MacClancy, J. (ed.) *Sport, Identity and Ethnicity*, Oxford: Berg, pp.1–19.

McNamee, M., Olivier, S. and Wainwright, P. (2007) *Research Ethics in Exercise, Health and Sports Sciences*, London: Routledge.

Madrigal, R. (1995) 'Cognitive and affective determinants of fan satisfaction with sporting event attendance', *Journal of Leisure Research* 27 (3), 205–27.

Malcolm, D., Jones, I. and Waddington, I. (2000) 'The people's game? Football spectatorship and demographic change', *Soccer and Society* 1 (1), 129–43.

Marshall, P., Walker, D. and Russo, N. (2010) 'Mediating the Olympics', *Convergence* 16 (3), 263–78.

Martinent, G., Campo, M. and Ferran, C. (2012) 'A descriptive study of emotional process during competition: Nature, frequency, direction, duration and co-occurrence of discrete emotions', *Psychology of Sport and Exercise* 13 (2), 142–51.

Matlin, M. and Gawron, V. (1979) 'Individual differences in Pollyannaism', *Journal of Personality Assessment* 43 (4), 411–12.

Messner, M., Duncan, M. and Cooky, C. (2003) 'Silence, sports bras, and wrestling porn: Women in televised sports news and highlights shows', *Journal of Sport and Social Issues* 27 (1), 38–51.

Miles, M. and Huberman, A. (1994) *Qualitative Data Analysis*, Thousand Oaks, CA: Sage.

Mills, C. and Hoeber, L. (2013) 'Using photo-elicitation to examine artefacts in a sport club: Logistical considerations and strategies throughout the research process', *Qualitative Research in Sport, Exercise and Health* 5 (1), 1–20.

Nau, D. (1995) 'Mixing methodologies: Can bimodal research be a viable post-positivist tool?', *The Qualitative Report* 2 (3), available at http://www.nova.edu/ssss/QR/QR2-3/nau.html (accessed 09/05/14).

Neil, R., Hanton, S., Fleming, S. and Wilson, K. (2014) *The Research Process in Sport, Exercise and Health: Case Studies of Active Researchers*, London: Routledge.

Neuendorf, K. (2001) *The Content Analysis Guidebook*, London: Sage.

Neuman, W. (2000) *Social Research Methods: Qualitative and Quantitative Approaches* (4th edn), Boston, MA: Allyn and Bacon.

Nixon, H. and Frey, J. (1996) *A Sociology of Sport*, Belmont, CA: Wadsworth.

Ntoumanis, M. (2009) *A Step-by-Step Guide to SPSS for Sport and Exercise Studies* (2nd edn), London: Routledge.

Olive, R. and Thorpe, H. (2011) 'Negotiating the "F-word" in the field: Doing feminist ethnography in action sport cultures', *Sociology of Sport Journal*, 28 (4), 421–40.

Oppenheim, A. (1992) *Questionnaire Design, Interviewing and Attitude Measurement*, London: Pinter.

Palmer, C. (2000) 'Spin doctors and sportsbrokers: Researching elites in contemporary sport – A research note on the Tour de France', *International Review for the Sociology of Sport* 35 (3), 364–77.

Papathomas, A. and Lavallee, D. (2013) 'Self starvation and the performance narrative in competitive sport', *Psychology of Sport and Exercise* advanced online publication, doi: 10.1016/j.psychsport.2013.10.014.

Perkins, K., Columna, L., Lieberman, L. and Bailey, J. (2013) 'Parents' perceptions of physical activity for their children with visual impairments', *Journal of Visual Impairment & Blindness* 107 (2), 131–42.

Phillips, E. and Pugh, D. (1994) *How to get a PhD*, Buckingham: Open University Press.

Podlog, L., Wadey, R., Stark, A., Lochbaum, M., Hannon, J. and Newton, M. (2013) 'An adolescent perspective on injury recovery and the return to sport', *Psychology of Sport and Exercise* 14 (4), 437–46.

Pol, L. and Pak, S. (1994) 'The use of a two stage survey design for gathering data from people who attend sporting events', *Sport Marketing Quarterly* 3 (3), 9–12.

Poynter, R. (2010) *The Handbook of Online and Social Media Research*: Chichester: Wiley.

Reber, A. (1995) *Penguin Dictionary of Psychology*, London: Penguin.

Ridley, D. (2012) *The Literature Review: A Step-by-Step Guide for Students*, London: Sage.

Roberts, J., Jones, R., Harwood, C., Mitchell, S. and Rothberg, S. (2001) 'Human perceptions of sports equipment under playing conditions', *Journal of Sport Sciences* 19 (7), 485–97.

Rosenthal, R. and Jacobsen, L. (1968) *Pygmalion in the Classroom*, New York: Rinehart and Winston.

Rovio, E., Arvinen-Barrow, M, Weigand, D., Eskola, J. and Lintunen, T. (2012) 'Using team building methods with an ice hockey team: An action research case study', *Sport Psychologist* 26 (4), 584–603.

331

Sands, R. (2002) *Sport Ethnography*, Champaign, IL: Human Kinetics.

Saunders, M., Lewis, P. and Thornhill, A. (2000) *Research Methods for Business Students* (2nd edn), Harlow: Prentice Hall.

Scanlan, T., Stein, G. and Ravizza, K. (1991) 'An in-depth study of former elite figure skaters: III. Sources of stress', *Journal of Sport and Exercise Psychology* 13 (2), 103–20.

Scelles, N., Durand, C., Bonnal, L., Goyeau, D. and Andreff, W. (2013) 'Competitive balance versus competitive intensity before a match: Is one of these two concepts more relevant in explaining attendance? The case of the French football Ligue 1 over the period 2008–2011', *Applied Economics* 45 (29), 4184–92.

Schreier, M. (2012) *Qualitative Content Analysis in Practice*, London: Sage.

Seidman, I. (1991) *Interviewing as Qualitative Research*, New York: Teachers College Press.

Sharpe, L. and Hodge, K. (2014) 'Sport psychology consulting effectiveness: The athlete's perspective', *International Journal of Sport and Exercise Psychology* 12 (2), 91–105.

Shoham, A., Rose, G. and Kahle, L. (1999) 'Practitioners of risky sports: A quantitative examination', *Journal of Business Research* 47, (3) 237–51.

Silk, M. (2005) 'Sporting ethnography: philosophy, methodology and reflection', in Andrews, D., Mason, D. and Silk, M. (eds) *Qualitative Methods in Sports Studies*, Oxford: Berg, pp.65–103.

Silverman, D. (2006) *Interpreting Qualitative Data*, London: Sage.

Smith, A. and Stewart, B. (2001) 'Beyond number crunching: Applying qualitative techniques in sport marketing research', *The Qualitative Report* 6 (2), available at http://www.nova.edu/ssss/QR/QR6-2/smith.html (accessed 09/05/14).

Smith, A., Stavros, C., Westberg, K., Wilson, B. and Boyle, C. (2014) 'Alcohol-related player behavioral transgressions: Incidences, fan media responses, and a harm-reduction alternative', *International Review for the Sociology of Sport* 49 (3–4), 400–16.

SNCCFR (1996–2000) *Premier League Fan Surveys*, Leicester: Sir Norman Chester Centre for Football Research.

Sparkes, A. (2000) 'Illness, premature career-termination, and the loss of self', in Jones, R. and Armour, K. (eds) *Sociology of Sport: Theory and Practice*, Harlow: Longman, pp.13–28.

Sparkes, A. (2002) *Telling Tales in Sport and Physical Activity*, Champaign, IL: Human Kinetics.

Sparkes, A. (2009) 'Ethnography and the senses: Challenges and possibilities', *Qualitative Research in Sport and Exercise* 1 (1), 21–35.

Sport England (2002) *What We Do – Evaluating the Regional Economic Impact of Sport (2002–03)*, London: Sport England.

Stein, A., Mitgutsch, K. and Consalvo, M. (2013) 'Who are the sport gamers? A large scale study of sports video game players', *Convergence* 19 (3), 345–63.

Stone, B. (2009) 'Running man', *Qualitative Research in Sport and Exercise* 1 (1), 67–71.

Sugden, J. (1996) *Boxing and Society*, Manchester: Manchester University Press.

Sugden, J. and Tomlinson, A. (1999) 'Digging the dirt and staying clean: Retrieving the investigative tradition for a critical sociology of sport', *International Review for the Sociology of Sport* 34 (4), 385–97.

Tainsky, S. and Babiak, K. (2011) 'Professional athletes and charitable foundations: An exploratory investigation', *International Journal of Sport Management and Marketing* 9 (3/4), 133–53.

Theobald, W. and Dunsmore, H. (2000) *Internet Resources for Leisure and Tourism*, Oxford: Butterworth-Heinemann.

Thomas, J. and Nelson, J. (2010) *Research Methods in Physical Activity* (6th edn), Champaign, IL: Human Kinetics.

Turner, J. (2013) 'A longitudinal content analysis of gender and ethnicity portrayals on ESPN's SportsCenter from 1999 to 2009', *Communication & Sport* 1 (1), 1–27.

Turnnidge, J., Côté, J., Hollenstein, T. and Deakin, J. (2014) 'A direct observation of the dynamic content and structure of coach–athlete interactions in a model sport program', *Journal of Applied Sport Psychology* 26 (2), 225–40.

UK Sport (1999) *Major Events, The Economics: A Guide*, London: UK Sport.

Van der Roest, J., Spaaij, R. and van Bottenburg, M. (2013) 'Mixed methods in emerging academic subdisciplines: The case of sport management', *Journal of Mixed Methods Research* advanced online publication, doi: 10.1177/1558689813508225.

Vazou, S., Ntoumanis, N. and Duda, J. (2005) 'Peer motivational climate in youth sport: A qualitative inquiry', *Psychology of Sport and Exercise* 6 (5), 497–516.

Veal, A. (2006) *Research Methods for Leisure and Tourism: A Practical Guide* (3rd edn), Harlow: Prentice Hall.

Veal, A. and Darcy, S. (2014) *Research Methods in Sport Studies and Sport Management: A Practical Guide*, London: Routledge.

Vincent, W. (2005) *Statistics in Kinesiology* (3rd edn), Champaign, IL: Human Kinetics.

Wakefield, K. and Sloan, H. (1995) 'The effects of team loyalty and selected stadium factors on spectator attendance', *Journal of Sport Management* 9 (2), 153–72.

Walliman, N. (2001) *Doing Your Research Project*, London: Sage.

Walseth, K. (2007) 'Sport and belonging', *International Review for the Sociology of Sport* 41 (3/4), 447–64.

Wann, D. (1994) 'Biased evaluations of highly identified sports spectators: A response to Hirt and Ryalls (1994)', *Perceptual and Motor Skills* 79, 105–6.

Wann, D. (1997) *Sports Psychology*, Upper Saddle River, NJ: Prentice Hall.

Wann, D. and Branscombe, N. (1993) 'Sports fans: Measuring the degree of identification with their team', *International Journal of Sports Psychology* 24 (1), 1–17.

Waring, M., Warburton, P. and Coy, M. (2007) 'Observation of children's physical activity levels in primary school: Is the school an ideal setting for meeting government activity targets?', *European Physical Activity Review* 13 (1), 25–40.

Watson, B. and Scraton, S. (2001) 'Confronting whiteness? Researching the leisure lives of South Asian mothers', *Journal of Gender Studies* 10 (3), 265–75.

Weiss, R. (1995) *Learning from Strangers: The Art and Method of Qualitative Interview Studies*, New York: Simon and Schuster.

West, A., Green, E., Brackenridge, C. and Woodward, D. (2001) 'Leading the way: Women's experiences as sports coaches', *Women in Management Review* 16 (2), 85–92.

Weyers, J. and MacMillan, K. (2009) *How to Write Dissertations and Research Projects*, Upper Saddle River, NJ: Prentice Hall.

Witz, A. (1990) 'Patriarchy and professions: The gendered politics of occupational closure', *Sociology* 24 (4), 675–90.

Worsley, P. (1992) *The New Introducing Sociology*, London: Penguin.

Wright, K. (2005) 'Researching internet-based populations: Advantages and disadvantages of online survey research, online questionnaire authoring software packages, and web survey services', *Journal of Computer-Mediated Communication* 10 (3), article 11, available at http://onlinelibrary.wiley.com/doi/10.1111/j.1083-6101.2005.tb00259.x/full (accessed 13/05/09).

Yiannakis, A. (1992) 'Toward an applied sociology of sport: The next generation', in Yiannakis, A. and Greendorfer, S. (eds) *Applied Sociology of Sport*, Champaign, IL: Human Kinetics, pp.3–21.

Yiannakis, A. (2000) 'The relationship of theory to application in the sociology of sport', in Jones, R. and Armour, K. (eds) *Sociology of Sport: Theory and Practice*, Harlow: Longman, pp.114–33.

Yin, R. (1994) *Case Study Research: Design and Methods* (2nd edn), London: Sage.

Yin, R. (2008) *Case Study Research: Design and Methods* (4th edn), London: Sage.

Zajonc, R. (1965) 'Social facilitation', *Science* 149, 269–74.

Index

guidelines for treatment of 141–2; in/voluntary 138–40; increasing responses from 169–70; informed consent of 138–9; observation in ethnography 228; online surveys and 161; social media ethics 241–3; threatening questions 163; voluntary/involuntary participation 138–40 *see also* ethics in research

performance, operationalising 94–5

Perkins, K. (2013) 284

personal interests and experience 47

phenomenology 23, 185

Phillips, E. 88, 320

physical activity promotion 194

physical education: Korean teachers and 204

Podlog, L. 130

Pol, L. 172

Pollyanna effect 164

popular issues as question sources 46–7

positivism: definition and characteristics of 19–20; Hallman's study and 24; literature review and 62; post-positivism 21–2; use in research 32

poster presentations 305–7

Poynter, R. 160, 161

presentation to audiences 304–5

private papers/letters/diaries: content analysis 214

Pro Quest 67

problems: understanding with research 5, 11

procedures and systems, creation of 5

proposals: required information 56–7; weakness of 56–7

PsychInfo 67

public record sources 213

publisher web pages 67

Pugh, D. 88, 322

qualitative research 32; assessment of 106–7; authenticity 107; basic points and questions 109; choosing 26–7; coding 231, 276–80; combining with quantitative 137; compared to quantitative 274; content analysis 210; credibility 107; definition and characteristics of 23–6; enhancing quality of 108; interviews 191–3; literature review and 62, 63–4; presentation of analysis 281; questionnaires 154; reliability 101–3, 106–7; research design and 134–5; rigour 107; sampling and 125–6, 128–30, 132; software and 282–3; stages of analysis 275–6; themes 276–80; trustworthiness of data 283–5; writing the report 295

Qualitative Research in Sport and Exercise 33

quantitative research 32, 271; assessing validity 103–4; choosing 26–7; combining with qualitative 137; common mistakes in 270; compared to qualitative data 274; conceptual frameworks 101–4; definition and characteristics of 23–6; dependent and independent variables 97; general research traditions and 30; intervening variables 98–9; literature review and 62, 63–4; nominal, ordinal, interval and ratio 96–7; operationalising concepts 93–5; questionnaires and 148, 154; relation between variables 99–100; reliability and validity 101–3; research design and 134–5; sample sizes 132; sampling techniques 126, 127–8; variables 113–15 *see also* data analysis; data collection

questionnaires 173–4; access 151; advantages and disadvantages 148–9; analysing the data 152–3; as appropriate method 147; closed and open questions 153–5; collection 172; compared to interviews 179; covering letters 170–1; definition and types 146; design of 152–9; face-to-face 146; filter questions 158; internet-based 149–52; for interviews 180–2; leading questions 163; list questions 157–8; non-respondents and 172; online 146, 159–61, 240; open/closed questions 162; order

340

and structure of 158–9; piloting 164–9; possible design problems 162–4; postal 146; primary research 8; ranking questions 157; research design and 134; response rates 149, 169–70; scales 155–7; at sporting events 171–2; student research 315; telephone 146; used with observation 208

race and ethnicity: interviews and 191; sampling techniques 129; *SportsCenter* study 212

Ravenscroft, N. 240

realism, knowledge and 23

reflexivity 108; autoethnography 123; qualitative analysis 285

reliability: forms of 101–2; interviews 189–91; threats to 102–3; with validity 103–4

reporting/writing 308; abstracts 13, 290, 298; acknowledgments 290; appendices 298; conclusions 276, 290, 297, 298, 322; dissemination of research 36, 40; ethnography 231; further communication of 307–8; general presentation 302–3, 322; intended audience for 289–90; introduction 293–4, 298; language and style 299–300; layout and technical requirements 290; literature review 290, 294, 296–7, 298, 300–1; methodology 290, 294–6, 298, 301; posters 304–5; presentation to an audience 304–5; quotations and 76–9; references 70; references/bibliography 290, 297–8; role of tutors and 318–21; self-assessment of 300–3; structure of report 291–8, 298; viva voce defence of 303–4; the writing process 41, 289–91

research: abstracts of 14; academic and non-academic 2–3; characteristics of 4; conclusions 40; definition of 3; disciplinary approach 9–10; drawing conclusions 36; empiricism 94; exploratory/descriptive/explanatory 7–8; finding your approach to 31–2; keeping heart in 41;

measurement and control 20–1; misconceptions about 10–11; 'originality' 11; planning process of 40–1; primary and secondary 8; pure and applied 8; purpose of 5; reading 15; reading others' writings 11–15, 32–3; stages of 35–40; theoretical and empirical 9; topic selection 36, 37; types of 6–9 *see also* data analysis; data collection; methodology; qualitative research; quantitative research; reporting/writing

research design 36, 142; action research 121–2; autoethnography 122–5; case studies 119–21; cross-sectional/survey 116–17; data collection methods 134–5; ethics and 137–41; ethnography 122, 135; experimental 113–15; focusing the question 321; grounded theory 121; longitudinal 118–19; measuring variables 113–15; planning your methodology 112–13; qualitative or quantitative data 134–5; sampling 126–33; stages of 38–9; time series 117; triangulation 135–6; writing your report and 295 *see also* student research

The Research Process in Sport, Exercise and Health (Neil) 42

research question 36; CAFE considerations 51, 52–3; checklist 54–5; development 54, 58; development sources 45–9; focusing 38, 49–56, 58–9; importance of 45; literature review and 62; objectives 54–5, 58–9; originality and re-thinking 47; the proposal 54–7

Roberts, J. 279, 280

Roest, Van Der, J. 27

Rosenthal, R. 140

Rovio, E. 122

Rowe, D.: *Sport Beyond Television* (with Hutchins) 77, 78

running, music technology and 237

Saleh, S. 94

sampling: bias 131; case studies and 132–3; cluster 128; convenience 129; ethnography and 225–6;

Related titles

FROM ROUTLEDGE